ENTREPRENEURIAL JOURNALISM IN GREATER CHINA AND SOUTHEAST ASIA

Exploring startup journalism and digital media platform trends in China, Taiwan and Southeast Asia, this book offers a practical insight into how to launch and run successful news operations as digitisation spreads through the region.

Drawing from a range of case studies of news and journalism startups, including Malaysiakini, Hong Kong Free Press, The News Lens of Taiwan, Thailand's The Standard, Ciwei Gongshe of China, Indonesia's IDN Media, Sabay of Cambodia and Frontier Myanmar, this book provides tips on how to launch a news media startup, how to find funding and how to sustain and scale the enterprise. Blending a theoretical approach with core business and newsgathering expertise, the author offers an engaging overview of contemporary entrepreneurial concepts and their vital relationship in finding new markets for journalism today.

Entrepreneurial journalism in greater China and Southeast Asia is an invaluable resource for both students and professionals interested in new media, startups and the Asian media market.

Judith Clarke worked as an editor and correspondent for *Asiaweek* magazine in the 1980s and taught and researched journalism at Hong Kong Baptist University from 1990 to 2020. Her research focused on news in Southeast Asia, particularly Cambodia. She set up and taught HKBU's postgraduate course in entrepreneurial journalism.

ENTREPRENEURIAL JOURNALISM IN GREATER CHINA AND SOUTHEAST ASIA

Case Studies and Tools for Media Professionals

Judith Clarke

LONDON AND NEW YORK

The cover image credit is Getty Images.

First published 2022
by Routledge
2 Park Square, Milton Park, Abingdon, Oxon OX14 4RN

and by Routledge
605 Third Avenue, New York, NY 10158

Routledge is an imprint of the Taylor & Francis Group, an informa business

© 2022 Judith Clarke

The right of Judith Clarke to be identified as author of this work has been asserted in accordance with sections 77 and 78 of the Copyright, Designs and Patents Act 1988.

All rights reserved. No part of this book may be reprinted or reproduced or utilised in any form or by any electronic, mechanical, or other means, now known or hereafter invented, including photocopying and recording, or in any information storage or retrieval system, without permission in writing from the publishers.

Trademark notice: Product or corporate names may be trademarks or registered trademarks, and are used only for identification and explanation without intent to infringe.

British Library Cataloguing-in-Publication Data
A catalogue record for this book is available from the British Library

Library of Congress Cataloging-in-Publication Data
A catalog record has been requested for this book

ISBN: 9781138283084 (hbk)
ISBN: 9781138283091 (pbk)
ISBN: 9781315270432 (ebk)

DOI: 10.4324/9781315270432

Typeset in Bembo
by Deanta Global Publishing Services, Chennai, India

Access the Support Material: Routledge.com/9781138283091

CONTENTS

Preface   vi

1 Entrepreneurialism, journalism and Asia   1

2 Finding your niche and getting your journalism startup on the way   19

3 Money to start up   36

4 Technological and journalism skills for your startup   52

5 Funding your journalism enterprise – income   66

6 Sustaining and scaling your enterprise, ethical issues   91

7 Case studies   106

Index   213

PREFACE

The idea for this book came about when I was assigned to write a syllabus for and teach classes in entrepreneurial journalism at Hong Kong Baptist University in 2012. The academic staff felt at the time that journalism students were less and less likely to find a conventional job in media. Around us new journalism businesses were flourishing, and one choice for our graduates would be to start their own outlet. We were giving no tuition in this important contemporary aspect of the profession. On setting up the course, it became apparent that there were few texts and even fewer reference books on the subject. Those that existed mostly addressed western situations. With our student body encompassing not only Hong Kong but mainland China, Taiwan and Southeast Asia, there was a clear need for more information on entrepreneurial journalism and a reference work for teaching the topic.

Research showed that in our region, despite political and economic difficulties, many entrepreneurial journalists were entering the field. Thirty outlets were studied for this book, and my thanks go to all the interviewees who gave me so much of their time to help me put their stories together as case studies for others who would like to follow in their footsteps. My thanks also go to the students, now graduates, and friends who worked with me, in particular Jiranan Hanthamrongwit, who helped with the Thai interviews, and Gabi Xu Wen and Wallis Wang Xueyang, who helped with those in mainland China. Thank you, too, to my colleagues, friends and family who encouraged me. Without so much support the book wouldn't have been possible, but I am solely responsible for any mistakes in its pages.

Judith Clarke
Hong Kong, June 2021

1
ENTREPRENEURIALISM, JOURNALISM AND ASIA

Introduction

This book is about digital startups in the journalism business in China (including its once-colonised Special Administrative Regions, Hong Kong and Macau), Taiwan and Southeast Asia. Its aim is to show just how lively and diverse the scene is despite the many constraints journalism entrepreneurs face. It covers all aspects of the business of journalism in the digital age and presents many examples from the region. Its goal is to encourage those who are starting out as independent digital journalism providers or are thinking of doing so, and to support those already on the way.

Entrepreneurial journalism

Background and emergence

Even today the combination of the words "entrepreneurial" and "journalism" jars for traditional journalists, who see their role as telling the public the truth rather than making money. Yet in fact, as US researcher Jane B. Singer writes, the connection is fundamental: "[e]ntrepreneurialism gave birth to Western journalism, from the earliest periodical printers to the 19th-century publishers who turned fledgling news initiatives into empires" (Singer 2018, 356). The link just got distorted in the 150 years those empires boomed.

In the early days, newspapers, like most other products, made money from sales. From the 1830s the emerging advertising business, seeking to reach potential customers for the new manufactured goods of the Industrial Revolution, found them the perfect channel to do so, and thus provided them with incomes often many times those they derived from readers. With well-off audiences the preferred target, advertising boosted conservative newspapers in the wealthier

DOI: 10.4324/9781315270432-1

markets of the world into big businesses. They could improve their product with ever-more sophisticated machinery and pay professional journalists well to provide attractive content for mass audiences. Small papers and publications that appealed to poorer audiences fell by the wayside, while the reader became a consumer without any role in producing the news other than to pay for it (Curran & Seaton 1997, 33–38). The arrival of radio and television in the 20th century only entrenched this "advertising model" because they needed even more expensive facilities, though the influence of broadcast meant governments took a role as regulators and, in some places, as providers themselves.

At the end of the 20th century critics had plenty to complain about. The big commercial publications and broadcasters were accused of pandering to consumers and advertisers through "market-driven journalism" that focused on sensationalism and trivialisation (McManus 1994). What's more, the major companies, mostly American and European, were growing bigger through aggressive takeovers, reducing their numbers and threatening a "media monopoly", as US academic Ben Bagdikian (2000) pointed out. The only sign of entrepreneurialism in the business was among the small élite running these huge media conglomerates. Then the whole industry was unexpectedly turned on its head by developments apparently beyond its control: the advancement of technology and, linked to it, the emergence of an invigorated entrepreneurial scene.

Entrepreneurialism had been at the centre of economist Joseph Schumpeter's concept of "creative destruction", in which new, innovative firms appear that disrupt old oligopolies, eventually destroying their markets (Schumpeter 1987). American entrepreneurship specialist Bruce Kirchhoff (1994) took up the idea and developed his theory of "dynamic capitalism", where some small firms grow into "ambitious" or "glamorous" companies whose new products win market share from old corporations and create new wealth – and become big companies themselves waiting for new small ones to do the same to them, a continual process.

Economists Thurik, Stam and Audretsch (2013) linked "dynamic capitalism" with the new information and communication technologies (ICTs). The old "managed economy", as they call it, suited big enterprises and economies of scale. The new ICTs had started appearing from the 1940s with the invention of the transistor, and continued with the integrated circuit of the 1950s, the microprocessor of the early 1970s, the personal computer of the 1980s and the internet of the 1990s, all quietly but progressively disrupting not only the developed industrial economies but eventually the whole world. They created new markets with products that could be sold at high prices because they had no competition and because the prosperity they created made price less of a factor in demand. They enabled communication across boundaries, breaking down national and international entry barriers to business and making outsourcing efficient, thereby necessitating company restructuring. They brought the old communist command economies into the world market, producing a level of globalisation unseen before.

The new entrepreneurial economy that emerged had innovation at its core and was "characterized by a convergence of institutions and policy approaches designed to facilitate the creation and commercialization of knowledge through entrepreneurial activity" (Thurik, Stam & Audretsch 2013). The old behemoth capitalist corporations were "disrupted" by new outfits that started from tiny beginnings but used novel ideas and attracted huge investment – the likes of computer pioneers Microsoft and Apple, search engine Google, online shop Amazon and the social media outfit Facebook. These companies, based in the US, rapidly and almost exponentially increased in value, making their owners and shareholders rich and creating capital for investment in more new companies in America and beyond. In 2021 it was reported that global venture investment amounted to US$125 billion, the highest ever (Teare 7 April 2021).

The news industry didn't see it coming. There was some concern in the 1990s because audiences were already declining, but with many startups failing in the dot.com bust of 1999, the sector was lulled into thinking that change would be limited. As the 2000s proceeded, however, it soon became clear that digitisation was a real threat. The new ICTs not only improved technology and equipment, they made the instruments of the business much smaller and cheaper, opening up to competition. Now, "anyone could be a journalist" and write a blog or upload information for users to view free, including the expensively obtained content of the old media. Advertisers, seeing the increasing number and types of outlets and the diverse technology they used, grew less confident in print and broadcast but were unwilling to pay the same high fees for digital media, where the multiplicity of sites and pages fragmented audiences and made it impossible to gauge effectiveness. The advertising-supported model, on which media empires had grown over the previous century and a half, had collapsed.

Those still in the industry set out on a desperate search for a "new model" that would breathe life into the media business again, and at first it seemed like a hopeless quest as more and more digital outlets provided information free. Then things took a sudden turn when a string of startups in the US began attracting big-time entrepreneurial funding. The tech blog Mashable, opened in 2005 by Scottish blogger Peter Cashmore, pulled in US$46 million in investment. The same year, society diarist Ariana Huffington and her partners set up the Huffington Post news site using unpaid writers, mainly journalists keen to get their names known and find a paying job. The outlet received US$37 million in venture funding (the partners sold it to AOL in 2011 for US$315 million). "Listicle"-site-cum-news-provider BuzzFeed, launched in 2006 by HuffPost partner Jonah Peretti, attracted investment of US$496.3 million. Others that followed included Vice Media, owner of VICE, a Canadian magazine that started out as print but moved online, which received US$1.4 billion in funding between 2011 and 2017, and Vox, a multi-outlet news platform founded in 2011 on the basis of an older site, which brought in a total of US$306.7 million in funding over the next four years. (Figures in this paragraph are from Crunchbase.)

The commercial success of these companies gave rise to the notion that "entrepreneurial journalism" was the model that was going to save the media business, though probably not the dinosaurs of the earlier period.

The nature of entrepreneurial journalism

While the new stars attracted most attention, what was emerging under the heading of entrepreneurial journalism was a whole range of media. Early analysts noted that there were two distinct new types. One was a "craft" or "storytelling" mode, where journalists focused on narrow areas of coverage, more like traditional journalism and what we would call today niche media. The other was a "service-oriented" mode, where information from many sources was transmitted via a variety of platforms and sold as variable bundles at variable prices (Sirkkunen & Cook 2012; Picard 2014), and included curation and aggregation sites (Carlson & Usher 2016). Within these categories were many different ways of setting up in the media business. Researcher Nicole Cohen (2015) says the spectrum ranged from the public's "most revered version" – "the venture capital-backed startup whiz", typically a man who moves from an established journalism career – to "the more marginalized, feminized end", that is, "the growing pool of freelance journalists, or solo operators living by selling bits and pieces of work". In between there were multiple levels of size, type and profitability.

For journalists this was a sea change. Over the previous century and a half, they had been salaried professionals whose jobs were to report and edit, and they were protected from the commercial decisions of their employers by the separation of the newsroom and the business side ("church and state"). While this custom helped discourage advertiser influence over coverage, it had its downside. Journalism academics Jeff Kaye and Stephen Quinn think it might have contributed to the failure of "old" media to adapt to the digital world:

> the commercial and editorial sides of the business had minimal understanding of each other's work and did not combine skills and knowledge to create innovative new information-related products that readers, viewers and online users would value enough to pay for.
>
> *(Kaye & Quinn 2010, 128)*

Unsurprisingly, few journalists were prepared for or even inclined towards this role. American journalist and trainer Mark Briggs, who wrote the first book on the topic – *Entrepreneurial journalism: how to build what's next for news* – said they just had to get used to the idea. "If you've worked in journalism, you probably think of money as a dirty word", he wrote. "Time to face facts: If you want to be an entrepreneur, you're going to have to make friends with money" (Briggs 2012, 34). A scary thought for many.

The classic perception of an entrepreneur is one who goes all out to make money from a new idea, attracting investment and aggressively expanding business with the goal of becoming a major company. However, the literature on entrepreneurship tells us that this is not the only definition. Kirchhoff's research found plenty or entrepreneurs who were not interested in innovation or growth and were satisfied with survival and earning just enough to cover the owner's needs (Kirchhoff 1994, 71). European academics Emanuelle Fauchart and Marc Gruber followed up by identifying three different types of company founder. There were the classic "Darwinians", whose main goal was to make money, but they also found "communitarians", who went into business because their interests were of use to the community, and "missionaries", who saw themselves as changing society (Fauchart & Gruber 2011).

So journalism entrepreneurs don't have to fit the money-minded stereotype usually connected with the startup world, something that academic studies have shown to be the case. American news production scholar Nikki Usher found that they often prefer to set up as nonprofits with the aim of using new tech capabilities and channels to challenge the traditional ways of doing journalism and to improve it (Usher 2017). That perception was reinforced by a study by two more US academics, Summer Harlow and Monica Chadha, who tried to fit Fauchart and Gruber's typology to journalism entrepreneurs in India. They found that very few suited the three existing categories at all. Instead, "[t]heir motivation for founding a startup is re-inventing journalism in a way that it maintains its original ethos yet becomes sustainable, profitable even, attracts readers, and avoid the pitfalls of mainstream media" (Harlow & Chadha 2018).

In fact, there has been scepticism about the whole idea of entrepreneurial journalism as the new way forward for the news business. Cohen (2015) comments that the "precarity" of the profession produced such a "climate of insecurity" that, in desperation, many saw "few options other than proposing entrepreneurialism as journalism's silver bullet". Fellow academics Tim Vos and Jane Singer (2016) found in a study of writings on the topic in the US media that most were positive towards it, but this was because it was seen to be the only possibility, the key to making big money again, and few discussed what the term actually meant. It remained a vague concept.

Moreover, by the end of the second decade of the 21st century, the shine of the big-time entrepreneurial stars was already fading. HuffPo had been merged as part of AOL into Oath, itself part of US media giant Verizon Media, and then was bought by BuzzFeed in a 2020 deal that gave Verizon a minority stake in BuzzFeed (Allsop 20 November 2020); both media outlets downsized their staff from 2019 to 2021 (Gabbatt 9 March 2021). Mashable got sold in 2017 for US$50 million, far less than the US$250 million it had earlier been valued at, and fell from favour with its readers. Vox and VICE were reported to be finding it hard to hit their revenue targets and shedding staff (Jarvey 8 May 2019; Hazard Owen & Scire 15 May 2020).

At the same time, confidence in new media was declining. Social media, which had become so important to the development of online news by making distribution easier and cheaper than ever before, not only grew into powers unto themselves but enabled the spread of fake news and hate speech. Audiences looked for trusted brands, helping bring about a comeback for some well-respected "legacy" media – the reliable *New York Times* made a success of online subscriptions (7 million in late 2020), *The Washington Post* revived after Amazon founder Jeff Bezos bought it in 2013, British public broadcaster the BBC became a vast worldwide commercial brand and *The Guardian*'s committed liberal views persuaded readers to support it (1 million subscribers and regular contributors at the end of 2020). They have all gone online and taken up the entrepreneurial methods pioneered by the digital-native outlets, capitalising on their longstanding reputations and professionalism. There is little difference between old and new in terms of how they operate.

The term "entrepreneurial journalism" has taken a beating in the decade and a half since it was latched on to as the future of the business. Inspired by the appearance of a few big-money outlets, it soon seemed outmoded as many non-money-minded journalism startups appeared that went on to survive well enough without becoming hugely profitable. But, even if it's lost its revolutionary shine, it remains very relevant today, something distinct from "digital journalism" or "startup journalism", which give little recognition to the importance of business. For the purposes of this book, then, the term "entrepreneurial journalism" refers to journalism startups opened in the digital era which are independent (that is, not run by governments nor largely government supported) and, as far as possible, operate as businesses and respect professional standards.

The region

Background

Communism and authoritarianism notwithstanding, all countries of the region have embraced free markets, propelling some into spectacular development. After Japan's rise to economic power in the 1960s, four other Asian countries/territories – South Korea, Taiwan, Hong Kong and Singapore – followed suit and became "little dragons" or "little tigers", reaching living standards on a par with the developed world by the 1980s. Tiny enclave Macau also grew wealthy through its casinos, and Islamic sultanate Brunei prospered from its oil deposits. Three more countries that got on the development ladder in those days – Indonesia, Malaysia and Thailand – are today middle-income states. China has had perhaps the sharpest trajectory into economic development, from the isolationist Cultural Revolution era of the 1960s to the world's hi-tech manufacturing centre today – all under a government that still calls itself communist. Vietnam, which has also remained communist, has been freed from its cold-war isolation but remains poor, though it is already following China's lead as a manufacturing hub.

The Philippines, once one of the wealthier countries of the region, declined somewhat during the 1980s, but today is on the cusp of the middle rank.

Four nations have less-developed-country (LDC) status. Formerly communist Cambodia, whose corrupt democracy has moved into dictatorship in the last two decades, is now largely reliant on China, and landlocked Laos, still ruled by a communist government and dominated by neighbouring Vietnam and China, both hope to move up to the next ranking in the 2020s. Timor-Leste, whose long war of independence from Indonesia left it in ruins, and Myanmar, ruled by its army for 50 years before opening up in the 2010s only to revert to military rule after a coup in early 2021, both seem likely to remain LDCs for the foreseeable future. For all the countries of the region, however, the COVID-19 pandemic affected economic growth.

The region has also moved firmly into the global entrepreneurial economy. Leading the way, rather unexpectedly at first, was China, where huge venture-capital-funded internet tech companies started appearing in the 1990s – Sina, Sohu, Netease and Baidu, as well as international blockbusters Alibaba and Tencent. Many more have followed, notably the late-blooming media giant ByteDance, opened in 2012 and reportedly valued at nearly US$400 billion in early 2021 (China Money AI 2 April 2021). Singapore, Indonesia and Vietnam have also developed into hubs for successful entrepreneurial startups. Gaming companies VNG of Vietnam and Singapore's Garena, now called Sea, were the first unicorns (companies valued at US$1 billion or more). Sea, which now focuses on e-commerce site Shopee, has listed on the New York Stock Exchange and is valued at US$100 billion (Le 8 February 2021). Other Southeast Asian companies that have become unicorns are Singapore-based ride hailer Grab (which has received more than US$10 billion in funding and operates through much of the region), e-commerce site Lazada, also of Singapore and now part of Alibaba ($4.2 billion), Indonesian travel company Traveloka (US$1.2 billion), as well as Indonesia's Gojek, originally a courier service but much diversified (US$5.3 billion in investment) and e-commerce site Tokopedia (US$2.8 billion), now merged into the giant company GoTo which has been valued at US$18 billion (ASEAN UP 6 August 2020; Crunchbase; Tani 17 May 2021).

Investment has come from afar – American venture capital (VC) is very active in the region, as is Japan's SoftBank – but also from the neighbourhood. China's new conglomerates have been prominent in regional startups, both in China itself and in Southeast Asia, as have Singapore's government-linked companies and the many regional family-based corporations as well as specialised investment companies. The importance of the entrepreneurial economy to Indonesia was clear when in 2019 then-newly re-elected President Joko Widodo appointed the founder of Gojek as his education minister and those of two other local startups to his special staff. The biggest year for VC funding in Southeast Asia was 2018, but after a lull due to the COVID-19 outbreak, in 2021 the press cited industry reports as saying results from the first quarter indicated that the annual figure was on track for a new record (Bernama 27 May 2021).

If economies are booming, politics has remained predominantly authoritarian. Freedom House rates much of the region as "not free" and most of the rest as "partly free", the only "free" territories being Taiwan and Timor-Leste (see

Table 1.1). China's Xi Jinping, who came to power in 2012 and extended his presidential term potentially indefinitely in 2018, carried out a purge of his opponents and has kept an ever-tighter lid on freedom of expression, even curbing the country's tech giants in 2020. Authoritarian rule spread to Macau at its official takeover in 1999 and to rebellious Hong Kong from 2020, where many opposition figures were jailed under various offences including a new Beijing-imposed National Security Law. The ruling parties of Vietnam and Laos have also firmly stifled dissent, as has Cambodia's, the formerly communist Cambodian People's Party.

Singapore's People's Action Party has monopolised power since 1959, sidelining opposition through laws and regulations. Malaysia's entrenched ruling élite, though shaken by a 2018 election loss, has moved back into position through parliamentary manoeuvring. In the Philippines, President Rodrigo Duterte, though elected, exercised a controversially personal rule marked by a policy of extrajudicial execution of people suspected of being connected with drugs. Thailand's military, which had alternated power with elected governments for more than 20 years, reasserted itself in 2014 and looked set to remain in power after winning a biased election in 2019. Myanmar started on a road map from decades under military rule towards democracy in the 2000s, with elections in 2015 and 2020 ousting military parties in landslide votes for the National League for Democracy, but found itself under the generals again after a coup in 2021. Indonesia left behind the authoritarian rule of longtime president Suharto in the late 1990s and has since established a largely democratic government though limited by Islamic fundamentalism and the continued influence of old élites.

Democracy may be in abeyance at present, but there have been many steps towards it. Genuine elections have taken place not only in the "free" territories of Taiwan and Timor-Leste but also the Philippines, Indonesia, Thailand, Hong Kong, Myanmar and Malaysia. There have been democracy victories, at least temporarily, such as Thailand's uprisings in 1973 and 1992, the "people power" movements in the Philippines that overthrew Marcos in 1986 and Joseph Estrada in 2001, the Indonesian revolt that got rid of Suharto, and the Sunflower Movement in Taiwan that led to a change of government in 2014. Many failed, though, including the 1988 and 2007 insurrections against military rule in Myanmar, the 1989 Tiananmen demonstrations in Beijing and the Hong Kong Umbrella Movement of 2014 and its successor protests in 2019–2020. But the democratic spirit remains. As the third decade of the 21st century began, youth-led pro-democracy protesters in Thailand, Hong Kong, Taiwan and Myanmar were linking up in solidarity as the "Milk Tea Alliance" and sharing tactics (Pajai 11 February 2021).

In international politics, US influence dominated the region in the period of decolonisation after World War II, especially during the Vietnam war, but China, suzerain to much of Southeast Asia in historical times, reasserted itself in the 21st century. Beijing pursues a policy of bringing Taiwan fully into its fold and, elsewhere, operating President Xi's "Belt & Road Initiative" (BRI),

TABLE 1.1 General statistics

Country/territory	Population 2019* (millions)	GDP per capita, current prices 2020† (US$)	Freedom (political rights & civil liberties) 2020#		Corruption levels 2019^	
			Score (0 free, 100 not free)	Rating##	Score (0 most corrupt, 100 least)	Rank (out of 198)
Brunei	0.43	23,120	28	NF	60	35
Cambodia	16.49	1,570	25	NF	20	162
China	1,443.78	10,840	10	NF	41	80
Hong Kong	7.44	45,180	55	PF	76	16
Indonesia	270.63	4,040	61	PF	40	85
Laos	7.17	2,570	14	NF	29	130
Macau	6.4	38,770	N/A	N/A	N/A	N/A
Malaysia	31.95	10,190	52	PF	53	51
Myanmar	54.05	1,330	30	NF	29	130
Philippines	108.12	3,370	59	PF	34	113
Singapore	5.8	58,480	50	PF	85	4
Taiwan	23.60	26,910	93	F	65	28
Thailand	69.63	7,300	32	PF	36	101
Timor-Leste	1.29	1,460	71	F	38	93
Vietnam	96.46	3,500	20	NF	37	96

Note: Figures only go up to early 2020 to avoid the distortion of the COVID-19 pandemic.

* Source: United Nations, except Taiwan, population figure from government 2019 yearbook. https://eng.stat.gov.tw/public/data/dgbas03/bs2/yearbook_eng/y003.pdf

† Source: IMF. https://www.imf.org/external/datamapper/NGDPDPC@WEO/OEMDC/ADVEC/WEOWORLD

Source: Freedom House, https://freedomhouse.org/countries/freedom-world/scores.

F = Free, PF = Partly Free, NF = Not Free.

^ Source: Transparency International's Corruption Perceptions Index 2019. https://www.transparency.org/en/cpi/2019/results/idn

offering generous financing for infrastructure and other major projects in an effort to extend its sway. An effort by Washington to form the free-trade Trans-Pacific Partnership, or TPP, was scuppered when then-president Donald Trump pulled out in 2017, but the Comprehensive and Progressive Agreement for Trans-Pacific Partnership (CPTPP) went ahead without the US in 2018 and was signed by 11 countries including Brunei, Malaysia, Singapore and Vietnam. However, the broader Regional Comprehensive Economic Partnership (RCEP), a trading pact, was signed in 2020 and due to start in January 2022. It brings together ASEAN (the Association of Southeast Asian Nations, comprising all countries of Southeast Asia except Timor-Leste), China, Japan, South Korea, New Zealand and Australia. When Joe Biden became US president in 2021, he quickly showed renewed interest in the region by forming first the Quadrilateral Security Dialogue, or Quad, with Australia, Japan and India, and then AUKUS, a security agreement with Australia and Britain.

Entrepreneurial journalism in the region

The region's press began with the newspapers of 18th- and 19th-century colonisers and missionaries, and was taken up in the late 19th and early 20th centuries by wealthy individuals as well as independence and revolutionary movements. Unlike the lucrative mass media of north America and northern Europe, where the entrepreneurial model emerged, the news industry here was generally small and élite-focused, more done for political influence than for money (McCargo 2003, 12). An effort to professionalise the press and make it into a business, led by the Press Foundation of Asia in the 1960s, foundered largely due to the high costs of production (printing technology had to be imported and newsprint was expensive), which made newspapers unaffordable to many readers. Other contributing factors were lack of trained personnel and editors' tendency to aim their outlets at older, better-off readers and "use unattractive, bombastic writing" (Lent 1982). Broadcast started out in government hands in most places, the main exception being the Philippines, though Hong Kong's official channel operates as an adjunct to the commercial stations. Dominance of the traditional media by government and ruling parties and their linked companies or by wealthy establishment figures is the norm.

Table 1.2 gives an overview of the media situation at the end of the second decade of the 20th century.

The western watchdogs, in line with the low ratings for political and civil freedoms, score most of the region's media freedom poorly. The global press freedom rankings of the French observer Reporters Without Borders (Reporters Sans Frontières, or RSF) put only Taiwan, Timor-Leste and Hong Kong in the top 100 (total: 180), while the three communist countries (China, Vietnam and Laos) are in the bottom ten. Freedom House, which no longer does a separate press ranking but assesses internet freedom for 65 countries and territories, gives low ratings all round though it excludes five places covered in this book

TABLE 1.2 Media freedom and digital development

Country/territory	Internet freedom 2020*		Press freedom 2021†			Mobile-cellular subscriptions per 100 inhabitants#			Percentage of individuals using the internet^			Social media penetration‡ Jan 2020 (%)	Facebook users 2020§	
	Score (0 least free, 100 freest)	Status**	Score (0 freest, 100 least free)°	Rank (out of 180)		2000°	2010°	2019°	2000°	2010°	2019°		Millions	% of popn§§
Brunei	N/A	N/A	50	154		29	112	133	9	53	95	95	0.40	93.0
Cambodia	43	PF	47	144		1	57	130	0	1	41+	58	7.81	47.4
China	10	NF	79	177		7	48	122	2	34	54+	91	1.33++	0.1++
Hong Kong	N/A	N/A	30	80		82	196	289	28	72	92	78	5.36	72.0
Indonesia	49	PF	37	113		2	87	126	1	11	48	64	136.96	50.6
Laos	N/A	N/A	71	172		0	64	61	0	4	26+	43	3.06	42.7
Macau	N/A	N/A	N/A	N/A		33	209	345+	14	55	86	84	0.41	6.4
Malaysia	58	PF	39	119		22	120	140	21	56	84	81	25.52	80.0
Myanmar	31	NF	46	140		0	1	114+	0	0	24+	41	22.20	41.1
Philippines	64	PF	46	138		8	89	155	2	25	43	67	71.76	66.4
Singapore	54	PF	55	160		70	146	156	36	71	89	88	4.47	77.1
Taiwan	N/A	N/A	24	43		82	121	123	28	72	89	88	19.19	81.3

(Continued)

TABLE 1.2 Continued

Country/ territory	Internet freedom 2020*		Press freedom 2021†		Mobile-cellular subscriptions per 100 inhabitants#			Percentage of individuals using the internet^			Social media penetration‡ Jan 2020 (%)	Facebook users 2020§	
	Score (0 least free, 100 freest)	Status**	Score (0 freest, 100 least free)°	Rank (out of 180)	2000°	2010°	2019°	2000°	2010°	2019°		Millions	% of popn§§
Thailand	35	NF	45	137	5	107	186	4	22	67	75	46.00	66.1
Timor-Leste	N/A	N/A	29	71	0	43	110	0	3	27†	31	0.39	30.2
Vietnam	22	NF	78	175	1	126	141	0	31	68	67	66.72	69.2

* Source: Freedom House, Freedom on the net 2020 (only 65 countries/territories are scored). https://freedomhouse.org/report/freedom-net

** F = Free, PF = Partly Free, NF = Not Free.

† Source: Reporters Without Borders, 2021 World press freedom index. https://rsf.org/en/ranking

° Rounded to nearest whole figure.

\# Source: ITU, Mobile_cellular_2000–2019. https://www.itu.int/en/ITU-D/Statistics/Pages/stat/default.aspx

⁺ 2018 or 2017 figure.

^ Source: ITU, Percentage of individuals using the internet. https://www.itu.int/en/ITU-D/Statistics/Pages/stat/default.aspx

‡ Source: We Are Social & Hootsuite, Digital 2020: global digital yearbook. https://datareportal.com/reports/digital-2020-global-digital-yearbook. NB: China doesn't allow western social media but has its own set.

§ Source: Internet World Stats. https://www.internetworldstats.com/stats3.htm#asia

§§ Percentages based on population figures in Table 1.

†† Facebook is banned in China, though it can be illegally accessed through VPNs.

including RSF's top three, while two of the three communist nations (Laos is one of the excluded) merit the lowest designation – "not free" – along with Myanmar and Thailand.

But this lack of press freedom has not prevented the region following the remarkable transformation of communication brought about by digitisation, a parallel to and partial reason for its general development. Table 1.2 shows that at the turn of the 21st century only a handful of better-off places – Hong Kong, Singapore and Taiwan – had widespread use of mobile phones and the internet, while in poorer neighbours – Cambodia, China, Indonesia, Laos, Myanmar, Thailand, Timor-Leste and Vietnam – usage was very low and in some places close to zero. However, by 2010 the field was levelling out, particularly in the case of mobile phones, and in 2019, though differences remained, everywhere but Laos had at least one mobile phone per person and the lowest internet penetration was around a quarter of the population (Laos and Timor-Leste). In eight countries/territories, including Vietnam, at least two-thirds of people were online.

There have been two keys to this turnaround.

One is the spread of fibre-optic networks. Once systems had been built in the wealthier parts of the world, the businesses laying cables naturally turned to other regions to expand. They have linked Asia to the world and brought faster connections not only to the major conurbations of the region but deep into rural settings. By 2019 there were 22 systems in our region, with 5 more planned by 2022 (Submarine Telecoms Forum 2017). These supported the massive expansion not only of broadband for offices and homes but, more importantly for the later starters, of 3G and 4G networks. A 2015 report by the mobile phone operators' organisation GSMA found that, by 2014, 3G covered 72 per cent of the Asian population, including many rural areas (GSMA 2015). By 2020, 3G accounted for less than 20 per cent of connections in the Asia Pacific, with 4G soaring to 60 per cent coverage and 5G beginning to take off, though impeded by the coronavirus pandemic (Stryjak & Pedros 2020).

The other key has been the growing availability of smartphones, which connect people directly to mobile internet using 3G and 4G, allowing latecomers to the internet to skip the broadband-desktop stage of development. Table 1.2 shows ITU figures only for mobile subscriptions, covering all kinds of phones, but it can be guessed that the smart type have taken up a majority share of the market in recent years. The fastest change came in Myanmar, which only started affordable 3G smartphone services in October 2014 and yet had 30 per cent smartphone penetration only a year later (Trautwein 20 November 2015). GSMA predicts that the region will have two of the three most-connected markets by 2025 – China (no. 1) and Indonesia (no. 3) – with neighbouring India no. 2; it estimated that these three will account for more than 40 per cent of connections in the world at that point (Stryjak & Pedros 2020).

This massive expansion in connectivity and user interface provided a perfect platform for social media to take off in our region, which caught up quickly with the rest of the world (though China bans western platforms and has its own versions). It is interesting to note from Table 1.2 that in many places the percentage of individuals using the internet is close to social media penetration – sometimes the latter are higher, probably due to different data-gathering methods – but they show how dominant social media are in online life. This has been particularly so for the younger generation, who use their access both for social connection and entertainment as well as, as researchers Lars Willnat and Annette Aw found in their Asian student survey, for political participation (Willnat & Aw 2014). Facebook stands out as more popular than all the others. Table 1.2 shows that it reaches just about every internet user, except in China. In some countries, Facebook is seen as the internet itself.

Governments' approaches to the development of digital communication have been varied. Some were determined to forge ahead in the new technology stakes, encouraging big business to get involved in the provision of telecoms infrastructure and equipment to give their populations a head start in the digital world – in the 1990s Singapore's "intelligent island state" and Malaysia's Multimedia Super Corridor were policies that committed those countries to digital advancement. But even in places that took a less proactive stance the pressure to allow their peoples to catch up on digital communication and to let business benefit from it meant that it was encouraged (Myanmar's military leaders prior to democratisation being the longest holdout) or, as in China, allowed to grow in controlled conditions. This resulted in the online media that sprang up often being able to operate without being subject to the rules and regulations of traditional print and broadcast. In many places, suppressed voices took the initiative to reach audiences directly on the internet in the 1990s and 2000s before governments had cottoned on: not only did Singaporeans and Malaysians develop opposition presences online but also the Myanmar dissident media in exile, the diaspora-supported Cambodian opposition and the Hong Kong pro-democracy camp.

That spurred officials to respond. One way was to take up digital channels themselves by modernising their outreach, with improved websites and social media presence. Another was to take legal action. Existing laws covering national security, sedition, official secrets and other matters were invoked, but almost everywhere legislation was updated or added to cover cyberspace. Defamation was extended to online communication by Indonesia's 2008 Electronic Information & Transactions Act, the Philippines's Cybercrime Prevention Act of 2012 and Myanmar's 2013 Telecommunications Act under its soon-notorious Article 66(d). Thailand expanded use of its longstanding lèse-majesté law, which criminalises criticism of the monarch, and banned online expression deemed upsetting to national security in its 2007 Computer Crime Act. Malaysia forbade "fake news" in 2018, though the law was repealed a year later, and Cambodia passed regulations at the time of the 2018 elections allowing the government to block sites deemed to be spreading fake news. Singapore passed the Protection from Online Falsehoods & Manipulation Act, or POFMA, in 2019, banning published statements that undermined national security or politics. In Vietnam, two sections of the penal code used liberally against online expression have been updated – Article 117, "propagandising against the state", and Article 331, "abusing internet freedoms" – and in 2019 the Cybersecurity Law allowed authorities to take down "toxic content".

Until recently not that many journalists have been in the region's prisons, with these repressive laws targeting dissenters in general. According to the Committee to Protect Journalists (CPJ https://cpj.org/data/), the only two countries to have journalists in jail on any scale in 2020 were China (47) and Vietnam (11) (the only other recorded figure was 2 in Cambodia. In 2021, though, Myanmar's military junta arrested 87 journalists in the four months following the February coup, charging 28 of them mostly under Penal Code Section 505(a), which criminalises comments causing fear or spreading false news (Reporting ASEAN, n.d.), while Hong Kong detained the outspoken news proprietor Jimmy Lai and five of his editorial executives on national security charges. However, governments are generally wary of arresting journalists because of the resulting bad publicity, and there are many instances of threats of legal action, accusations, charges that eventually lead nowhere, or cases where fines result rather than prison terms. Journalists also face physical intimidation, but the only place that has seen actual killings is the Philippines, with CPJ recording 9 from 2016 to 2020.

It's fair to say that journalists everywhere in the region risk crossing not only governments and unfair laws but powerful people, which can create a chilling effect on their work. However, it's also fair to say that these factors rarely stop them. The main reason is that many outlets cover topics that are uncontroversial – tech, business, lifestyle. These are also attractive to investors and advertisers and, while generally not threatening authority, can on occasion be used to address confrontational issues. For those that take up more risky remits, such as covering politics or pursuing investigative stories, reaction will depend on how powerful their support network is, often in the form of opposition parties or dissident voices. Many practise self-censorship at least for some of their coverage, risking outspoken stories only when they are really worth it, though some braver ones don't hold back and either end up as heroes, like Malaysiakini (see pp. 160–165) and others that revealed the massive 1MDB government scandal despite legal threats, or having to close, like China's Qdaily (see pp. 174–178). Nonetheless, the main reason for folding is failing to build up a good business.

There are no official figures for online media startups in our region. Some, like Malaysiakini, have been around for almost as long as the internet, but most have appeared in the last decade of digital expansion. Some are small concerns, such as Indonesia's Magdalene (see pp. 156–160) and Thailand's art4d (pp. 107–109), but others have grown into full-blown newsrooms, such as Malaysiakini, Taiwan's The News Lens and The Reporter (see pp. 187–190 and pp. 190–193) and Thailand's The Standard (pp. 196–200). For entrepreneurial journalists in the region, the situation is far from perfect, but the new tech and business milieu offers more opportunities than ever before. Some media startups are managing to take up a fourth-estate role, and even in the most controlled régimes there is space for independent, commercial journalism for those brave enough to risk it

– none of Myanmar's respected online outlets has closed despite military oppression. These and many other media startups in our region show truly extraordinary courage in standing up to authority. But many have non-controversial content, informing a niche audience or covering a non-sensitive topic. There are political risks, but this is always the case with journalism. The difference today is the real chance of making a working business, big or small, out of it.

References

Allsop, Jon (20 November 2020). The good and bad news of the *HuffFeed* deal. *Columbia Journalism Review*. Retrieved 5 March 2020 from https://www.cjr.org/the_media_today/buzzfeed_huffpost_acquisition_verizon.php

ASEAN UP (6 August 2020). The 6 unicorns of Southeast Asia. Retrieved 28th October 2020 from https://aseanup.com/tech-unicorns-southeast-asia/

Bagdikian, Ben (2000). *The media monopoly*. Boston, MA: Beacon Press.

Bernama (7 May 2021). VC funding in Southeast Asia set to see record year in 2021. Republished in The Edge Markets. Retrieved 5 June 2021 from https://www.theedgemarkets.com/article/vc-funding-southeast-asia-sets-see-record-year-2021

Briggs, Mark (2012). *Entrepreneurial journalism: how to build what's next for news*. Los Angeles, CA: SAGE Publications.

Carlson, Matt, & Usher, Nikki (2016). News startups as agents of innovation: for-profit digital news startup manifestos as metajournalistic discourse. *Digital Journalism*, 4/5, 563–581.

China Money AI (2 April 2021). China tech digest: Bytedance's valuation closes to $400bn; Volkswagen may buy carbon credits. *China Money Network*. Retrieved 5 April 2021 from https://www.chinamoneynetwork.com/2021/04/02/china-tech-digest-bytedances-valuation-closes-to-400bn-volkswagen-may-buy-carbon-credits

Cohen, Nicole S. (2015). Entrepreneurial journalism and the precarious state of media work. *South Atlantic Quarterly*, 114/3, 513–533.

Curran, James, & Seaton, Jean (1997). *Power without responsibility: the press and broadcasting in Britain*. 5th edition. London; New York: Routledge.

Fauchart, Emmanuelle, & Gruber, Marc (2011). Darwinians, communitarians, and missionaries: the role of the founder in entrepreneurship. *The Academy of Management Journal*, 54/5, 935–957.

Gabbatt, Adam (9 March 2021). BuzzFeed lays off 47 HuffPost workers less than a month after acquisition. *The Guardian*. Retrieved 8 April 2021 from https://www.theguardian.com/media/2021/mar/09/huffpost-layoffs-buzzfeed-jonah-peretti

GSMA Intelligence (2015). *Closing the coverage gap: a view from Asia*. Retrieved 10 August 2016 from https://www.gsmaintelligence.com/research/?file=e245c423854fcfd38eeae0a918cc91c8&download

Harlow, Summer, & Chadha, Monica (2018). Indian entrepreneurial journalism. *Journalism Studies*. DOI: 10.1080/1461670X.2018.1463170

Hazard Owen, Laura, & Scire, Sarah (15 May 2020). "Prior assumptions about our business no longer apply"; cuts pile up at Vice, Quartz, The Economist, BuzzFeed, and Condé Nast. *NiemanLab*. Retrieved 5 March 2021 from https://www.niemanlab.org/2020/05/prior-assumptions-about-our-business-no-longer-apply-cuts-pile-up-at-vice-quartz-the-economist-buzzfeed-and-conde-nast/

Jarvey, Natalie (8 May 2019). Disney discloses new $353 million write-down on Vice Media investments. *Hollywood Reporter*. Retrieved 15 September 2019 from https://www.hollywoodreporter.com/news/disney-posts-353-million-write-down-vice-media-investment-1209002

Kaye, Jeff, & Quinn, Stephen (2010). *Funding journalism in the digital age: business models, strategies and trends*. New York: Peter Lang.

Kirchhoff, Bruce A. (1994). *Entrepreneurship and dynamic capitalism: the economics of business firm formation and growth*. Westport, CT: Praeger Publishers.

Le, Thu Huong (8 February 2021). Vietnam's first unicorn is finally serious about its global gaming ambitions. *Tech In Asia*. Retrieved 5 March 2021 from https://www.techinasia.com/vietnams-unicorn-finally-global-gaming-powerhouse

Lent, John A.(1982). Asian newspapers: non-political trends. In Lent, John A. (Ed.). *Newspapers in Asia: contemporary trends and problems*. Hong Kong: Heinemann Asia. 1–18.

McCargo, Duncan (2003). *Media and politics in Pacific Asia*. London: Routledge.

McManus, John H. (1994). *Market-driven journalism: let the citizen beware?* Thousand Oaks, CA: SAGE Publications.

Pajai, Wanpen (11 February 2021). Junta to junta: as milk tea alliance brews in Myanmar, how far can it go? SEA Globe. Retrieved 4 March 2021 from https://southeastasiaglobe.com/milk-tea-alliance-myanmar/

Picard, Robert G. (2014). Twilight or new dawn of journalism? Evidence from the changing news ecosystem. *Journalism Studies*, 15/5, 500–510. DOI: 10.1080/1461670X.2014.895530

Reporting ASEAN (n.d.). In numbers: arrests of journalists and media staff in Myanmar. Retrieved 8 June 2021 from https://www.reportingasean.net/in-numbers-arrests-of-myanmar-journalists/

Schumpeter, Joseph (1987). *Capitalism, socialism and democracy*. London; Boston, MA: Unwin Paperbacks.

Singer, Jane B. (2018). Entrepreneurial journalism. In Voss, Tim P. (Ed.). *Journalism*. Berlin: Walter de Gruyter GmbH & Co.

Sirkunnen, Esa, & Cook, Clare (Eds.) (2012). *Chasing sustainability on the net*. Tampere: Juvenus. Retrieved 10 Aug 2016 from http://tampub.uta.fi/bitstream/handle/10024/66378/chasing_sustainability_on_the_net_2012.pdf?sequence=1

Stryjak, Jan, & Pedros, Xavier (2020). The mobile economy: Asia Pacific 2020. GSMA. Retrieved 27 October 2020 from https://data.gsmaintelligence.com/research/research/research-2020/the-mobile-economy-asia-pacific-2020

Submarine Telecoms Forum (2017). *Submarine telecoms industry report*. Issue 6, 2017/2018. Retrieved 2 June 2018 from https://subtelforum.com/products/submarine-telecoms-industry-report/

Tani, Shotaro (17 May 2021). Gojek and Tokopedia announce Indonesia's 'largest ever' merger. *Nikkei Asia*. Retrieved 5 June 2021 from https://asia.nikkei.com/Business/Technology/Gojek-and-Tokopedia-announce-Indonesia-s-largest-ever-merger

Teare, Gené (7 April 2021). Global venture funding hits all-time record high $125B in Q1 2021. Crunchbase. Retrieved 8 April 2021 from https://news.crunchbase.com/news/global-venture-hits-an-all-time-high-in-q1-2021-a-record-125-billion-funding/

Thurik, Roy, Stam, Erik, & Audretsch, David (2013). The rise of the entrepreneurial economy and the future of dynamic capitalism. *Technovation*, 33/8–9, 302–310. DOI: 10.1016/j.technovation.2013.07.003

Trautwein, Catherine (20 November 2015). Myanmar named fourth-fastest growing mobile market in the world by Ericsson. *Myanmar Times*. Retrieved 15 August 2016 from http://www.mmtimes.com/index.php/business/technology/17727-myanmar-named-fourth-fastest-growing-mobile-market-in-the-world-by-ericsson.html

Usher, Nikki (2017). Venture-backed news startups and the field of journalism: challenges, changes, and consistencies. *Digital Journalism*, 5/9, 1116–1133.

Vos, Tim P., & Singer, Jane B. (2016). Media discourse about entrepreneurial journalism: implications for journalistic capital. *Journalism Practice*, 10/2, 143–159.

Willnat, Lars, & Aw, Annette (2014). Conclusion. In Willnat, Lars, & Aw, Annette (Eds.). *Social media, culture and politics in Asia*. New York: Peter Lang. 276–299.

2
FINDING YOUR NICHE AND GETTING YOUR JOURNALISM STARTUP ON THE WAY

Introduction

With the flexibility of the internet, journalism startups can take many kinds of shape, form, size or nature, but your challenge is to find the right formula that is both different from or better than others and has a chance to find an audience in the environment you live in. You may already have a great concept, or you may have a few possibilities to try out, or you may be very flexible. Whatever the situation, some careful planning will help clarify your idea, decide how to make it work and help anticipate obstacles.

It's an entrepreneurial buzzword, but everyone needs a "niche". A French word originally meaning a cove or recess often used to display a statue, today it signifies a comfy place where your business fits snugly. Your niche could be a whole new genre or an innovative approach, but it could also be just a tiny change in the design of a site or a tweak in distribution methods, just doing something a little different from what is already being done to give you an edge in the market. Once you've decided on your niche and what you're going to do, you must quickly get your content into place and distribute it.

Motivation, values and mission statement

Thinking about your reasons for starting up and the principles behind your work will ground your business, helping refine your niche and guiding your operation. This reflection will provide material for your mission statement, which can be clearly posted on your site to inform readers what you stand for.

The first step is to address the kind of journalism you want to do. Malaysiakini (see pp. 160–165) emphasises in its "about us" page its commitment to independence: "We achieve this independence by allowing editors and journalists the full

DOI: 10.4324/9781315270432-2

freedom to practise professional and ethical journalism, without interference of the shareholders, advertisers or government". Frontier Myanmar, on its equivalent page, says it is "an unbiased voice" to "inform and entertain" with "high-quality journalism" and aims to be balanced in the country's polarised market: "We focus on delivering fresh, in-depth reporting from all corners of Myanmar, making space for a range of voices and opinions, and setting high editorial standards, while seeking to bring unheard and moderate voices into the national dialogue" (see pp. 131–135). Indonesia's IDN Times, founded and run by brothers Winston and William Utomo, is one of the country's most successful outlets for young people (see pp. 143–146). The siblings have a long, clear mission statement on their "about us" page where they lay out their vision – "to democratize access to accurate, balanced, useful, and positive information and ultimately, to become the voice of millennials and Gen Z in Indonesia and bring positive impacts on … society."

The next step is to consider your own values and goals. In Cambodia, businessman Chy Sila, who founded Sabay ("Happy"), suffered through the country's decades of genocide and war, and now his mission is "to make people happy", especially the younger generation. "We really want to make a difference, we want to change, in a positive way", he says (see pp. 178–181). For IDN Times's Utomo brothers, equality and diversity are key. On their "about us" page they lay out "eight values that we believe in", which are "gender equality, unity in different races and ethnicities, unity in different religions, unity in different worldview, anti sexual harassment, anti bullying, anti stereotyping, and redefining beauty". Fellow Indonesian outlet Magdalene (see pp. 156–160) similarly wants to make society more inclusive:

> Magdalene is a manifestation of our vision of online media that offers fresh perspectives that transcend gender and cultural boundaries. We accommodate the voices of feminist, pluralist and progressive groups, or anyone who is not afraid to be different. We want to be a bridge, not hostile.

In Hong Kong, Will Cai Hua, founder of The Initium, wanted his publication to be a Chinese equivalent of *The New York Times* for Chinese people everywhere outside China (see pp. 181–184). The site's high specs include a toggle function between simplified and traditional characters so that it can be read by all.

Finally, financial goals need attention. You may be in this business to make good money but even if you aren't you shouldn't forget about it. British researcher Andrew Youde (2017) reminds us that "making a profit" should be on the list of aims and objectives of any small startup, otherwise it's not going to grow. Your ideas on this will inform your business plan (see below).

Finding your niche: audience and field of coverage

Media economist Robert Picard points out that the financial control of the industry originally lay with journalists, but in mass media days it moved into the hands of investors and advertisers. Today, however, with the huge choice of information sources, it is the audience who are in charge (Picard 2010, 70–73). The most crucial aspect of your business is making it attractive to users, who will be your key to making an income.

General news may be the most obvious option because it will appeal to a broad range of people, but few startups can survive on it. Many established outlets are already doing it well and it's costly to keep enough staff to be able to compete. That's not to say it's impossible. A number of outlets covered in this book have made a go of it: Malaysiakini, The Malaysian Insight (see pp. 184–187), The News Lens (see pp. 187–190), IDN Times and many more Indonesian startups cover news or some aspect of it. But they all had a head start, whether being early on the scene or filling a gap in mainstream media or aiming at a different audience. DAP News in Cambodia got off the ground running by beating the opposition on the story of the day (see pp. 128–131). The Myanmar media that grew in exile during military rule in the 1990s and 2000s could supply news the government outlets were ignoring, but once back inside the country from 2012 the competition among private daily media all covering the same stories was cutthroat while the official outlets undercut everyone on price, creating a funding crisis. One experienced Cambodia journalist learned the hard way: he set up a daily news site with very good intentions but just couldn't generate enough stories on his own to keep going. Luckily for him, his old job welcomed him back.

So what else to cover? Picard points out that journalists must provide value for their audience, who will lose interest otherwise. "Value is created by news products that inform, entertain, and stimulate, but also by providing audiences with knowledge and understanding that helps in decision making and solving the challenges of their lives and professions," he says (Picard 2010, 60). Good advice comes from Jeff Kaye and Stephen Quinn, writing in 2010 but with equal relevance today.

> [A]udiences appear most willing to pay for content that is *unique* and not readily available elsewhere …; is *fresh and frequently updated*; is *authoritative* and comes from a *trusted* source in a relevant *niche* area; and is *actionable*. With the last point, the story must help the reader *make or save money, improve their professional career or health, or develop a personal interest such as a hobby*.
>
> *(Kaye & Quinn 2010, 71; my italics)*

This can be done in several ways. One approach is to seek a particular section of the population that is not otherwise well served by media. For many startups that demographic is the younger generation – millennials, Gen X, Gen Y, Gen Z – who before the digital age were largely ignored by the media. Sabay and IDN Times, as well as fellow Indonesian outlet Hipwee and Thai news site The Standard (see pp. 196–200), have tapped into younger people's vibe by providing novel and light-hearted news via mobile phones using infographics and video.

That can be combined with extending geographical location. Indonesian outlets are now vying to attract young people in areas beyond Jakarta and Java, people who previously had little choice of media. In China, aggregator Qutoutiao – "Fun Headlines" – is using artificial intelligence to provide personally targeted entertainment for the younger generation in "Tier 2" and "Tier 3" cities who are less well served than their counterparts in the major metropolises.

Another approach is to seek more focused audiences. Singapore's theAsianparent serves an international audience of young middle-class families, and its parent company has attracted more than US$7 million in funding, while in Beijing, True Run Media, founded by an American resident, produces two outlets for the same kind of audience in English and Chinese. International site Coconuts targets the young, international English-speaking set in the region's major cities (see pp. 124–128). In Myanmar, Frontier made it its business to attract foreign resident professionals and educated local people who appreciated investigative journalism and were willing to fund it. No startup aimed at the older generation was found in the region, but it's not an impossibility. In the US, the AARP (American Association of Retired Persons) is one of the country's most profitable media companies, top in audience for print and digital magazines with 38.6 million readers bringing in ad revenue of more than US$174 million annually (Fischer 12 November 2019). The "boomer" generation may not be so apparent in Asia, but with median ages in populations in the region easing upwards it is a potential market.

Then, as Picard points out, there are two tried-and-tested ways to find niche audiences: localisation and specialisation (Picard 2010, 117).

The first has come to be called "hyperlocal". This is one of the buzzwords of the entrepreneurial journalism revolution: many local traditional media have declined due to digitisation, leaving a gap that can be filled by a variety of online outlets. Kaye and Quinn point to the possibilities: hyperlocal reporting can combine professional and amateur journalism, can use data such as maps and records and can "create highly relevant local news for residents in small, specific geographical areas" (Kaye & Quinn 2010, 46). It can even bring a bit of power to neighbourhoods. Janet Jones and Lee Salter (2012, 100) write about how hyperlocals in Britain became more daring than traditional journalists and challenged authorities, rectifying the bias of official public relations information. This kind of outlet exists in our region – even Vietnam and China have very active blogospheres. One challenge for a business venture of this type is the competition from social media, where groups can be set up for communities of any size, from a whole town to a single building, run by an administrator who invites posts from participants and does it all free. However, you can trump such groups by providing professional journalism covering local events and people, making money out of advertisers in the area.

As for specialisation, there are two areas that have provided niches and sub-niches and sub-sub-niches for journalism startups the world over. Both are politically non-sensitive and have income potential.

The first is tech. With new ICTs, products are being developed and brought to market frequently, each supposedly better than the last, and it's not only investors who are looking for information but consumers in their millions. Indeed, early star Mashable covered tech news, and one of the original big-time entrepreneurial media today in the US is TechCrunch, whose founder Michael Arrington made its name when he got the scoop on Google's YouTube purchase in 2006; the company was, like HuffPost, bought out by AOL in 2011. There are many such outlets in our region. Singapore-based Tech in Asia calls itself "the largest English-language technology media company that focuses on Asia". Founded in 2011 on the basis of an earlier site, its prospects were so good that, according to its Crunchbase entry, it attracted six rounds of funding totalling US$17 million up to 2017. At that point it experienced difficulties, but was reported to be back on track by 2020. In Thailand, Blognone, built up by engineer Isriya Paireepairit, grew from a hobby blog in the early 2000s to the country's top tech site and is now part of star startup Wongnai (see pp. 110–112). Stratechery is a one-man site run from Taiwan by American Ben Thompson, whose insights from long experience working for the tech giants in the US make his industry newsletter attractive to subscribers.

The other hit topic is business. The legacy media that survived the digital downturn best were in this area – *Financial Times*, *The Wall Street Journal*, *The Economist* and the agency Bloomberg. All charge their readers for access and give little or no information away. Because of these behemoths, which cover not only international but local business, it's difficult for a small startup to compete, but again there are sub-slices of subject areas that can provide meaty content. e27, founded in Singapore in 2007, has a niche focus on the region's entrepreneurial startups. It received a total of US$3.5 million in investment between 2013 and 2016 and appeared to go through troubled times at that point, but is now back on its feet. DealStreetAsia was the brainchild of Joji Philip, a business journalist from India who followed his wife when she was posted to Singapore; he sought a gap in the market for a new online media outlet and decided to target an audience of investors with a narrow focus on business deals. Assembling a staff of freelancers across Asia, he launched in 2014, attracted capital investment and sold out in 2019 to the Japanese giant Nikkei Inc., owner of the *Financial Times*. Meanwhile, Qdaily of China rose to success by zoning in on news about the world's top tech companies, widening their net as their audience grew (see pp. 174–178).

There are also many special interest groups, whether hobby or professional, which could support a media outlet. One such covered by research for this book was Thailand's art4d, an architects' magazine started as print in the 1990s for the well-off design sector and used many innovative means to get its audience on board. In the same country, film journal Bioscope, set up by two leading lights in the industry as a classy print outlet, attracted a good audience of movie buffs. Its eventual takeover by a TV station helped it go online but with the world of film being turned on its head by streaming services it couldn't survive and closed in 2020 (see Chapter 8 pp. 1–3).

Another direction is to focus on a kind of journalism that will produce original stories of general interest. Many journalists long to do in-depth and investigative work that can make a difference to people's lives. However, it takes not only money but time to produce this kind of work, so it's difficult to get a reliable stream of content, and your reporting can get you and other people into trouble. It will bring in an audience, though, and the key is to secure funding. The Reporter of Taiwan has made a success of it (see pp. 190–193), while Hong Kong Free Press (see pp. 139–143), Hong Kong Citizen News (see pp. 135–139) and another Hong Kong outlet, FactWire, also do exposés, and all are donor-funded. Another type is data journalism, which uses the mass of public information available online to produce original stories. This needs some technical resources and skill, but the business can be spun off into profitable private contracts that involve processing and presenting data. In Indonesia, Katadata has made numbers its business (see Chapter 8 pp. 3–7), as has Lokadata, once an independent site but taken over by a local conglomerate (see pp. 153–156), while in-depth outlet Tirto has a supporting number-crunching company in Binokular (see pp. 202–205).

Building your brand

When Google and Facebook appeared, their names didn't seem like names at all. They were awkward, childish and meaningless, very unlike those of the staid companies of the past whose names came from their function or their owners (e.g. General Electric Company, British Telecom, Bertelsmann). The new names emerged with the entrepreneurial era, identities for Kirchhoff's (1994) "ambitious" or "glamorous" companies that would disrupt the world's economy. The cue was taken by the Chinese tech giants – Netease, Tencent, Alibaba, Bytedance and so on. When the new entrepreneurial journalism outlets appeared in the US, they chose names that were catchy and cool: HuffPost, Mashable, BuzzFeed, Gawker, TechCrunch, Slate, VICE, The Verge and more.

Many wonderfully quirky names can be found in our region. Some have little meaning. With Hong Kong's 100 Most, the latter word is a near-transliteration of the original Chinese word (meaning "hair"), a reference to the 100 focuses listed in each issue, according to its Wikipedia entry. Similarly nonsensical is the Singapore blog Yawning Bread. China has Ciwei Gongshe (Hedgehog Commune – see pp. 122–124) and Huxiu ("Tiger's Sniff"), the latter apparently an allusion to an English poem. Others contain some reference to their content. Taiwan had Media Farmers, where readers could go to "water" news "plants" to make them grow (it hasn't survived ...). In the Philippines, Bulatlat is a special word with no equivalent in English – its meaning is explained on p. 112. Malaysia has Cilisos, the Malay spelling for chili sauce, a nod to its hot and spicy information (see pp. 118–121). Meanwhile, Coconuts is a light-hearted reference to the regional fruit and its insinuation of being a bit crazy. Hong Kong's The Initium came from the Latin for "the start", which, according to Wikipedia, refers to Mencius's idea that, "The sense of concern for others is the starting point of humaneness".

But for more serious outlets conventional names are just as acceptable, especially with the legacy media making a comeback. That kind of name gives a sense of reliability and trustworthiness. In our region, Malaysiakini (meaning Malaysia Today), China's Jinri Toutiao (Today's Headlines), international outlets Asia Times and The Diplomat (see Chapter 8 pp. 13–16), Thmey Thmey (New News) of Cambodia (see pp. 200–202), Taiwan's The Reporter and The Standard of Thailand have followed that trend. Going a little further with their focus are the multi-sited The News Lens and The Malaysian Insight, which looks behind the news. Business and tech sites tend to reflect their subject matter, examples of the former being Caixin (Economic News Fortune) and DealStreetAsia, and, of the latter, Tech in Asia, the Philippine gadget site Unbox and Thailand's Blognone.

Then there are names that show your mission: VERA Files (Truth Files) in the Philippines (see pp. 206–210), Prachatai (Free People) of Thailand, Frontier Myanmar, Hong Kong Free Press and Hong Kong Citizen News. Others depict the cause they represent. Magdalene, a serious outlet for women, refers to the maligned follower of Jesus Christ, Mary Magdalene, and New Naratif (see pp. 169–174) aims to publish new and different in-depth content. Hong Kong's Passion Times and Stand News are outspoken supporters of democracy. Thailand's Isranews Agency (see pp. 146–149) and Indonesia's Tirto are named after revered national journalists. Other names derive from a place, usually a whimsical reference like Saigoneer, Urbanist Hanoi and Mekong Review (see pp. 165–169), which cover lifestyle and literature. But there's also The Irrawaddy, set up as an exile outlet in Thailand using the old spelling for Myanmar's main river and not changing, despite pressure from the authorities, to its military-created replacement, Ayeyarwady. Other names indicate soft lifestyle content – Singapore's TheSmartLocal (see pp. 194–196) and Cambodia's Sabay ("Happy") and Khmerload ("Khmer download") (see pp. 149–153).

Before you make a decision on a name, check not only that it isn't already in use but that it resonates in all the languages your audience may know. This can be done with an ordinary internet search, which should cover all the languages you are using, but ask friends or contacts to check on idioms and slang. An internet search should also be done to check for names that are similar.

Once you have your name, you need to get it known. US researcher Cohen (2015) emphasises that "self-marketing" is a key strategy for entrepreneurial journalists to build their brand. This may not sound palatable to people with a long journalism background – surely a good outlet will stand on its own merits without commercialisation? In the era of entrepreneurial journalism it very likely won't: media sites can't expect people to intuit their existence, recognise what they are and find them without guidance. Those in business advocate "product thinking", that is, treating your journalism as if it were any other commodity for sale. In the US, Northwestern University's Knight Lab has written a series of articles encouraging this approach. "Finding and maximizing the audience for our product is no longer the job of other people, like marketing and circulation departments", writes Professor Rich Gordon. "Now it's journalists – social media managers, audience development specialists, engagement editors, etc – who are doing the equivalent work on digital platforms" (Gordon 23 November 2020).

Convert your mission, values and goals into promotional content for use on your site and in your communications of all types as your own brand. Devise a short description of your outlet and design a logo. Build a contact list and start sending out information (for newsletters, see below pp. 94–95). Attend every event where you might come across people who can help you get the word out.

Research

Indian journalist Mudit Mohilay wrote in Tech in Asia about how he rushed into his sixth startup – all five earlier efforts had failed – with an idea for a news-in-brief site called The Clippings. He set it up quickly, using a group of interns, and then found not only that the model he was using was unsuited to the market but another company was already doing pretty much the same thing. His startup collapsed, leaving him in debt (Mohilay 14 December 2017).

First job: check out the competition. You can do this with a basic keyword search and a look at index sites like Alexa and Similarweb, which offer free trials. What you find should give you some idea of what's already working well and show you how to position yourself in the market. If you find a very similar site, you will need to work out if there is space for the two of you or whether you need to make some adjustments or move to a Plan B. Other possibilities are to try to outdo the competition or cause enough disruption that they buy you out, possibly making you a profit.

Next do a little market research. Even a very informal poll among friends and relations can help because they are likely to tell you what they think. If you have access to a wider audience, such as students or colleagues, or if you already have a contact list, try a survey. "One quick question" via email or social media or in an online meeting will likely get a good response. Choose the question carefully so that it's attractive to answer as well as useful to you. To take it further, use an online questionnaire service like SurveyMonkey, which is well-recognised by users. Draft your questions with even more care. They should be simple and thoughtful and should anticipate all possible answers. Make them clear and ensure they focus on the points you want information on because it's very easy to lose track. Keep question numbers down so you don't burden your respondent, and give a time estimate; people are more likely to do a two-minute task than a ten-minute one. For those who complete the questionnaire and pass it on, you can offer a small reward, such as merchandise, if you have it, or an online voucher or discount coupon or access to your product. It's a good idea to test-run the survey with a few people you know well enough to give you initial feedback. However, while the results of your research may be useful, don't assume that everything is true – people change their minds – or that the information is scientific.

A survey of this type serves as a point of contact with your audience, or potential audience, rather than a supplier of factual information.

Another way to test the waters is a trial run. Post some of your work to a social media platform either under your own account or under one set up for your own outlet, or to a blog service or third-party site provider, or even set up a basic website of your own. You will not only be able to gauge reaction but to find people who are interested in you. Rodolfo Rico, who worked with a Latin American media accelerator called Media Factory, advises: "Before you develop a perfect product, test interest in the idea. In the digital world, trying is cheaper. Create a landing page for your idea, invite people to register and learn about it", and then use the feedback to decide whether to launch or not (Rico 2014).

With so much information and so many decisions to make, another useful research tool at the preparatory stage is brainstorming. Throw around ideas with your partner or team, if you have them, or with family or friends or with other professionals. You should limit this circle if your idea is original and promising, but if you are happy to discuss it, or if you are at a very nascent level, you might look further afield. Of great help to this process are events where people with experience in the field give talks or seminars. Splice Media are very good at this, inviting speakers from all over the region to their Splice Beta events with the aim of inspiring media startups. Originally held in Chiang Mai in 2019, in 2020 the coronavirus outbreak forced it to move online, and the founders put on a whole month of talks, which are available online free (see Chapter 8 pp. 9–13).

Content sourcing

It's easy to forget, with so many other things to think of, that getting publishable material is one of the most challenging aspects of a media startup. Anyone setting up a journalism outlet must be careful to choose not only content that will attract an audience and bring in an income, but must be consistently gettable. While Ariana Huffington had a phalanx of willing writers to provide endless good content without payment when she started Huffington Post, few journalists today are willing to work for nothing. For most news startups, budgeting for a team of reporters and editors, however small, is basic to ensuring new and original content of a professional standard.

Your full-time team can be supplemented by outside journalism. Most outlets take the services of freelancers, that is, professionals who work on their own. They may operate their own sites but live by selling their work to others, usually by the item but sometimes on a retainer that covers a period of time. They provide a way to supplement regular staff and to extend and diversify content, especially if you have a wide remit, such as those covering the whole of Asia – Asia Times has 100 experienced freelancers on its books and The Diplomat has about 30 part-timers and a similar number of freelancers. Mekong Review survives entirely off a group of highly regarded contributors. You could also do deals with other publications that complement your coverage, especially if your sites use different languages and you have translation capacity.

Another potential outside source of quality content is the big international news agencies. They charge high fees for their very professional services but may do a deal for at least part of their feed for media startups. The French news agency Agence France Presse has supplied some outlets in our region but the concessionary fees are still not cheap (details of cost are not made public). The Thomson Reuters Foundation, which has a team of 55 full-time journalists and 350 freelancers covering under-reported stories round the world, lets small media use its content by arrangement, as does the Global Investigative Journalists' Network (GIJN). Other major international news media credited by startups in our region include the BBC, Japanese news agency Kyodo and Germany's broadcaster Deutsche Welle. The problem with this kind of arrangement is that the same stories are likely to be published elsewhere.

With so much information available online today, it's possible to find content by searching social media or community platforms. While much of what appears in these places is reposted from other sites, you might spot original material that is suitable for you. However, republishing needs care. Copyright holders must agree and be acknowledged and, in some cases, paid, and there should also be rigorous checking for accuracy and originality. In 2020 the sprawling US-based community site Reddit partnered media monitoring site NewsWhip to help make its content searchable for journalists (Carey-Simos 30 September 2020). NewsWhip and others also offer paid search services for social media platforms, which may be worth exploring if you have enough money. All too often, however, the speed and ease of taking material from other sites without any formal arrangement is tempting, especially if the story is good or you lack content from elsewhere. For a discussion of ethical issues, including plagiarism, see Chapter 6.

An alternative to professional reporting is User Generated Content, or UGC. In the form of "citizen journalism", or "anybody can be a journalist", or "community journalism", this was one of the biggest innovations of digital communication, a potential new media democracy. Popularised by Dan Gillmor's 2004 book *We the media: grassroots journalism by the people, for the people*, its underlying point is that the audience have more knowledge than journalists do. It envisaged people without journalism training using technology to make up for their lack of professional knowledge and skills. The main problem with putting it into practice was that it was difficult to make money from (Jones & Salter 2012, 51).

The earliest successful UGC site was OhmyNews of South Korea, whose motto was "Every citizen is a reporter". Founded in 2000, it attracted up to 14 million hits a day and was heralded as a new model for journalism. Four-fifths of its content came from its 700,000 users, and they were paid according to reader feedback, though amounts were small. At one point it even had an international site in English with 6,000 uploaders. It wasn't entirely UGC: the amateur content had to be professionally overseen and edited by a staff of journalists, and these professionals also provided the rest of the stories. It brought in good income, mainly from advertising, and became profitable from 2003. However, the Global Financial Crisis in 2008 caused it to lose advertising and, with losses mounting and many new competitors in the field, it closed the English site and moved to a subscription model (Jones & Salter 2012, 51–52; Kaye & Quinn 2010, 75–77).

UGC still presents one of the easiest ways to get affordable content, if you can handle it. It seems like a slam dunk: the audience know the kind of information they want and will have an interest in providing it. But it's not that simple. A German study found that readers were interested in UGC when it came from knowledgeable people, and they still valued professional journalism on regular topics (Zeng, Dennstedt & Koller 2016). Moreover, UGC nearly always needs professional monitoring and editing not only to make it presentable but to ensure it is accurate and is not publicity material, propaganda or, worse, fake news or hate speech. Indonesian sites are particularly keen on UGC – Hipwee claims 50 per cent of its content is from users, and IDN Times almost as much. In both cases, the strategy is to nurture talented content producers rather than random postings, and, as with OhmyNews, edit the work before publication. IDN already has some automation and is hoping to use AI for the full process. Any plan to ask for reader contributions needs careful preparation to specify standards and ensure they are respected.

Business model and business plan

Anyone who starts up a journalism outlet has to think about the business model it's going to run on. Picard (2011) gives a definition for this very vague term:

> Business models conceptualize the underlying business logic of an enterprise. They reveal company competences, how a firm creates value through its products and services, what sets it and its offerings apart from the competition, how it undertakes its operational requirements, how relationships are established and nurtured with customers and partner firms, and how it makes money.

In other words, how all aspects of your startup dovetail to work financially. Besides your goals, your audience, your resources, your distribution methods, your team and its skills, your business model needs to take into account the business and media climate, the financial situation, the tastes of your audience, local trends and even unexpected conditions, as the coronavirus pandemic has made us aware.

One important business model for startup media is the nonprofit. This doesn't mean not making a profit – indeed, it's vital to make more revenue than expenditure – but that all profit goes back into the company rather than to owners and shareholders, who would expect interest or dividends as a form of return on investment. In some countries, this is a kind of charity status, allowing donations to be exempt from tax, which encourages people to give more. Thus in the US you find highly respected media like PBS, ProPublica and the International Consortium of Investigative Journalists that support themselves through public donations and grants from foundations. Business experts are sceptical of this model. Picard (2014) acknowledges its usefulness in reducing pressure on making a profit and allowing community media to produce content that is not commercially sustainable, but he points out that nonprofits have to face the same market conditions as anyone else and their lack of business acumen may mean they operate ineffectively. Donations and grants are often one-offs, too, rather than regular income. Kaye and Quinn (2010, 54) wonder how nonprofits can develop a sustainable business model that doesn't rely on continuing donations.

In most territories in our region, nonprofit charity status is generally not available for media, and tax exemptions are rare, but a number of journalism businesses operate in effect as nonprofits. Most prominent is The Reporter of Taiwan, which is under the auspices of a foundation. Others include the Philippines's VERA Files and Bulatlat, as well as Prachatai of Thailand. Hong Kong does provide the option of registering as a "company limited by guarantee", that is, it is owned by guarantee holders who are not entitled to any of the profits, though there is no tax exemption for donations. Hong Kong Free Press and Hong Kong Citizen News have registered this way – Daisy Li Yuet Wah of HKCN calls her outfit a "social enterprise". New Naratif of Singapore has registered in Britain under a similar status. All are still surviving several years on, showing that the nonprofit model can be sustainable in certain circumstances. Alan Soon of Splice Media, however, feels that commercial is the way to go: "You know, we're proudly for-profit because we want to demonstrate that if you can find a community to serve, in a space like media, you can build something that's monetisable."

As you start out your startup, a business plan will be necessary to give both yourself and those you want to do business with (such as investors or donors) an idea of how you will survive financially. Andrew Youde (2017) helps with the types of expenditure you need to consider. "Fixed" costs remain the same however much business you're doing. They include office rent, insurance and utilities. "Variable" costs are those that depend on the amount of business being done, and cover such items as salaries, journalists' time working on stories, travel costs and freelance payments. Other variables appear as you grow: sales and marketing (including web hosting and content promotion), loan financing, professional services (accountants, solicitors, copyright protection) and general office costs.

The difficulty with media is that forecasting when your product is journalistic content seems little more than crystal ball gazing. The best way to go about it is by researching media sites that are running well – look at the examples in this book, ask friends in the business or find info online. For advertising income, you can check with social media and ad companies (for more on this, see Chapter 5). What you must build is some reasonable evidence that your business can be a going concern. Once you've made some estimates, aim in your calculations for a "break-even point", which will show when you can start to make a profit. Jumpstart magazine gives a formula: total fixed costs divided by contribution margin, which is the sales price per unit less the variable cost per unit. To make it work you must include all costs you expect to run up (Ravi 24 March 2021).

Finally, a "SWOT" analysis of your planned business can help identify promising aspects and stumbling blocks. On paper or screen divide a square into quarters and label each with one of the "SWOT" components: Strengths, Weaknesses, Opportunities and Threats. Poring seriously over this diagram and doing some brainstorming will force you to consider all aspects of your proposal. The process should result in your being able to capitalise on the positive aspects and deal with the negative ones. Again, this will help in any submission you make for funding of any type.

There is nothing to stop you changing your plans or even your whole business model as you move forward – many outlets researched for this book did so. And it's worth working on a Plan B and even a Plan C so that you are prepared for change when the need arises.

Distributing your work

If marketing your brand is important, successful distribution is essential. Today search tools and social media make digital distribution and audience accumulation possible. Their complex algorithms will bring your posts to the attention of people who are interested in your kind of content worldwide and provide the means to keep getting your work out, not to mention help you make money.

According to the Reuters 2020 digital news survey, Facebook is the most popular social media channel for news in the five territories of our region it looked at, coming top in Hong Kong, Malaysia and the Philippines and second in Singapore and Taiwan (Newman 2020). It is used by diverse audiences – young and old, all educational levels, all communities. Its importance became clear when it cut news story sharing in Australia during the 2021 spat over a new law requiring it to pay news companies: traffic inside the country dropped by 15 per cent immediately (Benton 18 February 2021). But other social media attract more specific audiences. Instagram, used for news in all five territories Reuters surveyed in our region by 8–20 per cent of respondents, focuses on pictures and is becoming more popular among millennials for news. Microsoft's LinkedIn is for the business community, Google's YouTube (also scoring well in the Reuters survey) is for videos of all types, Bytedance's TikTok (known as Douyin in its home country, China) is for short videos and appeals to a very young audience (Instagram Reels has been introduced as a competitor). Twitter is less popular in our region than in the west, but is used by many journalists, who can often be important in passing on your work to others.

If you just send out your work in these ways it will spread "organically", that is, by natural sharing, and the key is to have a good following. If you want greater reach, you can pay for distribution services. You can "boost" posts on Facebook, Instagram and Twitter to send your item out to a wider suitable audience – chosen by the platform but which you can specify to a certain extent, with more options on Facebook than the others. Since the costs depend on what options you choose, it's worth checking first with the channel to see what they're going to charge. Instructions can be found on the relevant platform "help" sites.

Facebook also offers Instant Articles, "a faster, Facebook-native way of distributing the content that publishers already produce for their own websites", according to the platform. If you sign up for IA, you format your articles as HTML documents (you can add your own design, make templates and so on) and they will, after scrutiny for banned content and posting via IA, load four times faster on a click than they do via a web link and, according to the platform's introduction, be 44 per cent more likely to be opened. You will have to submit ten articles for review first to get approval, but there is no cost. However, IA's added speediness and accessibility come at a price because there is no external link, meaning your customers stay in FB and need not go to your own site at all.

Instant messaging channels often bring in people who use digital less because you can use them on pre-3G phones. Once you have formed a group, content can be posted in much the same way as on social media, but it is more targeted. WhatsApp (maximum number for a group: 256) is the most used in general in the region bar China, where it is banned. The Reuters survey finds it the most popular of the social media and messaging systems for news in Singapore and second in Hong Kong and Malaysia, while Facebook's other channel, Messenger (up to 250 in one group), was used by a third of respondents in the Philippines and 8–11 per cent in the other four territories. Line, the messaging app that came out of the 2011 Fukushima tsunami, is used in Taiwan (where, according to the Reuters survey, it is the most popular) and parts of Southeast Asia and can accommodate up to 5,000 group members. Signal (maximum 150 in a group) and Telegram (up to 200,000) are good for more sensitive information because their privacy is very strong. Because of its huge numbers, the latter has been much used by protest channels such as Hong Kong's LIHKG, though the difficulty in controlling membership may lead to security being compromised.

Stories can be posted on multiple social media, but should be tailored to each one in ways that will suit the audience and lead them to seek out more of your work. For Facebook, pictures are important, but text is just as much part of it. A study reported in late 2020 found that posts that displayed the story and allowed you to click on it to go to the site did better than those with just a photo and a link (Kalim 11 November 2020). For Twitter you need some short, attention-grabbing hashtag words and an intro line, while for Instagram and YouTube obviously visuals come firs, and for TikTok some entertainment value is important. TikTok has its own "university" page with instructions on how to get started. YouTube has its Creator Academy with instructions on how to set up your own channel.

If you're in China, western social media are prohibited but there is a dizzying array of local possibilities. Tencent's WeChat is by far the most versatile, working like a combination of Facebook and WhatsApp with its own payment facility. Started as a messaging app in 2011, it was originally a more secure means of communication than other forms, but has since become just as subject to surveillance as any other. But, with WeChat's success, many more have followed suit to offer you similar ways to get your work out, including the Twitter-like Weibo, the question-and-answer site Zhihu, aggregator Jinri Toutiao, Douyin, Tencent's video platform Youku and so on. It was in China that Chaping found a clever method of distribution based on timing: founder Tao Weihua posted just one article a day, releasing each on the dot of one minute to midnight, keeping his audience waiting for his words of wisdom until the very last minute of the day (see pp. 115–118).

In the case of search engines, the challenge is to get your content to pop up at or near the top of any relevant search – in practice, on Google because it is by far the most-used search engine, with more than 90 per cent of searches done through its portal (Statcounter November 2020). Thus search engine optimisation or SEO, in which key words in a piece of work are identified as likely to be sought in search queries, has become a major factor in content creation. You can do it yourself with help from Google's own instructions (on its developers' site), which go from beginner to advanced, while outlets like Moz, Yoast and Search Engine Watch (the marketing industry go-to) provide a lot of helpful free information as well as paid services. Today most content management systems (CMSs) include SEO, doing part of the brain-numbing work for you, and Google gives it free if you use its AMP (see p. 72), though you still need to experiment with choices. You do this by writing different headlines and keywords for a story and seeing whether they come up when you enter search terms. Whichever method you use, don't delay because it can take between one and six months for Google to implement the process.

Users found through SEO are likely to be more valuable than those found through social media because they are actually looking for something specific – they have "high intent" – rather than just roaming for information. Analytics specialist Parse.ly shows in its 2020 report that referrals through search went up by more than 50 per cent over the year while those from social media dropped – Facebook was still in the lead but its share declined (What's New In Publishing 17 March 2021). Moreover, the unreliability of Facebook's algorithms has made SEO more interesting to journalists, though of course Google can change its algorithms too. Google has become more journalist-friendly by highlighting original reporting in its searches through its "beyond the headlines" link on its news page to bring up original and investigative journalism (Guaglione 18 November 2019). Hong Kong Citizen News, which has its own data-savvy tech contractor who can do the work and automate the process, prefers SEO to get both stories and pictures known. This gave them an advantage over other news sites in 2018 when Facebook changed its algorithms to downplay news. "We noticed that there was a certain percentage drop [in] referrals from Facebook", said chief editor Daisy Li. "But they were up triple from SEO."

One more way to get your work distributed is to partner other people, sites or institutions. The Asia News Network includes at least one news outlet, in most cases the leading English-language daily, from every country in East and Southeast Asia. Started and partly supported by the Konrad Adenauer Foundation of Germany, it provides a network of otherwise unconnected media who can share their stories. Although the group is closed, other similar sharing partnerships can be set up via funders or journalism organisations. This can work well when stories are local but have human interest appeal or need translating.

Writing newsletters has become one of the most important ways to get your work out to readers, and is addressed below in Chapter 6. But it's worth starting out early on with this method to bring yourself close to your audience. As you build up contacts through social media and other means, such as a "sign-up" form on your site, you can provide a more personalised message to your readers via email, which has now returned to prominence as a way to keep in touch. In line with the traditional newsletter, sent out to a specialist audience for a fee, it can even become your whole product, like tech blog Stratechery of Taiwan.

Getting ready for business

It's important to consider how to make your business legal. If you're starting at a very basic level and making little or no money, especially if you are still working in another job and just posting on social media or a blog platform, you won't need to do anything. But once you start to make an income you will have to register as a company to make sure you can get bank accounts to facilitate payments. There may be a choice of company type as in Hong Kong (see above) or there may only be a commercial option. Also in many places in our region you have to register as media with the government as well. If there is any doubt, consult an expert.

References

Benton, Joshua (18 February 2021). In Australia, Facebook's ban on sharing news stories has sent publishers' traffic tumbling. NiemanLab. Retrieved 20 March 2021 from https://www.niemanlab.org/2021/02/in-australia-facebooks-ban-on-sharing-news-stories-has-sent-publishers-traffic-tumbling/

Carey-Simos, George (30 September 2020). Reddit partners with NewsWhip to help journalists and media uncover great stories. WERSM. Retrieved 5 November 2020 from https://wersm.com/reddit-partners-with-newswhip-to-help-journalists-and-media-uncover-great-stories/

Cohen, Nicole S. (2015). Entrepreneurial journalism and the precarious state of media work. *South Atlantic Quarterly*, 114/3, 513–533.

Fischer, Sara (12 November 2019). The boomers' media behemoth. Axios. Retrieved 24 February 2020 from https://www.axios.com/the-boomers-media-behemoth-412b5106-f879-477d-806d-6130148956bf.html

Gillmor, Dan (2004). *We the media: grassroots journalism by the people, for the people.* Sebastopol, CA: O'Reilly Media.

Gordon, Rich (23 November 2020). Yes, product thinking can save journalism. Six reasons why news media need product thinkers. Knight Lab. Retrieved 20 March 2021 from https://knightlab.northwestern.edu/2020/11/23/product-thinking-can-save-journalism-product-management-news-media

Guaglione, Sara (18 November 2019). Google news feature to spotlight in-depth articles. *MediaPost*. Retrieved 17 December 2020 from https://www.mediapost.com/publications/article/343471/google-news-feature-to-spotlight-in-depth-articles.html

Jones, Janet, & Salter, Lee (2012). *Digital journalism.* London: SAGE Publications.

Kalim, Faisal (11 November 2020). Publishers could be "missing out on valuable reach and traffic": links posts outperform photo posts on Facebook, study finds. Whats New In Publishing. Retrieved 17 December 2020 from https://whatsnewinpublishing.com/publishers-could-be-missing-out-on-valuable-reach-and-traffic-links-posts-outperform-photo-posts-on-facebook-study-finds/

Kaye, Jeff, & Quinn, Stephen (2010). *Funding journalism in the digital age: business models, strategies and trends.* New York: Peter Lang.

Kirchhoff, Bruce A. (1994). *Entrepreneurship and dynamic capitalism: the economics of business firm formation and growth.* Westport, CT: Praeger Publishers.

Mohilay, Mudit (13 December 2017). What I learned about market research after my 6th startup failure. Tech in Asia. Retrieved 9 November 2020 from https://www.techinasia.com/talk/no-market-research-sixth-startup-failure

Newman, Nic (2020). Reuters Institute digital news report 2020. Reuters Institute for the Study of Journalism. Retrieved 18 July 2020 from http://www.digitalnewsreport.org/

Picard, Robert G. (2010). *Value creation and the future of news organizations: why and how journalism must change to remain relevant in the twenty-first century.* Lisbon: Formalpress/MediaXX1.

Picard, Robert G. (2011). *Mapping digital media: digitization and media business models.* Open Society Foundations. Retrieved 30 September 2016 from https://www.opensocietyfoundations.org/reports/digitization-media-business-models

Picard, Robert G. (2014). Twilight or new dawn of journalism? Evidence from the changing news ecosystem. *Journalism Studies*, 15/5, 500–510.

Ravi, Reethu (24 March 2021). Break-even analysis: how to figure out whether your startup will be profitable. *Jumpstart*. Retrieved 30 March 2021 from https://www.jumpstartmag.com/break-even-analysis-how-to-figure-out-whether-your-startup-will-be-profitable/

Rico, Rodolfo A. (2014). What I learned as a media factory entrepreneur. IJNet. Retrieved on 20 March 2020 from https://ijnet.org/fa/node/1798

Statcounter (November 2020). Search engine market share worldwide. Retrieved 15 December 2020 from https://gs.statcounter.com/search-engine-market-share

What's New In Publishing (17 March 2021). Parse.ly's 2020 content analytics report: what publishers need to know. Retrieved 20 March 2021 from https://whatsnewinpublishing.com/parse-lys-2020-content-analytics-report-what-publishers-need-to-know/

Youde, Andrew (2017). The business of journalism. In Marsden, Paul (Ed.). *Entrepreneurial journalism: how to go it alone and launch your dream digital project.* London; New York: Routledge. 22–39.

Zeng, Michael A., Dennstedt, Bianca, & Koller, Hans (2016). Democratizing journalism: how user-generated content and user communities affect publishers' business models. *Creativity and Innovation Management*, 25/4, 536–551.

3
MONEY TO START UP

Introduction

The job of this chapter is to look at methods of getting funding to start your outlet off. They run from the very basic – using your own money – to investment of various sizes and types to crowdfunding and donations. These methods may also be used for financing further down the line.

Bootstrapping, aka self-funding

This is the quickest startup route, especially for keen journalists with less interest in business. It's simple and cheap, doesn't bother anyone else and you have complete control. You can win yourself a following on social media or third-party platform like Medium or Substack (see pp. 73–74) or by using the free version of a content management system to set up a site (see pp. 53–55). That won't cost you more than your time and the price of your phone or laptop and internet connection. This route is appealing for those who have already made their name in the profession, but it's also attractive for beginners who need to get a foot on the ladder while holding on to their day job until they have found the right formula. It takes hard work, dedication and enthusiasm to go it alone, but perhaps that's all you need to make a business work.

Minh Bui Jones, long a journalist in Australia, set up the quarterly Mekong Review in 2015 almost on the spur of the moment when a literary festival in Cambodia opened a chance to launch the kind of publication he'd been mulling for some time. Sales from the first print issue funded the next and it's still going today on subscriptions and sales (see pp. 165–169). If you have some of your own savings to plough into your venture, even better. In Taiwan, The News Lens's founders Joey Chung and Mario Yang couldn't find a funder when they planned their outlet so they put in US$100,000 of their own money for the launch. Once they had something to show, investors were much easier to find (see pp. 187–190).

Avoid using consumer debt. Most banks in our region are loath to lend to small businesses and are even less keen on media, so it's hard to get a loan anyway. Credit cards allow easy debt but impose high interest rates on borrowing beyond the repayment deadline. Loan company interest rates are prohibitive. If you need money and your idea has potential, it would be better to check out the options described below. Finding the resources to launch and expand is not too difficult in fact, and opportunities for big-time support become possible.

Investors

Angels

Hong Kong venture capitalist Derek Kwik characterises angel investors as "FFF" – "friends, family and fools" – that is, anyone willing to take a punt on you out of love, trust, pity or sheer recklessness. You can expand the pool beyond your own circle by joining networking groups to seek out other monied risk-takers. Usually this type of investment comes early in your startup's days, that is, as seed funding, and is small-scale, at most US$125,000. It may be a gift but for those seeking returns it can be in the form of equity (a share in your company's ownership) or debt (a loan), and the terms are very easy. Leadership expert Derek Lidow (2014, 51) points out that some major American companies started out on family funding, naming computer maker Dell, Bill Gates's Microsoft and Turner/CNN (set up by Ted Turner but now part of WarnerMedia, owned by communications conglomerate AT&T).

Kwik points out the advantages of angel funding: it materialises quickly, has few complexities and is flexible enough to support diverse situations. Moreover, the investee has control of the money, has few conditions to fulfil, and may not be pressed for results. "At this seed level stage, the investor most likely does not have a controlling stake in return for their investment so they are really just coming along for the journey", says Kwik. He notes the downsides too. First, the amount is usually too small to cover anything beyond basic setup costs, so further input will be needed for growth, probably from other sources. Second, there is rarely any value-added in the form of the advice and expertise professional investors supply, albeit as part of their plan to make money out of you. Third, it could lead to tension in your relationship with the investor and others close to you. An "angel" may become distinctly unangelic on seeing their investment decline, and if a loan is involved may want the money back sooner than planned. Overall, Kwik recommends, for entrepreneurs in general as well as for media startups, that you use your own savings and angel investment to start with because they will get you going so that you have something to show to more serious investors.

Some of the outlets interviewed for this book started off with angel support. Will Cai Hua, founder of The Initium, an in-depth news outlet in Chinese for

Chinese outside China, has been happy to plough a reported US$11 million of his own money into the project (see pp. 181–184). In Malaysia, journalist Jahabar Sidiq started up The Malaysian Insight with S$1.5 million (US$1.1 million) from his friends – "people I went to school with", he says. He calls the input "debt-equity", that is, if he can't pay them back they can take over his business, but that hasn't happened yet (see pp. 184–187). Cambodian-American educator Quach Mengly was happy to fund the startup in 2012 of Thmey Thmey, a news outlet that has become successful due to its credibility; he dropped out later to start up his own TV station but the outfit has been able to replace him with other investors, though they won't identify them (see pp. 200–202).

Venture capitalists and other investors

As noted in Chapter 1, it was venture capital that kickstarted the entrepreneurial era for media. In today's startup world, VC is the engine for fast-track company growth, and it's becoming a way of life: Crunchbase reported that in 2020, despite the pandemic, global venture funding was 4 per cent up on 2019 (Teare 13 January 2021).

VCs are professional investors who establish funds comprising their own and/or other people's money to invest in young companies they think have a chance of "disrupting" an industry. It's a high-risk strategy. Figures commonly cited have 80 per cent of VC-invested companies failing completely, with most of the rest doing no more than covering their costs. What makes it all worthwhile is the tiny percentage that do make money and particularly the even tinier proportion of "home runs" that really make the big time. American and European VCs invest in our region, but there are also many from within the region itself. Some are the vehicles of family-owned companies or big corporations like Japan's SoftBank, others are the corporate venture capital (CVC) arms of state-owned enterprises (SoEs), such as those in China, which are investing all over the world, but also in Southeast Asia, led by those of Singapore's "government-linked companies" or GLCs (Widyasthana 15 December 2020).

The investment process has a formal structure. It starts with seed funding, and, if that works well, moves to a number of investment rounds – series A, series B and so on, perhaps as far as series G or beyond – each one increasing in value as the company grows. The goal for "exit" is the IPO (Initial Public Offering), when the company launches its shares for sale on a stock market and "goes public", allowing anyone to buy its equity. This process may bring a windfall to the founders and investors. More recently an alternative has become popular, the Special Purpose Acquisition Company, or SPAC, where a well-trusted team raises funds for an IPO for a shell company and then looks to acquire another company to put into it. This is quicker than the regular IPO and has a built-in investor base (Metinko 3 December 2020), though is not yet popular in Asia.

VC investment is usually made in return for a stake in the company, but can also be in loan form, known as venture debt. The latter gives the investee the advantage of keeping control of the startup, but the money must be repaid with interest even if things go wrong. The equity option does mean handing over part of your company, but your partners will likely help you develop it and in troubled times can't ask for their money back. Most deals are structured to release the investment in tranches on the achievement of agreed milestones as the company develops.

The term "incubator" for an early investor came about at the beginning of the internet boom when there were no mature startups. The value of this type of investment would be up to US$1 million, comprising capital and other resources such as mentoring time, office space, products and services. As the startup scene flagged, the term "accelerator" appeared, referring to an investor who would put in a larger value – US$1 million to US$2.5 million in cash and resources – to boost a startup towards new rounds of financing and even to an IPO. But, says Derek Kwik, investors were often too trusting of startups and, as experience built and they saw how often failure came about due to poor execution, they became more cautious. With startups flooding the market, cash is handed out with greater caution and services figure more prominently in deals these days. "This has been an evolution of sorts", says Kwik. "Now investors and startups are both smarter and the transactions are structured to manage the inherent risk." While companies tend to favour investment at different stages of company growth, with bigger investors coming in on later rounds as the investee becomes more valuable, the incubator/accelerator difference has become blurred.

There are many ways to link up with investors. Check Crunchbase to see who has invested in media in our region, enquire through personal contacts or specialist sites, such as e27's Connect, which is accessible through subscription. You can also find networking events in most major cities. Putting your idea to them might be just a matter of catching someone's attention with a quick, catchy description – the "elevator pitch" that sums things up in a punchy way – but you may be invited to give a formal presentation. Some pointers for this appear in Box 3.1.

BOX 3.1 MAKING A PITCH

If you're seeking funds from an investor, a donor or the public, you're going to have to show them what you're doing and why they should support you. This will be your business plan presented as a pitch deck. The "elevator pitch" gives you only a couple of minutes to make your case, which is a good exercise in prioritising your information.

1. Your pitch should be tailored to each funder you approach. Do your due diligence on your target supporters. What is their main business? What do they normally invest in? What stage of a company's development do they prefer? For instance, according to a Technode article, the

> Chinese tech giant Tencent, a big investor in this region, focuses on gaming, but outside this sector will take only a 20 per cent stake in a company. Moreover, they generally go for early-stage investment in mature markets but in Southeast Asia prefer larger companies at a later stage (Udemans, Cohen & Artman 13 January 2020). If your project suits your potential funder's profile, emphasise its fit; if it's outside their normal remit, work on persuading them to make an exception.
> 2. You should cover your strategy, financials, marketing plan and so on, but focus clearly on what you're offering and why it's going to be successful (i.e., who is going to use your product and how you'll get an income). You should also be clear about what you want. Although the disruption so loved by entrepreneurs is more and more difficult to bring about as markets get saturated, emphasise what is new and different in your niche. You should also show that you and your team are capable of executing your project.
> 3. Use good presentation skills. These are useful for so many areas of study and work that you probably shape up well already. If you use a slide deck, make sure the design is simple, the important ideas stand out and that there is not too much detail, especially if you don't plan to use it (but have everything at your fingertips in case a question arises and perhaps provide a printed report). Avoid technical language or jargon; if you have to use it, explain it clearly. Prepare well so that you can spend more time looking directly at your audience – do not read off the slide. If you provide your deck in .ppt or .pdf format, make sure all the information is visible and all your links work.
> 4. Act naturally. "Tell a story", says Hong Kong venture capitalist Derek Kwik, who has read upwards of 15,000 business plans. "Everyone wants to hear a story, not a presentation." That can also be done informally – a chance meeting, an invitation to coffee, a follow-up online video chat – to give yourself more opportunity to get your idea over.

China and Southeast Asia are hot regions for VC investment, but, with governments sensitive about news and journalists less interested in making big money, news media are not often the target of major investors. In China the big sums have gone to platforms, including ByteDance's short-video app Douyin and its Tencent-backed rival Kuaishou, as well as ByteDance's news aggregator Toutiao and its competitor Yidian Zixun, now also a unicorn. Journalism outlets that do attract funding are usually those covering non-controversial areas and with diverse means of making money. An example is Hupu, a sports information company that also does entertainment, retail and much more and is a partner itself in a sports investment fund. It has had at least five funding rounds totalling nearly

US$332 million, according to Crunchbase. However, the tech giants also invest in new media and there are smaller investors who have also stepped in, though, as the cases of Chaping and QDaily (see pp. 115–118 and 174–178) show, not always without problems.

In the rest of the region, the main scene for major media investment is Indonesia, with its huge pool of previously underserved young people. The digital media market took off in the 2010s, with local investor GDP Venture taking the lead in buying out some companies and investing in others. Established (traditional) media conglomerates are close behind along with overseas investors from Singapore (including Willson Cuaca's East Ventures, also a big investor in Tech in Asia and scores of other companies in the region) and elsewhere, including German conglomerate Bertelsmann's Asian investment arm and China's ByteDance. The financial interest in the country's media has led to a very competitive sector, with new sites setting up their own specialist outlets to compete for valuable niche audiences via a variety of platforms. Singapore has three standouts – Tickled Media, Tech in Asia and e27 – which have had investment from the government and other local investors as well as from around the region. Meanwhile, Taiwan's VC-funded media outlet, The News Lens, was on Series D in 2020, bringing its total investment to US$13 million – after its initial failure to attract any funding at all.

In the other countries and territories of our region, media markets are more sluggish due to government pressure, slow economies or saturation, so VC-funded outlets are rarer. Entertainment site Khmerload of Cambodia has managed to start down the investment path, though its CEO, In Vichet, acknowledges that it's not easy. "Some venture capitalists are not very keen on media … because they say it's hard to get a good exit", he says. His businesses, both media and other arms, have now had three rounds of funding from US-based VC 500 Startups (a massive fund that has also invested in Vietnam's Saigoneer and Hong Kong's 9Gag meme site and has two regional sub-funds, 500 Durians for Southeast Asia and 500 TukTuks for Thailand), a new Phnom Penh-based (but Singapore-registered) investor called Belt Road Capital Management and Thai TV conglomerate True (see pp. 149–153).

Not all companies reach IPO status, and only two media companies that have done so in our region were found. One was Indonesia's Arkadia Media, which has a stable of outlets headed by news site Suara.com, and went to IPO in 2018; in 2020 it received investment from the Media Development Investment Fund (see below). The other was the quirky Most Kwai Chung of Hong Kong, which puts out 100 Most. Set up in 2010 as a print magazine distributed through convenience stores, it had one outside investor, a local newspaper that took up 10 per cent of its equity, and became highly popular with the younger generation, supporting the Umbrella Movement in 2014. It opened new outlets as it grew. It became known for its creative advertising, including a coffee ad with local superstar Leon Lai Ming. In 2018 it registered in the British Virgin Islands and went to IPO in Hong Kong, where it was 2,900 times over-subscribed – a record. The company made HK$53.5 million (US$6.86 million) from the exercise and reported good profits in 2019, though its share price had dropped at the end of 2020 (Li 25 June 2016; He 28 March 2018; Most Kwai Chung share offer prospectus and 2019 company report).

There are other exits. One is to be sold to another company – Thailand's Blognone and Bioscope did this (see pp. 110–112 and Chapter 8 pp. 1–3), also Singapore's DealStreetAsia, bought by Nikkei. However, the most common result for media is a company that continues to operate efficiently and keeps its investors as shareholders.

Specialist investors

Three American-based investment outfits specialising in media development are active in our region. Two are "impact investors" – interested not only in making money but in doing some social good. The other is an investor that offers a lot of value-added in expert support. Their terms are less demanding than regular VCs and they are often in it for the long haul, but they still insist that their investees stay on track to get their business in order and make money.

Media Development Investment Fund (MDIF)

This was founded in 1995 as Media Development Loan Fund (MDLF) by Serbian editor Sasa Vucinic (now of North Base Media – see below) and the late *Washington Post* journalist Stuart Auerbach. "Together they had the idea of launching a 'media bank' to help journalists in countries with a history of media oppression build sustainable news businesses, strong enough to stay independent of governments, political parties and oligarchs," says the website. The Fund is registered in New York as a not-for-profit corporation with public charity status and is overseen by a board of directors with seven members, all with media and/or investment backgrounds. Its 39 staff are headed by CEO Harlan Mandel. Today MDIF calls itself an impact investor.

Like most VCs, MDIF gets its resources from other investors. The outfit has strict rules for its funders: they must have a good reputation, follow a set of ethical guidelines and not expect undue influence over decisions. Thus most investors are foundations, government aid agencies and ethical funds from the US and Europe. The site lists "a selection" of 18, including Hungarian-American hedge-fund billionaire George Soros's Open Society Foundation (OSF), eBay founder Pierre Omidyar's Luminate (see below), the Swedish development agency SIDA and its Swiss counterpart SDC, US-based sustainable investor Arjuna Capital and German gender-focused nonprofit Dreilinden. Investors can put their money into a specific MDIF fund (two were current in early 2021 – the MDIF General Fund and MDIF Media Finance – and another, the private-equity Emerging Media Opportunity Fund, EMOF, closed in 2019) or they can buy flexible "Free Press Investment Notes" or lend directly to MDIF on negotiable terms. MDIF doesn't reveal its full list of investors, nor does it say how much each has put in or got back. Figures on its site show that by the end of 2020 it managed a portfolio with US$114-million-worth of assets and had returned US$57.4 million to investors.

MDIF works in developing and less-free countries in Latin America, Africa, Eastern and Southeast Europe and Asia. Its site says that up to 2021 it had invested US$240 million in 128 independent media businesses in 44 countries "where access to information is under threat".

One of its major schemes in our region was the SIDA-funded Myanmar Media Program (MMP), started in 2015 and renewed in 2019 to run to late 2022. Reported to have had US$2.4 million in its first term, it supported a dozen national and local outlets "with intensive mentoring and various forms of tailored technical assistance aimed at improving their business and management capacity". In the second term it added to the programme "two dozen" more outlets on a "less intensive" basis. However, the MMP had to be abandoned after the February 2021 military coup. Its initial success led to the setting up in 2019 of the Southeast Asian Technical Assistance Initiative, or SEATAI, a business coaching scheme funded by Luminate (see below).

MDIF also has a long history of supporting individual media. This has mainly been in the form of equity investment, often long-term – it invested in Indonesia's independent radio network KBR68H from 2000 until exiting recently, has held 29 per cent of Malaysiakini's shares since 2002 (see pp. 160–165) and, according to news reports, invested through EMOF in Arkadia Digital Media to the tune of US$750,000 with an additional loan of US$250,000 (The Jakarta Post 12 July 2020). MDIF's site says it is currently investing in the Cambodian Center for Independent Media, an independent online and radio news provider, as well as Philippine social news network Rappler and three Indonesian outlets: legal information provider Hukumonline, data-crunching outlet Katadata (see Chapter 8 pp. 3–7) and Arkadia's news outlet Suara.com. In 2021, MDIF Ventures was launched as an angel fund with Asia as a focus.

The value-added that MDIF brings to its investees, according to its director of communications Peter Whitehead, is a team who provide "intensive management advice assistance" – one-on-one consultancy, group training, workshops and conferences – carried out by their in-house experts or, if they can't cover an area themselves, outside professionals. "We aren't always looking simply to get the maximum financial return", Whitehead said in an interview. "We bring specifically … a media strategy. Whether it's, say, ad sales or it's product development, it would be very much focused, because our experience is only in media."

Any media outfit in the region that fits the entry criteria – in short, being independent, legally registered and supportive of democratic principles – can apply. What MDIF is looking for when considering applications, says Whitehead, is a commitment to business: "We very much want to work with organisations that actually want to become a self-sustaining entity". Even if an outlet is run by a top journalist it will get rejected if it can't develop a workable business plan, though MDIF can help with one if necessary. Although this section is about launch funding, MDIF prefers applicants who have a track record of a year or so. However, it does consider promising new startups, and will provide grants and assistance to help them get to a point where they are ready for investment (this was the situation with Magdalene of Indonesia – see pp. 156–160).

North Base Media

Like MDIF, NBM is a media-focused investor based in the US and was founded by Sasa Vucinic, but that's just about all the two have in common. NBM is very much the new kid on the block (founded in 2014) and it's much smaller, with only five staff. Vucinic is a managing partner and his co-founder and co-managing partner is Marcus Brauchli, a long-time *Wall Street Journal* correspondent and editor and former *Washington Post* editor. Stuart Karle, a lawyer who was COO at Reuters, is general counsel, while Turi Munthe, who once led the photojournalists' network Demotix, is venture partner; an admin person completes the staff. Its focus is on emerging markets but it has invested in the US and Japan, and it's interested not only in all kinds of media outlets but in media tech startups as well, companies that will help deliver content to audiences in an optimum way on new platforms.

NBM operates like any other VC. "We're not saying, you know what, we'll settle for low returns because we're doing good for the world", Brauchli said in an interview.

> When we bring in investors we say to them, you can expect competitive returns ... We think that what we're doing has an inherent social good, but we don't want anybody thinking that they're putting money with us and they're going to get lower returns.

NBM's own investors are mostly media-connected: Graham Holdings (which formerly owned *The Washington Post*), Bloomberg Beta (the VC arm of Bloomberg), Singapore Press Holdings and NZZ (publisher of the Swiss newspaper Neue Zürcher Zeitung), as well as some wealthy media-connected families. NBM doesn't publish details of its finances, but DealStreetAsia, a former recipient of its funding, said in 2019 that the firm's second fund had reached a first close at US$15 million (Nguyen 12 April 2019).

The outfit got started when Vucinic went to Washington to apply for support from the International Centre for Journalists for a planned crowdfunding platform. Brauchli was on the ICFJ board and thought the proposal was too narrow. He met Vucinic for coffee "and the more I talked to him, the more I thought, well, this is an underutilised asset ... We can do something big and different." Brauchli himself had some entrepreneurial experience when he was posted to Shanghai in the 1990s and, with a couple of friends, set up a bar that spun off an internet company (one of their investors was Victor Koo, the founder of YouTube/Netflix lookalike Youku, which grew into a giant and got bought out by Alibaba). It was against the rules for *WSJ* journalists to run an outside company so Brauchli had to get out, but on his return to the US he spent some time in Silicon Valley talking to people involved in tech startups. He saw the US as a saturated market and knew more could be done in other parts of the world.

NBM may not be an impact investor officially, but its operations gave them a chance to do some good anyway. "For me the attraction of doing this isn't really so much about trying to be a businessperson and make money, it's more about using capital to create new things", Brauchli says. "I'm much more interested in creating things that have impact and that are successful and serve needs and create useful products or engaging products for people. High quality. To me, that's the mission." The value-added NBM brings is the experience of its founders: "We offer guidance and ideas and connections", says Brauchli. They can put their investees on the other end of the phone with some of the biggest names in western journalism.

You can't apply to NBM – if they're interested, they will find you. "What we do is we scour for what we think are the most interesting media companies in places ... where people are just getting access to smart phones and data", says Brauchli. They prefer countries with bigger populations, and India has become an investment focus for them, with Vucinic moving to Mumbai. As a small company they keep costs down by investing lower amounts in early-stage startups. "We're not majority owners of things", Brauchli goes on. "We take minority stakes ... We don't come in at a later stage because when they get successful, they need more money, and then we stop being useful to them."

North Base's investment in TheNewsLens seems to break some of those rules. Taiwan has a small population and NBM funded the outlet not only at the start but carried on through to Series C, though by then as one of many participants. Brauchli notes that TNL has been singularly successful: "I think you can safely say ... a significant portion of people under 30 in Taiwan look at The News Lens at least once a month". The fund has also invested in the Philippines' Rappler, getting in before Omidyar's fateful investment (see below) – NBM did due diligence and followed regulations to ensure its deal was legal, Brauchli says, and has had no trouble. Other companies it's invested in are the millennial-attracting IDN Media of Indonesia (see pp. 143–146), which, Brauchli points out, already has an audience half as big as *The Washington Post*'s, and DealStreetAsia, which it exited on the site's sale to Nikkei in 2019.

Luminate

An impact investor like MDIF, Luminate is not a separate entity but part of the Omidyar Network, the foundation started by eBay founder Pierre Omidyar and his wife Pam. ON's mission is to help create "new models, tools, ideas and policies that build power for everyday people, strengthen communities, and promote a society in which we all can thrive as equals", according to its website. To this end it has a hybrid structure, being both a limited liability company and a private philanthropic foundation, and can give grants to and invest in both for-profit and nonprofit organisations. Pierre Omidyar has a special interest in media. He once ran an investigative news outlet in Hawaii, and his company First Look Media helped finance and produce *Spotlight*, a film about the *Boston Globe*'s investigation into the Catholic church's sex abuse scandal; it won the Academy Award for best picture in 2016. ON has also supported the International Consortium of Investigative Journalists (ICIJ), which has produced revelations about the hidden wealth of the rich and powerful through the Panama Papers, Paradise Papers and Pandora Papers. Omidyar also set up The Intercept, a hard-hitting journalism site led originally by investigative journalist Glenn Greenwald (Sullivan 4 April 2017).

Once an ON department, Luminate was spun off in 2018. It is overseen by a board headed by Pierre Omidyar and is run by Stephen King, a former director of the BBC's media foundation arms. Helping the media is only one of its jobs – its other specialist areas are civic empowerment, data & digital rights and financial transparency. It has, according to its "about us" page, "supported 296 organisations in 17 countries with over $378 million in funding". The reason for hiving it off, according to King in an interview published in Alliance Magazine, was to focus more on supporting freedoms at a time of growing authoritarianism and to provide programmes that were more tailored to individual situations (Milner 26 March 2019).

Luminate has the same dual structure as its parent, allowing it to both invest for profit and give grants. According to its website: "Common types of funding we have used in the past include but are not limited to: unrestricted and restricted grants, direct equity, deferred equity instruments such as Simple Agreements for Future Equity (SAFE) or convertible notes and debt". Grants may be given to media outfits when they can do public good, according to the site, but "[w]e are also interested in for-profit investments in media organisations developing new, scalable business models that will improve their sustainability and remove reliance on advertising". Luminate goes further than other supporters in that it will also get involved in "strategic litigation" and go into partnerships with international organisations to protect freedom of speech and of the press.

In our region, one of Luminate's biggest media investees has been MDIF, to whom it gave US$645,234 for its SEATAI programme in 2020 (see above). Otherwise most support has gone to Myanmar: a total of US$940,000 went to the Yangon School of Journalism between 2014 and 2019, another US$250,000 went to the Poe Pyin Programme, a British government-funded NGO that made a TV series to raise rights awareness, and an undisclosed sum to the online news magazine Frontier Myanmar (Luminate doesn't reveal amounts given to for-profit outlets). The only other individual media beneficiary in the region has been Rappler. That investment, amounting to US$1 million and made by ON before Luminate was set up, got the Philippine online outlet accused of having foreign ownership, which is forbidden (Hepworth 16 January 2018); Luminate ended up donating the money to Rappler.

Like NBM, Luminate does not accept unsolicited applications. "We identify potential partners through our own research and diligence, plus our extensive global network", it says on its website. It takes into consideration the fit with its goals and values and with the diversity of its portfolio, as well as how well the target organisation functions and how effective it is.

Crowdfunding

With crowdfunding, many supporters donate small amounts that can add up to a large sum. Like the kinds of investment mentioned above, it is possible to raise funds this way before or at the launch of your startup, or a little way down the line, and the exercise can be repeated. The main thing is to have a niche where there is a desperate need for information. A crowdfunding exercise will give you a good idea of how well-liked you are, and, if you are well-liked, it may allow you to proceed without having to seek out investors. The Press Gazette of the UK calculated that from 2012 to 2021 the 30 most successful crowdfunded journalism projects raised US$21 million between them (Majid 22 January 2021). Only one, however, was in our region – Hong Kong's Factwire. In fact, only Hong Kong outlets have made this method work on any scale in our part of the world, though it may be possible for nonprofit media in other places to try it out.

The two established international crowdfunders that support journalism are San-Francisco-based Indiegogo and New York-based Kickstarter, founded in 2008 and 2009, respectively. In 2020, Kickstarter said on its site that 19 million people had pledged a total of US$5.4 billion for 192,506 projects through its mechanism, while Indiegogo claimed to have 9 million backers in 223 countries and territories who had raised more than US$1 billion for 650,000 projects.

Kickstarter is particular about the projects it supports – they must create something to share with others, they cannot be charities, they cannot offer equity – and its aim is getting startups on the way rather than raising continuing funding. It does have journalism as one of its focuses, however. According to a NiemanLab report, it has a journalism support team to help with campaigns, though few projects raised more than US$100,00 and over half got less than US$10,000. The star was Britain's Tortoise, specialising in "slow journalism", which brought in US$585,000 (Schmidt 5 November 2018). The platform is officially only open to Hong Kong and Singapore in our region, though in late 2020 it listed nearly 200 journalism projects in Asia, most for travel journalism and one-off documentaries. Indiegogo is more flexible. It allows all kinds of fundraising, including for charities and for equity, and supports applicants with a variety of help from before the campaign until way past its finish date. It has been particularly active in China (Wiggers 9 January 2019).

What's very worthwhile about these sites for anyone setting up a business is the huge amount of advice they provide. Kickstarter's "creator handbook" and Indiegogo's "essential guide to crowdfunding" are goldmines of general tips on fundraising strategies, team building, connecting with your audience, budgeting, timing and so on. Two things to remember, however: platforms take a fee (Kickstarter 3–5 per cent, Indiegogo 5 per cent) as well as up to 5 per cent for payment processing, and if you fail to reach your target your money may be returned to donors.

Crowdfunding for media has had its problems. Three American media-specialist platforms – Spot.US, Contributoria and Beacon – failed in 2015 and 2016 (DeJarnette 3 October 2016). Then in 2018 came one exercise that caused donors to question the whole idea. The innovative Dutch news site De Correspondent, which had started in 2013 and made its income from its 19,000 members at home, mounted an international crowdfunding campaign to raise US$2.5 million for a global English-language version called The Correspondent, apparently to be based in the US. To cover the cost of the exercise, it received US$1.8 million from Luminate (see above), a Dutch foundation and the philanthropic vehicle of Craigslist founder Craig Newmark. In the US it was boosted by high-profile figures in journalism, and in just 30 days donations amounted to US$2.6 million. But in 2019 the company announced it would appoint only one full-time journalist in the US and not set up an office there. That news disillusioned its American supporters. The outlet apologised and offered refunds, saying the initial plan to set up a US newsroom had been changed but the decision was not communicated. The English site opened in September 2019 from its base in Amsterdam but closed in late 2020 (Engaged Journalism Accelerator n.d.; Goligoski & Pilhofer 24 January 2019; Hazard Owen 17 September 2019; Hazard Owen 10 December 2020).

There are now many crowdfunding platforms in our part of the world, but journalism is an unusual area for them to cover. However, Hong Kong's Fringebacker, which was founded in 2013 and has raised money for projects from an Antarctic expedition to a candidate for chief executive, has provided a way for three media outlets to raise startup funds.

The investigative news agency Factwire set up its first Fringebacker campaign in 2015 before launching, raising US$600,000 plus, more than one-and-a-half times its original goal. Founder Ng Hiu Tung, an award-winning journalist who had worked for local media including the main commercial TV station TVB, says that this large sum allowed the outlet to give fair salaries to its ten journalists at a time when media pay was going down in general. Factwire published a string of exposés, such as the appointment of officials to semi-government bodies without proper procedure, problems with a new air traffic control system at Hong Kong's international airport and bid-rigging in the construction industry. FactWire raised two further crowdfunded rounds in 2017 and 2018 and has moved to a subscriber model.

Hong Kong Free Press is another Fringebacker success story. Its founder, Tom Grundy, ran a blog called Hong Wrong and saw the need for an independent English-language news outlet at a time when student protests in the Umbrella Movement of 2014 were generally covered in a hostile manner. Grundy's initial call for funds on Fringebacker produced far more than he had expected – a total of US$77,000. A second round followed with an increased target and, though it wasn't reached, more money came in than in round one. A third call for funding went out in February 2018 just before Lunar New Year – a time when people are used to handing out cash gifts. Realising HKFP was likely to be able to survive on donations, Grundy planned his own crowdfunding platform to save on costs, receiving a grant from Google News Initiative in 2019 to develop it and let others use it (see pp. 139–143).

The third outlet to have started up on crowdfunding is Hong Kong Citizen News, an outlet staffed by a group of experienced and well-trusted journalists. After the success of the other two crowdfunding exercises, they also did a prelaunch Fringebacker campaign in 2017, raising the equivalent of US$346,000. This, along with some large donations from well-wishers, set them up for a good start, giving them time to get a subscription scheme going to which they tried to get their crowdfunders to sign up (see pp. 135–139). However, after the Beijing crackdown on protesters and the opposition in Hong Kong in 2020, further crowdfunding exercises seemed unlikely and the outlet looked to direct donors and subscribers.

Crowdfunding as a means to make a large sum to launch an outlet or take it to stage two is not an easy path. Preparing for a campaign takes skill, effort and time. It also needs money to produce high-quality presentation materials as well as gifts such as low-value branded merchandise – though cash can be saved by offering limited subscriptions or just a personal thank you from the founders. But working on the crowdfunding application will at least force you to focus on what your outlet is and how it can connect with your audience, giving you a kind of pitchdeck, and you may well garner some readers and end up with some cash.

References

DeJarnette, Ben (3 October 2016). What Beacon's failure means for crowdfunded journalism. *MediaShift*. Retrieved 22 September 2017 from http://mediashift.org/2016/10/beacons-failure-means-crowdfunded-journalism/

Engaged Journalism Accelerator (n.d.). How The Correspondent crowdfunded $2.5m in 29 days. Retrieved 26 November 2020 from https://engagedjournalism.com/resources/the-correspondent-crowdfunding-rob-wijnberg-unbreaking-news-the-daily-show

Goligoski, Emily, & Pilhofer, Aron (24 January 2019). The Correspondent became the most participatory journalism crowdfunding project in history without one story on its site. Here's how. The Membership Puzzle Project. Retrieved 26 November 2020 from https://membershippuzzle.org/articles-overview/the-correspondent-crowdfunding

Hazard Owen, Laura (17 September 2019). After a $2.6M crowdfunding campaign, The Correspondent will have just one full-time journalist in the U.S. Retrieved 26 November 2020 from https://www.niemanlab.org/2019/09/after-2-6m-crowdfunding-campaign-the-correspondent-will-have-just-one-full-time-journalist-in-the-u-s/

Hazard Owen, Laura (10 December 2020). The Correspondent, De Correspondent's English-language site, is closing down on Dec. 31. NiemanLab. Retrieved 13 February 2021 from https://www.niemanlab.org/2020/12/the-correspondent-de-correspondents-english-language-site-is-shutting-down/

He, Laura (28 March 2018). Publisher of Hong Kong satirical magazine 100Most soars as much as tenfold on market debut after record demand. *South China Morning Post*. Retrieved 17 November 2020 from https://www.scmp.com/business/companies/article/2139220/most-kwai-chung-hong-kongs-most-oversubscribed-ipo-stock-soars

Hepworth, Shelley (16 January 2018). Another independent voice is silenced in Duterte's war on the media. *Columbia Journalism Review*. Retrieved 1 September 2020 from https://www.cjr.org/analysis/rappler-duterte-philippines.php

Li, Xueying (25 June 2016). New players diversify Hong Kong media scene. *The Straits Times*. Retrieved 17 November 2020 from https://www.straitstimes.com/asia/east-asia/new-players-diversify-hong-kong-media-scene

Lidow, Derek (2014). *Startup leadership: how savvy entrepreneurs turn their ideas into successful enterprises*. E-book. San Francisco: Jossey-Bass.

Majid, Aisha (22 January 2021). Alternative ways of funding journalism: crowdfunding has raised $21m+ and seeded some major titles. *Press Gazette*. Retrieved 18 March 2021 from https://pressgazette.co.uk/alternative-funding-journalism-crowdfunding/

Metinko, Chris (3 December 2020). SPAC vs traditional IPO: investors see benefits of blank-check companies. Crunchbase. Retrieved 16 March 2021 from https://news.crunchbase.com/news/spac-vs-traditional-ipo-investors-see-benefits-of-blank-check-companies/

Milner, Andrew (26 March 2019). Interview: Stephen King, CEO of luminate. *Alliance Magazine*. Retrieved 25 November 2020 from https://www.alliancemagazine.org/interview/interview-stephen-king/

Nguyen, Thi Bich Ngoc (12 April 2019). North Base Media reaches $15m first close for second round. *DealStreetAsia*. Retrieved 25 November 2020 from https://www.dealstreetasia.com/stories/north-base-media-reaches-15m-first-close-for-second-fund-130491

Schmidt, Christine (5 November 2018). 2018 has been a record-breaking year for journalism Kickstarters (though only about 1 in 5 actually get funded). NiemanLab. Retrieved 26 November 2020 from https://www.niemanlab.org/2018/11/2018-has-been-a-record-breaking-year-for-journalism-kickstarters-though-only-about-1-in-5-actually-get-funded/

Sullivan, Margaret (4 April 2017). Omidyar Network gives $100 million to boost journalism and fight hate speech. *Washington Post*. Retrieved 25 November 2020 from https://www.washingtonpost.com/lifestyle/style/omidyar-charity-gives-100-million-to-boost-journalism-and-fight-hate-speech/2017/04/04/aebb013c-193d-11e7-855e-4824bbb5d748_story.html

Teare, Gené (13 January 2021). Global VC report 2020: funding and exits blow past 2019 despite pandemic headwinds. Crunchbase. Retrieved 16 March 2021 from https://news.crunchbase.com/news/global-2020-funding-and-exit/

The Jakarta Post (12 July 2020). MDIF invests $750,000 in Indonesian digital media company Arkadia. Retrieved 24 November 2020 from https://www.thejakartapost.com/news/2020/07/12/mdif-invests-750000-in-indonesian-digital-media-company-arkadia.html

Udemans, Chris, Cohen, David, & Artman, John (13 January 2020). Where Tencent invests: infographic. Technode. Retrieved 26 November 2020 from https://technode.com/2020/01/13/where-tencent-invests-infographic/

Widyasthana, Sandhy (15 December 2020). Rise of the SOE: why startup M&A is a key part of a state-owned digital ecosystem. e27. Retrieved 17 March 2021 from https://e27.co/rise-of-the-soe-why-startup-ma-is-a-key-part-of-a-state-owned-digital-ecosystem-20201214/

Wiggers, Kyle L. (9 January 2019). Chinese entrepreneurs have raised over $150 million on Indiegogo since 2016. *VentureBeat*. Retrieved 26 November 2020 from https://venturebeat.com/2019/01/09/chinese-entrepreneurs-have-raised-over-150-million-on-indiegogo-since-2016/

4
TECHNOLOGICAL AND JOURNALISM SKILLS FOR YOUR STARTUP

Introduction

Technology has been the driving force in the transformation of media in the past three decades and it has not stood still. Anyone who sets up their own journalistic outlet doesn't have to be an expert but they do need to have a basic grasp of how to use and keep up with developments to produce better journalism and to make money from it. On the professional side, there must be some provision for support and training for gathering and producing content, especially if the outlet is run by people who haven't been journalists before.

Technology

Where media technology in the old days was so large, expensive and hard to get as to deter all but the wealthiest or most determined from entering the industry, today it is compact, affordable and accessible. However, it's not always easy to use. While everyone can set up a simple website, it's hard for an amateur to make it look good, get it working smoothly and fend off determined hack attacks. While some new technologies, such as livestreaming, are quickly mastered, specialist tech support is needed to do things like making apps and using artificial intelligence.

The International Center for Journalists (ICFJ) found in its 2019 global survey that tech is not a priority in newsrooms, with only 3–6 per cent of employees being tech professionals. The low number may be due to the likelihood that many newsrooms rely on outside contractors for their technical support. But there's another reason. The Reuters Institute's 2020 technology trends report found that three quarters of the media leaders spoken to in 32 countries couldn't retain tech employees because alternative employment paid much better (Newman 2020),

DOI: 10.4324/9781315270432-4

a situation noted by Katadata of Indonesia (see Chapter 8 pp. 3–7). The ICFJ report found that some other staff had tech skills, but not that many: only 12 per cent of managers and 8 per cent of journalists had degrees in a tech-related field. And even among the techies less than 40 per cent had such degrees, a full half of them having graduated in journalism or communications (ICFJ 2019).

Perhaps that's for the best because it's not worth jumping on to every tech bandwagon. In 2015, the "pivot to video" led many newsrooms to invest in the new technology and abandon all other – and they soon regretted it as audiences switched off (Moore 26 September 2017). A couple of years later, everyone was raving about podcasting, which did hold its ground but is not very profitable (though that may change – see p. 75). Then there was 360° photography, still being used in suitable situations but not the great breakthrough it was supposed to be. Virtual reality also arrived, a technology much-used in gaming, but not one that changed journalism, though it still has its uses. Use of technology varies hugely. Some people are still publishing in print, at least as one platform, while 5G is on the horizon, offering unknown possibilities. The lessons: weigh up the cost and effort of using the technology available, work out what suits your style and your audience and don't put all your eggs in one basket.

Content management systems

You may well want to start out on social media or third-party platforms like Medium, or even stay permanently there, but still the most-used permanent public interface is the website. For many outlets it's the basis of their online presence and the core to which their distributed content links back, and its design reflects and represents their identity. The program behind the website is called a content management system, or CMS.

WordPress is the most popular, claiming to run nearly two-fifths of the internet. Started in 2003 and owned by Automattic, it is open-source – that is, its source code is available for the public to use and develop. It offers many choices and options, from blogs to websites to domain names to e-commerce, from basic free versions to costly customised setups. It's reported that WordPress is used by such major media as Time Inc., *The New York Times*, Quartz and TechCrunch (wpbeginner 8 March 2019). Like most CMSs, WordPress does almost everything for you: it hosts your site, gets your domain name registered, provides myriad themes and customisable designs, updates software and security, syncs with social media, helps drive traffic to your site, sends you feedback on use (analytics – see Chapter 6) and does search engine optimisation, or SEO (see pp. 33–34). With paid versions you can remove the WordPress branding so it looks entirely as if it's your own site. Since it's open-source, there are thousands of plug-ins – add-on features – both free and paid, and more are added all the time.

And that means that setting up your own site can get complicated and difficult, especially with newsrooms clearly not prioritising tech matters. So, in consultation with a number of small- and medium-sized news organisations, WordPress developed Newspack, "a plugin that selects, streamlines and simplifies the use of other plugins best suited to newsroom needs", according to its FAQ. Launched in 2019 with the goal of providing "a foundation for a sustainable model for local journalism", it was developed with US$2.2 million in funding from Google News Initiative (GNI), The Lenfest Institute, The Knight Foundation and Civil Media (see below). Technical support is on tap 24 hours a day, and there's a Slack (see below) community to connect all users. Newspack is a hosted service, and the price depends on your site's income: you pay US$500 a month if your revenue is less than $250,000 a year, US$1,000 a month if it's between US$250,000 and US$500,000 a year and US$2,000 if it's more than that. At the end of 2020, 40 sites were live on Newspack and 50 more had signed up. About a third are outside America, among them Hong Kong Free Press (see pp. 139–143), Asia Times and Beijing-based TechNode.

Drupal and Joomla also offer free CMSs and paid versions. They have powerful functions, Joomla especially for commercial sites, but they require more technical expertise than WordPress. If you are going to choose one of these you should probably have the skills required or have already hired technical support, so there's no need to address how to use them here. Another choice is GitHub, the Microsoft-owned coding community, which uses open-source coding and completely free web hosting. It's not recommended for beginners because it needs a lot of technical knowledge, but may be worth exploring if you're interested in getting deeper into the topic.

Another option is a website builder, which allows you to construct your site using set templates without downloading any special software or using code. Squarespace provides basic site-building tools, content hosting, templates, SEO, analytics and all-day customer service. It has four plans for personal and business use ranging from US$12 to US$40 a month. The service includes a custom domain name and security and, for the more expensive plans, gmail address, analytics, payment systems and more. Also popular is Wix, which offers a free plan and paid ones from US$4.50 to US$24.50 a month and more if you want to have payments on your site. It's simpler than Squarespace and more suitable for beginners. Such site builders are less flexible than WordPress but easier to use. Singapore-based nonprofit Ghost also offers a CMS with many other services. Meanwhile, the old domain-name providers like GoDaddy and Namecheap offer web hosting as well.

With CMSs constantly changing as technology improves and tech companies compete, it's worth trying out several free versions and checking how they compare in suitability and cost. Later, when your site grows bigger, you will need to re-evaluate what is on offer. Every provider has a wealth of information and advice on how to do things. To get an idea of the process of setting up technically, Splice Media keeps on its site a diary of its ups and downs when it started in 2017; look for The Changelog (update note: Splice recently changed its CMS from WordPress to Squarespace) (see Chapter 8 pp. 9–13).

Take a little time to consider the design of your site, fitting this in with your branding (see pp. 24–26). A free site won't offer you many options, but colour and background picture are usually your choice, and you have a number of templates to select from. Your "about us" page should have your mission statement as well as details about your operation including ownership, how you raise funds and who your staff are, as well as contact information – social media, phone number and street address. Too many sites have incomplete information or no information at all, which hints at something to hide. An honest and full "about us" will inspire confidence and trust among your audience. Of course, there may be reasons you don't want to publicise some facts and figures, but be as complete as possible – New Naratif even publishes its accounts. And keep it updated.

Apps

Research done from 2015 to 2016 by US academics Jacob L. Nelson and Ryan F. Lei on 67 American news sites identified something rather interesting about apps. As news users migrated from desktops to phones, they were splitting into two kinds of audience: those who used mobile browsers and those who used apps. What was surprising was that there were five times as many of the former as the latter, but the latter spent 20 times as long on their apps as the former did on their browsers (Nelson & Lei 2018). Clearly, for a large news outlet like the BBC or CNN, having an app is a no-brainer. But it's an expensive and complicated thing to set up well. Is it worth a startup creating an app at or soon after its launch? There are sites that offer free app builders, such as Appy Pie, or a free basic version, such as that offered by Microsoft's Firebase, which can be used to set up a prototype for proposals or experimentation, but to get full functionality most pass the job to a professional. One downside to apps is that you are pretty much restricted for distribution to the major phone operating systems, which rake in revenue from their near-monopoly.

Whether you have an app or not depends to some extent on the local situation. In China, apps are common among big, rich media but, with private outlets highly circumscribed, small media tend to use WeChat as their platform. That is already an app, and one so well equipped it offers many functions including payment. In Indonesia and Cambodia, where the news industry is highly competitive, apps are plentiful; one outlet sets one up and the rest have to follow. Market leaders Khmerload and IDN Media are both planning super apps (see pp. 149–153 and 143–146). In other places startups have less pressure. In Myanmar the media business before the 2021 military coup was running on thin margins and apps didn't take off, and in Thailand too they just haven't developed. Nakarin "Ken" Wanakijpaibul, executive editor of Thailand's The Standard, says he is holding off producing an app because it needs a committed audience and his readers are not yet ready for that, though the plan is to produce one eventually and monetise it (see pp. 196–200).

Podcasts

Podcasts remain a cheap and reasonably easy way to connect with users. You need no major studio setup, have no pictures to worry about, and there's a chance to make money from ads, donations, subscriptions and merchandise. Anchor (bought by Spotify in 2020) still offers a free one-stop shop where you can use audio (and even video) recorded on your phone and add in background music and sound effects. Berlin-based SoundCloud offers another platform, though its main business is music and it's less user-friendly for podcast producers. Buzzsprout has a free service but also does paid packages with more capacity and has a Creator Program to support serious podcasters with potential. Other services include Soundtrap for Storytellers, a Spotify-owned podcast editor, which has a free one-month trial but after that requires subscription. The very versatile Hindenburg recording and editing software is recommended by many podcasters. It has a range of offerings from a basic version at a one-off US$100 to more professional levels, and can also be rented; it has a one-month free trial.

If you're keen to try podcasting, British journalist Mark Frary, writing in Index on Censorship, suggests choosing a weekly time slot and uploading it on a podcast platform (not just your own site). "Then, once it's out, reach as many people as possible by registering it in directories such as Apple Podcasts, using your own social media, message boards and mailing lists, and developing alliances with other relevant podcasts" (Frary 2017). An advice piece posted by IJNet has some suggestions for "pro-quality work on a shoestring": start with a detailed outline plan, including sounds to make the story come alive, then don't rush your takes, don't talk over your interviewee, don't be afraid to ask them to repeat and incorporate natural background noises. One extra good tip is to tell a good story and build suspense: "even in the shortest audio pieces, dropping hints and previews about what's to come creates narrative tension that will keep listeners plugged in" (Grimes 1 September 2017).

Livestreaming

Livestreaming's pioneer was Meerkat, founded in 2015, but it got into a bitter contest with Periscope, losing after just a year (Truong 5 March 2016). But even Periscope, bought by Twitter, has been eclipsed by services from other big tech companies, with the market now dominated by Facebook's Facebook Live and Instagram as well as Google's YouTube Live and also Twitch, which was acquired by Amazon in 2014. So easy are these to use that content appears in many shapes and forms, from people in their bedrooms to gaming contests to remote classrooms. For the media, though, livestreaming has become almost a necessity for important news events such as government press conferences, street protests and major celebrations.

All that's required to do something that until 2015 was the domain of big broadcasters is a smartphone and a wireless connection. Facebook Live is particularly popular because it will appear on the accounts of your followers without you doing anything at all and will be available for later viewing. However, this kind of content is not findable through search engines and has no connected monetising options. YouTube Live, on the other hand, is less easy to set up but productions can be searched for and, with Google being the owner, may get higher rankings in search. However, content is kept within YouTube's site and is used for its advertising. If you want higher quality, IBM Cloud Video, Vimeo, Brightcove and others offer paid services that also allow monetisation (Wilbert 13 November 2020).

Security

Running any media outlet involves some risk to both organisation and journalists. Everyone faces technical dangers, in particular hacking into the website or into communications.

ICFJ's two international reports on the state of newsroom technology show increasing use of security measures everywhere in the world, the main improvement in newsrooms in general being the greater popularity of secured messaging apps (ICFJ 2017, 2019). Facebook-owned WhatsApp has now become ubiquitous outside China both as a messaging tool and for delivering content, though it has been a nightmare to police for fake news. It provides end-to-end encryption, but there are concerns over its privacy level – it records not only your phone number but your metadata, which is not encrypted and can reveal who you messaged, when you messaged them and for how long. In 2021 it was threatening to share this user data with Facebook for advertising purposes. Many users signed up for the most secure alternative, Signal. An open-source app developed by the founders of WhatsApp, it not only encrypts content, which is stored only on your own phone, but hides details of both sender and receiver. Messages can be set to disappear at a chosen time (Ravi 14 January 2021).

Telegram has also become popular in our region outside China. Founded in St. Petersburg and, after moving several times, now based in Dubai, it was at one time involved in blockchain investment. Today, according to its site, it is a nonprofit funded by two Russian brothers. Free to use, it is cloud-based, so you can access it from different devices. Its encryption is not rated as highly as Signal's, and if you're not using Apple you have to actually turn it on. Telegram became popular during Hong Kong's pro-democracy protests in 2019, when whole channels of information were set up. But these demonstrated the weakness of any secure app for group messaging: you must check that those who join your group are not those from whom you wish to keep your information secret (some information in the above paragraph from Sha 11 June 2020). Eventually WhatsApp reined in its plans to share data and kept its dominant position in the market.

For email and documents, "PGP" (pretty good privacy) comes in the form of encryption software packages such as Gpq4win for Windows and GPG Suites for Macs. *The New York Times* uses Mailvelope, a browser extension for Chrome and Firefox that enables PGP. *The Guardian* has a key system, where your recipient has a "public key" that you can send your message to, and s/he will use a "private key" to unscramble it. VPNs (Virtual Private Networks) give you an intermediary server that hides your real IP address. Necessary (though illegal) for anyone in China to access overseas content, elsewhere they provide protection from hackers. However, the 2019 ICFJ report found that email encryption as well as (outside North America) VPN use had dropped by nearly half since 2017 (ICFJ 2019).

One way to secure your content is to use the Tor network, the "dark web", where anonymity is the norm. The BBC has put its content on Tor for countries where it can't distribute in the normal way such as Vietnam and China and provides advice for those who want to try it (Porter 24 October 2019). When it comes to security for potential sources who might be in danger, SecureDrop, an open-source whistleblower system managed by the Freedom of the Press Foundation, provides heavy-duty protection: it can only be accessed using Tor and has to be set up for each organisation on their own server. The information sent is downloaded in its encrypted form and only decoded offline.

Attacks can hit even the biggest outlets. According to an article by the Tow Center for Digital Journalism, the American nonprofit ProPublica had its staff email accounts flooded with so much spam that it became impossible to work, a method called "email bombing". All email had to be stopped, severely interrupting work flow. Other attacks include "doxxing", that is, exposing someone's private personal information in public, or "trolling", which involves stalking them online, or "ransomware", where data is stolen, encrypted and held hostage until payment is made (Renner 22 November 2017).

Organisational communication systems

Slack has made itself the go-to internal networking system for newsroom organisation. Launched in 2014, it claimed in early 2021 to have more than 12 million daily active users in 150-plus countries. It provides a single internal communication system that centralises all the information that would otherwise be sent out on a multitude of platforms. Messages can be sent out to everyone on the system or to "channels" of smaller subsets for, say, separate desks (newsroom sections) or projects. The information sent across the platform is searchable, attachments can be sent and stored, access can be gained by computer or phone and the system integrates with many other apps and services. It keeps staff in constant touch and has become the "digital water cooler" where people strike up informal conversations, even giving a voice to bottom-up complaints (Perlberg 15 July 2020). A free version is available that suits small teams (its limited archive search function is its major downside), while the Standard (US$6.67 per user per month paid annually) and Plus (US$12.50 per user per month paid annually) versions offer more sophisticated services for larger outlets. One problem for Asian users of this software is that it is not yet available in non-western languages.

Some criticise Slack as being too insecure (though it does seem to have upgraded – it was bought out in 2020 by software giant Salesforce) and used more for office gossip than anything else – suggested alternatives are

SpiderOak's Semaphor or the open-source Mattermost (Woodman 29 January 2018). Wrike is a newer option for larger teams – more expensive in its paid versions than Slack, but with more functions and designed originally more as an organising system than a communications channel. Another possibility is Notion, the "all-in-one workspace" as it calls itself. Designed to keep the whole company organised, it is particularly valued for its capacity for collaborative creativity and leadership (Pan 15 November 2019). Chinese tech giants offer two regional alternatives, both with free versions – ByteDance's Singapore-based Lark and Alibaba's DingTalk. There are simpler options. Tom Grundy of Hong Kong Free Press says he prefers the free calendar/organiser Trello as the newsroom workflow tool. He and his reporters use it to keep track of the stories of the day from approval through to finished version ready for publication.

Algorithms, artificial intelligence and machine learning

The ever-growing capability of computer technology has "disrupted" newsroom processes not only in the areas of distribution, business potential and production speed but for the finding, writing and editing of content itself. Major news organisations have been busy rolling out machine learning apparently to take on some journalistic functions – MSN was reported to be sacking 50 contract "news production workers" to replace them with AI (Baker 28 May 2020), the BBC used a Twitterbot to send out the results of the 2019 UK election (Mayhew 4 November 2019), while the Associated Press, Bloomberg and *Los Angeles Times* were among many outlets automating the delivery of thousands of formula stories (Cheung 21 November 2019). In our region, Indonesia's IDN Times has been using AI to partly process content and plans to develop it further to automate more of the whole operation. While the new technology is welcomed, it is also feared for its potential not only to replace journalists but, lacking constant human supervision, to skew the news by, for example, creating "filter bubbles", a term coined by online citizen engagement guru Eli Pariser in 2011 that refers to users being fed only matter that matches their own ideas and views, or fragmenting the public sphere into "sphericules" through individual feedback loops (Becket 2019; Helberger 2019).

The 2020 Reuters Institute technology trends report found that a good proportion of the 218 senior newsroom respondents it surveyed saw AI as "very important" for automated recommendations (53 per cent), commercial improvements like better subscription takeup and optimisation of payment systems (47 per cent) and newsroom automation such as tagging and transcribing (39 per cent). But only 16 per cent said using machine skills for newsgathering was "very important" and just 12 per cent thought so for "robo-journalism", the automated formula production of stories (Newman 2020). US researcher Matt Carlson studied journalists' reactions to a fully AI-produced publication and found them dismissive of computer production. They said news couldn't be written without the human touch, that is, "dissecting the drama of public life and the emotionality of quality news writing" (Carlson 2015).

A 2019 survey done by the London School of Economics and Political Science and Google News Initiative of newsrooms in 32 countries (including four in our region – Esquire Singapore, Malaysiakini, Hong Kong's *South China Morning Post* and *Tempo* of Indonesia) found AI being used well for functions like object extraction and automatic tagging, automated fact-checking, content moderation, speech transcription, ad targeting tools, propensity models (which predict how the user will respond to offers) and machine-generated content. Again basic reporting did not feature. Moreover, staff were put off using AI because of its costs, their own lack of skills and knowledge, scepticism of the technology and fear of job losses. Yet the report advises all newsrooms to at least start planning: "Its future impact is uncertain but AI has the potential for wide-ranging and profound influence on how journalism is made and consumed" (Becket 2019). If nothing else, the field is providing journalists with a bit more work: *The Wall Street Journal* created an "algorithmic beat" to report on AI's mistakes not only in news but in other sectors as well (Marconi, Daldrup & Pant 14 February 2019).

The bad news for startups is the common finding that small newsrooms usually cannot afford AI. It's possible that they may not need it, but in many cases it would be useful in finding and processing original content and encouraging user engagement. The best way to get on the ladder is to collaborate with other news media or nonprofit projects. At the other end of the scale, Taiwan's The News Lens has short-circuited the process by buying its own AI company (see pp. 187–190).

Blockchain

Only a couple of years ago, blockchain was the media technology of the future. Its attraction was its "distributed ledger" base that kept the original record of a document or transaction as well as every change made to it without allowing alterations, making it very secure. After it fuelled a dizzying market for cryptocurrencies like Bitcoin and Ethereum it was touted as the way forward for journalism. A report produced by the international press association WAN-IFRA in early 2019 looked into the pros and cons for the media: it was transparent and accountable; it could help news outfits establish credibility; it could track copyright violations and help monetise content; and it could stop advertising fraud (What's New in Publishing 23 January 2019).

The central actor in blockchain journalism was Civil, founded by Matthew Iles in the United States in 2016 on an initial US$5 million from ConsenSys, a blockchain company owned by Ethereum co-founder Joseph Lubin. Its goal was to set up "a blockchain-based media platform for trustworthy journalism owned and operated by the public", creating a decentralised network of independent newsrooms under its wing (Iles 2020). Its currency was to be the CVL, a blockchain-based token that was scheduled to raise another US$8 million in an Initial Coin Offering (ICO) in September 2018. The application procedure to buy

CVLs was made extremely complicated to discourage unethical investors, but it was almost impossible to make it work (Keefe 19 September 2018). The exercise raised only US$2 million, apparently 80 per cent from Lubin, but a US$3.5 million grant from ConsenSys allowed Civil to grow its newsroom numbers (Ingram 17 October 2018). Another ICO was tried in 2019 (Edmonds 5 March 2019) but Civil had to close in 2020. Said Iles in a valedictory letter: "We built innovative technology, supported award-winning journalists, and inspired many people all over the world with our vision for a more participatory media landscape. But ultimately, we failed to sustain ourselves independently" (Iles 2020).

The cost of technology

Most new tech comes with a cheap or free version, but unless it's from an outlet that supports journalism it's unlikely to provide much flexibility and more expensive versions will be required. Occasionally they can be bought for a single payment, but more and more often there is a monthly fee. Then there's just the basic cost of the connection and storage. Provision for these costs must be made in your business plan. Jahabar Siddiq of The Malaysian Insight (TMI) (see pp. 184–187) shows how it adds up for a nationwide news outlet: CMS licence, server space, IT services to keep it all going, operating systems and upgrades, apps, bandwidth for cloud content storage. "You think it's a one-off cost but it's never a one-off cost," he says. It all comes to as much as US$7,000 a month for TMI, and it's difficult to cut corners, Jahabar goes on: "You can't always think, oh, I'll just take minimum bandwidth because then you'll just clog up the site and people will have no access".

Journalism skills

Traditionally a craft job for those with the energy and inquisitiveness to find out what's going on in society and the literary skill to let people know about it in an interesting way, journalism has always been an open profession, one that, unlike law and medicine, doesn't need specified qualifications and professional memberships. A number of outlets examined for this book were started by journalism veterans – people like Daisy Li and her partners at Hong Kong Citizen News (HKCN), Prasong Lertrattanawisute of Isranews Agency, Sherry Lee of The Reporter in Taiwan, Sapto Anggoro of Tirto and Ellen Tordesillas and her colleagues at VERA Files. Others were set up by former reporters like Steven Gan and Premesh Chandran of Malaysiakini. Some, like the Utomo brothers of IDN Media and Chy Sila of Sabay, have come from a business background. Some have no experience at all – "Ken" of The Standard in Thailand qualified as a pharmacist. This is all to the good: tradition and experience remain, but the industry is always open to new ideas.

If journalism isn't like other professions, it has also moved beyond being a craft. Over the 20th century, universities, first in America and then elsewhere, took up the subject as an academic pursuit and today you can study for a journalism degree (or one in related subjects such as communication) in all the territories of our region. That doesn't mean all journalism students become journalists – many go into public relations or organisational communication, jobs where the skill of spotting what's interesting and then interesting people in what you've spotted is very useful, also where political sensitivity is of less concern. And it doesn't mean all journalists have journalism degrees – many graduated in language and literature or humanities.

If you want training in traditional journalism skills, or you want staff to be trained, there are many options, often with financial support or completely free. The Asian Center for Journalism at Ateneo de Manila University, supported by Germany's Konrad Adenauer Foundation, offers several distance-learning programmes for working journalists from the region. One is a two-year MA in Journalism, another is a six-month Diploma in Visual Journalism and then there are one-off short courses. All are taught in ways that allow overseas journalists to join, and financial support is available. Many other short-term courses are put on by specialist organisations like the US-based Internews or mature media like Thomson Reuters and the BBC, and also by NGOs, foundations and international organisations funding good governance. Google News Initiative (GNI) has its own Training Center offering fully online courses in basic skills and many more, including podcasts, though of course all using Google technology. To get news about such sessions, sign up to newsletters from the sites themselves as well as info hubs like Splice Media and the ICFJ's IJNet.

For entrepreneurial journalists, getting training in business and management can be a problem because going back to school to learn a new subject may not be practical. However, help can come from funders, who, once you have them on board, may arrange for training, give you inhouse advice or station someone in your company. The impact funders (see pp. 42–47) are particularly good at providing this kind of support. Recently Splice Media has opened its School of Splice for journalism startups (see Chapter 8 p. 12). There is also good advice in the books by Briggs (2012) and Kaye and Quinn (2010). Although these works are not new, the principles remain the same.

One much debated issue is whether journalists should learn computer skills. The 2019 ICFJ technology in global newsrooms survey found that nearly 40 per cent of journalists were dealing with CMSs and coding at least once a week, and more than 25 per cent on a daily basis, so you would think that web skills would be wanted. However, while newsrooms were offering training in video and audio, journalists really wanted to know more about "cybersecurity, podcasting, fact-checking tools and promoting work on social media", matters that would help them get their content out more reliably to more people in more formats; and more than two-fifths wanted training in AI when only 5 per cent of news organisations provided it (ICFJ 2019). It's possible that newsroom leaders don't see these skills as necessary for journalists. The latter can try doing it themselves with GNI, whose courses include machine learning.

When it comes to actual reporting, the biggest need for computer skills is for data journalism. With many sites already posting news of all kinds, often copied-and-pasted or reproduced with a little embellishment, competition for content is strong. Data crunching can produce original stories that can be investigative but can also be non-sensitive. It is also saleable, as Indonesian sites Katadata and Lokadata (see Chapter 8 pp. 3–7 and pp. 153–156) show. Perhaps many newsroom leaders haven't yet seen the potential: the ICFJ tech trends report says that nearly four-fifths of journalists surveyed wanted training in data analysis when only just over one-third of newsrooms provided it, and 65 per cent of journalists saw data journalism as important to engaging users compared to 55 per cent of managers (ICFJ 2019).

There are three stages to data journalism. The first is spotting a trend and extracting relevant data, usually in huge quantities, using "scraping" tools. The second is identifying previously unnoticed patterns in the data that could produce original news. The third stage is processing that data and presenting the result clearly, often through visualisation – a chart, diagram or illustration that brings home the full impact of the findings. All stages involve computer processing skills using such programs as Data Miner for scraping; SQL, Python and R for processing; and DataWrapper for visualisation, though there are many more, including Google Fusion, which can support parts or all of the process. The International Consortium of Investigative Journalists (ICIJ) lists all the tools it used for its FinCEN Files investigation into the role of global banks in large-scale money laundering (ICIJ 4 January 2021). All can be found online and are often free, but that doesn't mean to say they are easy to use.

In practice, this kind of journalism is not only difficult but time-consuming, with too few journalists having enough technical skills to do the work quickly, and few technicians able to pinpoint the journalistic treasure in the data. This may put off a lot of newsrooms. One way to tackle the problem is through collaboration. ICIJ's Pandora Papers investigation and many other revelatory stories were produced through its network of hundreds of journalists round the world using a common set of digital capabilities. WikiLeaks and other data dumps that prove too much for individual news organisations to examine fully get put online for anybody who has the time and skills to work through them.

In a media startup looking to produce its own stories, the best collaboration might be between the journalist and the computer specialist – a complete departure from past practices. Experience helps. Veteran editor Daisy Li of Hong Kong Citizen News had a group of friends working commercially on big data and suggested they do it for news. HKCN used the results of regular surveys to produce a story that showed how unpopular the territory's chief executive was after one of the tech groups used the raw data to find correlations. A study by local academics of the adoption of data journalism in Hong Kong by HKCN and others noted that the field was as yet undeveloped, possibly due to the high competitiveness of the market and the deteriorating political atmosphere. However, they found that one of the factors that encouraged its use was the presence of a designer on the team (programmers were also a choice in the questionnaire but not usually involved in the journalism process) (Zhang & Chen 2020).

References

Baker, Geoff (28 May 2020). Microsoft is cutting dozens of MSN news production workers and replacing them with artificial intelligence. *The Seattle Times*. Retrieved 8 December 2020 from https://www.seattletimes.com/business/local-business/microsoft-is-cutting-dozens-of-msn-news-production-workers-and-replacing-them-with-artificial-intelligence/

Becket, Charlie (2019). New powers, new responsibilities: a global survey of journalism and artificial intelligence. *LSE POLIS & Google News Initiative*. Retrieved 8 December 2020 from https://drive.google.com/file/d/1utmAMCmd4rfJHrUfLLfSJ-clpFTjyef1/view

Briggs, Mark (2012). *Entrepreneurial journalism: how to build what's next for news*. Los Angeles: Sage.

Carlson, Matt (2015) The robotic reporter. *Digital Journalism*, 3/3, 416–431. DOI: 10.1080/21670811.2014.976412

Cheung, Paul (21 November 2019). Journalism's superfood: AI? Knight Foundation. Retrieved 8 December 2020 from https://knightfoundation.org/articles/journalisms-superfood-ai/

Edmonds, Rick (5 March 2019). Civil tries a relaunch but blockchain and a complex 'constitution' remain. Poynter. Retrieved 8 December 2020 from https://www.poynter.org/business-work/2019/civil-tries-a-relaunch-but-blockchain-and-a-complex-constitution-remain/

Frary, Mark (2017). Power to the podcast. *Index on Censorship*, 46/3, 24–327. DOI: 10.1177/0306422017730789

Grimes, Andrea (1 September 2017). Lo-fi podcasting tips. *IJNet*. Retrieved 6 December 2020 from https://ijnet.org/en/resource/lo-fi-podcasting-tips

Helberger, Natali (2019). On the democratic role of news recommenders. *Digital Journalism*, 7/8, 993–1012. DOI: 10.1080/21670811.2019.1623700

International Center for Journalists (ICFJ) (2017). Survey: the state of technology in global newsrooms. Retrieved 6 October 2017 from http://www.icfj.org/resources/first-ever-global-survey-news-tech-reveals-perilous-digital-skills-gap

ICFJ (2019). The state of technology in global newsrooms. Retrieved 30 October 2019 from https://www.icfj.org/sites/default/files/2019-10/2019%20Final%20Report.pdf

ICIJ (4 January 2021). FinCEN Files data team shares tools, tips and songs that inspire. Retrieved 19 March 2021 from https://www.icij.org/investigations/fincen-files/fincen-files-data-team-shares-tools-tips-and-songs-that-inspire/

Iles, Matthew (2020). Ending the civil journey. *Civil*. Retrieved 8 December 2020 from https://civil.co/

Ingram, Matthew (17 October 2018). Civil's token sale fails to hit target. What now? *Columbia Journalism Review*. Retrieved 8 December 2020 from https://www.cjr.org/the_media_today/civil-token-sale.php

Kaye, Jeff, & Quinn, Stephen (2010). *Funding journalism in the digital age: business models, strategies and trends*. New York: Peter Lang.

Keefe, John (19 September 2018). How to buy into journalism's blockchain future (in only 44 steps). NiemanLab. Retrieved 8 December 2020 from https://www.niemanlab.org/2018/09/how-to-buy-into-journalisms-blockchain-future-in-only-44-steps/

Marconi, Francesco, Daldrup, Till, & Pant, Rajiv (14 February 2019). Acing the algorithmic beat, journalism's new frontier. NiemanLab. Retrieved 8 December 2020 from https://www.niemanlab.org/2019/02/acing-the-algorithmic-beat-journalisms-next-frontier/

Mayhew, Freddie (4 November 2019). BBC to use 'semi-automated journalism' for first time in covering 2019 general election. *PressGazette*. Retrieved 8 December 2020 from https://pressgazette.co.uk/bbc-semi-automated-journalism-first-time-covering-2019-general-election/

Moore, Heidi N. (26 September 2017). The secret cost of pivoting to video. *Columbia Journalism Review*. Retrieved 18 March 2021 from https://www.cjr.org/business_of_news/pivot-to-video.php

Nelson, Jacob L., & Lei, Ryan F. (2018). The effect of digital platforms on news audience behavior. *Digital Journalism*, 6/5, 619–633. DOI: 10.1080/21670811.2017.1394202

Newman, Nic (2020). Journalism, media, technology trends and predictions 2020. Reuters Institute for the Study of Journalism & University of Oxford. Retrieved 18 March 2021 from https://www.digitalnewsreport.org/publications/2020/journalism-media-and-technology-trends-and-predictions-2020/

Pan, Christina (15 November 2019). The future of work: 5 ways Notion is better than Slack. Medium. Retrieved 9 December 2020 from https://sfchris.medium.com/the-future-of-work-5-ways-notion-is-better-than-slack-e9361e84c28a

Perlberg, Steven (15 July 2020). Slack is fueling media's bottom-up revolution. *Digiday*. Retrieved 7 December 2020 from https://digiday.com/media/how-slack-is-fueling-medias-bottom-up-revolution/

Porter, Jon (24 October 2019). BBC News heads to the dark web with new Tor mirror. *The Verge*. Retrieved 7 December 2020 from https://www.theverge.com/2019/10/24/20930085/bbc-news-dark-web-tor-the-onion-browser-secure-censorship

Ravi, Reethu (14 January 2021). Switching to Signal? Here's what you need to know about the WhatsApp rival. *Jumpstart*. Retrieved 19 March 2021 from https://www.jumpstartmag.com/switching-to-signal-heres-what-you-need-to-know-about-the-whatsapp-rival/

Renner, Nausicaa (22 November 2017). The media today: journalists vs. hackers. *Columbia Journalism Review*. Retrieved 11 January 2018 from https://www.cjr.org/tow_center/the-media-today-journalists-vs-hackers.php

Sha, Arjun (11 June 2020). WhatsApp vs Telegram vs Signal: a detailed comparison of features and privacy. *Beebom*. Retrieved 7 December 2020 from https://beebom.com/whatsapp-vs-telegram-vs-signal/

Truong, Alice (5 March 2016). It's official: Meerkat has lost the live-streaming battle to Periscope. *Quartz*. Retrieved 12 January 2018 from https://qz.com/632017/its-official-meerkat-has-lost-the-live-streaming-battle-to-periscope/

What's New in Publishing (23 January 2019). 3 ways blockchain technology can benefit news publishers. Retrieved 8 December 2020 from https://whatsnewinpublishing.com/3-ways-blockchain-technology-can-benefit-news-publishers/

Wilbert, Max (13 November 2020). YouTube Live vs Facebook Live compared to online video platforms. *Dacast*. Retrieved 7 December 2020 from https://www.dacast.com/blog/youtube-live-vs-facebook-live/

Woodman, Spencer (29 January 2018). Five digital security tools to protect your work and sources. ICIJ. Retrieved 7 December 2020 from https://www.icij.org/inside-icij/2018/01/five-digital-security-tools-to-protect-your-work-and-sources/

wpbeginner (8 March 2019). 40+ most notable big name brands that are using WordPress. Retrieved 30 November 2020 from https://www.wpbeginner.com/showcase/40-most-notable-big-name-brands-that-are-using-wordpress/

Zhang, Xinzhi, & Chen, Minyi (2020). Journalists' adoption and media's coverage of data-driven journalism: a case of Hong Kong. *Journalism Practice*, 1–19. DOI: 10.1080/17512786.2020.1824126

5
FUNDING YOUR JOURNALISM ENTERPRISE – INCOME

Introduction

Once you've got your startup going, you must get working on making an income. The traditional media had few options – newsstand sales, subscriptions and advertising – but, once sorted, these channels could be lucrative. The digital milieu has many more avenues and much more flexibility, but it's harder to make money from them. As with seeking startup funding, you'll need entrepreneurial skills and ingenuity to identify and use the best ways to do business that suit your topic, your principles and your audience.

Advertising

The media lost its key financial nexus with advertising when the internet came along. Users entered media unpredictably from many different pages and not just a front page, and there was at first no way of knowing how well-viewed anything was. The development of algorithms changed that, making it possible to tell not only how many people were reading a particular ad but what kind of people they were – age, gender and location at minimum – and how they acted on it. Advertising benefited from the increasing sophistication of audience data either directly from users or third-party from the cookies embedded on sites, using that information to line them up automatically with relevant ads.

This seemed for a while to be bringing advertising back to centre stage as the media's mainstay income (Pachico 2017). But there were some big differences from the old days. Now the media's place as go-between for advertisers and customers is occupied by tech giants, with Google and Facebook hogging ad spend in most of the world, the former taking 53 per cent of all income and the latter 28 per cent according to figures cited by *The Guardian* (Meade 16

DOI: 10.4324/9781315270432-5

February 2021), while in China 60 per cent of digital advertising is in the hands of Baidu, Alibaba and Tencent (Lim 6 April 2021). Also, ad blockers were developed that reduced revenue potential for the media. The International Center for Journalists' (ICFJ) 2019 global survey of newsroom technology reported that in just over half of respondent outlets, advertising was no longer the top source of income as they diversified their revenue sources (ICFJ 2019). However, it remained important. A global industry report found that in 2020 more people than ever were spending their time on media, of which two-thirds were ad-supported – a figure that represented a decline but was still substantial (Mandese 19 January 2021).

However, the ad world is still undergoing change. In 2020 the coronavirus pandemic dampened the market, and concerns about targeting ads at individuals using personal information picked up from browsing was leading to the removal of third-party cookies – most major browsers had already got rid of them and Google Chrome was planning to do so in 2022. In 2021 Apple's new iOS 14.5 required apps on its App Store to obtain permission before tracking users on other sites, which they had been able to do up to that point to gain information to target advertising. This move particularly affected Facebook. Again the advertising world was thrown into turmoil.

First a look at the established options in advertising.

Display advertisements

Also known as banners, these appear in a fixed position on a page in a particular publication and are most like print ads, though the pricing is more complex. Academics Esa Sirkkunen and Clare Cook (2012, 91–95) explain the different methods. They can be paid by number of views in CPM (cost per mille), that is, per thousand views, a method usually used by corporate advertisers and advertising agencies for popular or quality niche sites. Then there is payment for the number of times users actually click on the ad, usually priced at a fixed CPC (cost per click). This is obviously less frequent than number of impressions though each is more valuable to an advertiser. Even more value comes from a user following up by filling in a form or buying something or similar, and this is charged at CPA (cost per action); it works best with sites that fit a particular taste such as sports outlets, so, while it can be lucrative in certain circumstances, it may not work for a news site except in combination with another company, such as travel offers in the travel section. The final payment method for banner ads is the periodically paid, that is, weekly or monthly, as in the traditional print/broadcast model. This works for advertisers more used to old media who prefer to pay for the prominence of position rather than the less predictable "per" payments. Sirkkunen and Cook (2012) point to this as an option for small media startups because it is easier to work with and more transparent.

Getting your ads: ad tech companies and programmatic advertising

Advertisers can be found individually by a little hard work among companies and organisations interested in your niche area, but they can also be located through advertising networks and agency groupings and the like. There are thousands of these operators, known as ad tech companies, but they are dominated by the two main go-between giants, Facebook and Google (which are addressed separately below). They work by aggregating available ad space and matching it with advertiser demand, taking the hard work out of your search for clients but also taking a share of the proceeds, usually a third to a half (Choo 14 January 2014). Mark Briggs divides them into two types. The big ones bundle large numbers of ad impressions from many sites and sell them more efficiently and at lower rates to advertisers or ad agencies. The smaller type Briggs calls "self-serve" networks, which you sign up to individually, with specialists known as "boutique" networks (Briggs 2012, 82–84).

As the numbers of sites and ads multiplied and automation became more sophisticated, programmatic advertising emerged. It started out as a way to use up ad inventory remainders by matching them up with suitable placements through bidding in real-time online auctions. It has turned into a general market covering thousands of sites based on their performance, bringing together on the one hand brands and agencies (the "demand-side platform", DSP), who put in their requirements in number of impressions, and on the other publishers, who offer ad space (the "supply-side platform", SSP). Ad networks buy up inventory, repackage it and resell it to advertisers. This process has produced ad exchanges, which deal with all kinds of ads.

Thus programmatic advertising has provided a very easy way for journalism startups to get on the advertising ladder without needing much expertise. However, it has led to the appearance of clickbait (ads that pull the reader in with attractive but over-hyped pictures and headlines with the aim of going viral) and intrusive videos that take over a user's screen. This spurred the growth in ad blocking. Google announced in 2017 that it would filter out invasive ads and allow publishers to charge people who used ad blockers, while Apple said it would stop the automatic playing of video on its Safari browser and Facebook cracked down on clickbait headlines (Uberti 6 June 2017). In 2018 the European Union's General Data Protection Regulation (GDPR) came into effect, protecting privacy by restricting third-party cookies. The ad industry's response was to improve the standards of ads and to target them better at people who should be interested, though in the eyes of publishers this put the initiative back in the hands of the consumer and diminished a promising revenue source in a difficult market (Moses 7 June 2017).

Programmatic advertising continued to dominate the market, though. Industry research cited by specialist media says its total value exceeded US$100 billion for the first time in 2019, with 85 per cent of ads in the United States,

90 per cent in the UK and 70 per cent in Germany being sold this way (Faw 25 November 2019; Bhattacharjee 26 February 2020; eMarketer Editors 10 January 2019). It was less used in Asia, and a survey done in the region found it took about 50 per cent of the ad market, though more than three quarters of respondents said it was available and adoption was "high" to "medium" (Rubicon Project & Campaign Asia 2020). For news publishers, however, automated ad placement still has its problems. One is that ad tech downgrades negative words in the interest of "brand safety" so that serious journalism, which often covers topics where such vocabulary is needed, may be disadvantaged (Parker 27 January 2021). Another is that ad placement is unpredictable, and may result in a clash with regular content on the page, though most services allow users some choice in categories that helps minimise this.

With privacy restrictions making things much more difficult for programmatic advertising, journalism outlets were facing the need to rely more on first-party data, that is, information provided directly by users rather than that gathered automatically from browsing and purchasing activities. Many outlets have been focusing more and more on getting users to sign up for subscriptions (see pp. 75–77) or memberships (see pp. 95–97), which both bring in legitimate data and promise direct income.

Affiliates

Affiliate ads are placed on your site to promote items your audience might be interested in, but, unlike regular advertising, no money changes hands until someone makes a purchase via your link, and then you get a pre-agreed cut of the payment. This is particularly suited to sites that have connections to easily marketed products such as beauty items, clothes and tech equipment, but any topic will do if you identify the kind of products your audience like. Some news media have bought up or created their own branches suited to this form of income. *The New York Times* (*NYT*) purchased the affiliate-financed review site Wirecutter in 2016, and in 2019 BuzzFeed, which has long relied on affiliate income, set up food site Tasty with recipes whose ingredients could be bought directly from Walmart (Smith 23 September 2019).

But even small sites can benefit from this kind of ad. Amazon has perhaps the biggest affiliate programme, but many major international brands have their own, such as Apple and Adidas, as do regional e-commerce outfits like Singapore's Lazada and some of China's big tech companies. There are also specialists like Awin, which has an entry-level service for newbies designed to help you find and build partnerships. The key is to choose one or more that have the right potential for your site. You can actually arrange your own ads directly with the original producer – the only costs are the creation of the ad and the setting up of the link. Some people highly recommend affiliate for both small and large media outlets because it is easy, cheap and controllable.

Paid content: native advertising, sponsored content and branded content

These forms of advertising have their roots in the "advertorials" of newspapers – pages that were laid out similarly to normal editorial but were in fact sponsored by outsiders, such as embassies celebrating national days or property developers launching a new project. They had the look of serious news rather than ads but they were clearly labelled as paid-for. But where advertorials provided a supplementary income for newspapers, the new version has become a major source of revenue for online outlets: ICFJ's reports on technology in newsrooms worldwide found in 2017 that 44 per cent of respondents were using "sponsored content", and in 2019, when they split the categories, a similar figure for for-profit outlets and even 28 per cent for nonprofit outlets (ICFJ 2017, 2019). Its advantage is that it provides media outlets with a much surer way to make money than regular ads while giving advertisers more engagement with readers.

There is some overlap and confusion between different types of paid content. British academic Andrew Youde (2017) provides some definitions. He says native is "advertising for a product which is produced in the format of your regular content ... the digital equivalent of an advertorial". He cites a *New York Times* investigation into women in prison to promote the Netflix series *Orange Is the New Black*. Sponsored, meanwhile, is "a conventional news story but with a named sponsor", in other words, one which is paid for by an outside entity and marked as such but doesn't mention the sponsor in the content itself, just carrying their label. "This approach yields less financial return than native advertising but it avoids readers potentially confusing ads for news," says Youde. Branded content is material written by the advertiser or prepared by the publisher with input from the advertiser and may vary from covering the advertiser to not having direct advertising at all.

Paid content has several benefits. Unlike the advertorial, it doesn't have to be confined to a separate section but can appear anywhere on the publisher's platform. Another is that it can't be turned off by ad blockers. Yet another is that the media site controls who advertises, where and when they advertise and usually the content itself. Ad agencies and content providers offer the service, but paid-for material is often written by the media outlet's own employees, who may be from a separate team or even part of a self-owned ad agency. Sometimes the journalists who work on regular content are put on the task, but there is usually some objection to this. Cambodia's Sabay found it had to divide its team into two, but Malaysia's Cilisos has everybody do everything because, they say, they have the same values for both functions (see pp. 178–181 and pp. 118–121).

Whatever path is followed, native and sponsored work should be clearly marked, but is not always so; sometimes that information may appear at the very bottom of the story or not at all. The key is putting together engaging but honest editorial content that is integrated into the whole look of the outlet while being prominently labelled as paid-for. The catch is whether the balance can really be achieved without compromising the outlet's integrity or that of the journalists who write it. Ethical issues with advertising are discussed in Chapter 6.

Search, social and CMSs

The most painless first step to making money is via the platforms you use to distribute your content. With a little work to make your posts attractive to your audience you can almost effortlessly earn money, mainly through these platforms' advertising, though it may not be a lot even if you have a large following because the intermediaries take much of the income.

Facebook allows you to monetise through newsfeed ads, instream ads (for videos), fan subscriptions, branded content (through connections with companies) and subscription groups, all with various eligibility requirements clearly explained on the site. Instagram, which has built itself up as a hub for influencer marketing, has been slower off the mark for media, but its IGTV was reported to be opening up to allow "creators" to get a share of sponsored posts that appear on their feeds or through brand collaboration (Williams 18 November 2020). WhatsApp and other messenger apps can be used to send out your content to paying customers, or to distribute branded content for clients. Twitter offers publishers a share of the income from the ads they attract. Through YouTube's Partner Program you can make money from ads, memberships, merchandise, premium subscribers and fans who want greater visibility on your feed. All these methods of monetisation are explained on the platforms as well as in numerous online videos.

There are some special programmes designed to bring in ads.

Google's AdSense, which supplies your site with targeted advertising, is a good place to start because it's very easy. To sign up you just need a Google account, a phone number and an address. You get a piece of software that does everything for you, though you can customise the placement and kind of ads you want. Its calculator suggests that a news site in the Asia-Pacific with 50,000 monthly page views could make US$3,432 a year. For greater reach and more income but needing a little more work, Google's Ad Manager, an agglomeration of several older services launched in 2018, encompasses thousands of ad networks including AdSense. An alternative is Google Accelerated Mobile Pages (AMP), set up in 2015, a distributed system whereby you reformat your pages using Google's AMPHTML (instructions are provided) so that they can be hosted on Google servers. Once done, your pages (and their ads) will load much faster (it's open-source so ads can appear on non-AMP pages as well) and will also pop up quickly on search. You also qualify for a higher ranking, though that privilege was set to end in 2021 amid concerns about the company's monopolistic tendencies (Jeffries 19 November 2020).

Facebook's counterpart programme is Instant Articles, also set up in 2015. IA provides a dedicated streamlined channel for individual media, as described in

Chapter 2 (see p. 32), but its disadvantage is that it keeps users within the platform to view stories rather than directing them to your actual site. For outlets for which Facebook is the chief source of traffic, IA can be a reliable earner. You receive a much greater share of ad revenue than from regular pages, and it helps you make money from branded content and subscriptions. However, the rules Facebook has developed to keep unethical content from its platform can be inconsistent. Posts can be removed suddenly and without explanation, or your whole account may be blocked for no obvious reason, cutting off your income. Some publishers in the region suspect that in non-English languages, Facebook's decisions are less reliable.

Automattic, which owns the CMS WordPress, offers WordAds, which places ads at the bottom of every post and page, as well as in other positions if you choose. You have to use it if you build your site on the free WP version because it's the only advertising allowed on it, though you have more flexibility if you take a paid service. It's been difficult to use if your site is not already quite big, but now self-hosted WP sites can sign up via the Jetpack Ads plugin.

Other platforms

Aggregators

News aggregators work by signing up with outlets whose stories' headlines and often first paragraphs get published in their news lists along with links to the originals. It's a way for media small and large to get their content to a wider audience, so usually the aggregating company doesn't pay sources on the grounds that the resulting increased traffic to the site is compensation enough. This has been a sore point with publishers, who complain that in practice many readers don't click at all on their sites (Kaye & Quinn 2010, 41–42; Elliott & Spence 2018, 70–72). When faced by a proposed Australian law that would require payment for aggregated content, Google News, the biggest aggregator, decided to pay its component news outlets there in late 2020 and also agreed to pay its French media in 2021. Facebook resisted pressure in Australia and even temporarily closed down its news sharing there, but ended up coming to an agreement with the government in early 2021 whereby it would negotiate with news providers for payment in return for some changes in the new law (Browne 21 January 2021; Statt 24 February 2021).

Some do pay as a norm, however. The biggest aggregator in our region is China's Jinri Toutiao (Today's Headlines), founded in 2012, which has shared its ad revenue with content providers since a plagiarism scandal early on in its existence (see p. 99), though the payment system is not very transparent (Zhang 2019). However, since it wants to encourage more content production (He 23 November 2017), small-time contributors do benefit. Japan's VC-invested aggregator SmartNews, founded in 2012, also shares revenue with its news partners according to how much their content is read on its free app rather than according to the ads they attract. It is only available in its home country and the United States so far. Apple's aggregator, Apple News, took the US audience by storm after Facebook pulled back on news in 2016 (Oremus 25 September 2018) and actually paid its publishers, but complaints emerged that revenue was limited because ads were not doing well (Willens 25 February 2019). The app is not available in Asia yet. Facebook was launching its own curator, News Tab, in early 2021 which would also pay its contributors, though it was only initially destined for use in Britain (Fischer 1 December 2020).

Publishing platforms

For a one-person or small journalism enterprise, signing up for one of a publishing platform is a good option not only to get your content out (see Chapter 3) but to secure payment as well.

Medium, set up in 2012 by Twitter co-founder Evan Williams and two others in San Francisco, received, according to Crunchbase, three rounds of VC funding totalling US$132 million between 2014 and 2016, but didn't seem to prosper. In the latter year it stopped taking advertising and in 2017 ended the system where publishers could use it to organise their own subscriptions, instead requiring visitors who wanted access to paid content to join the platform's own new membership scheme (Sutton 11 May 2018). It seems to have done better since then. Authors can choose whether to make their work free or put it behind the paywall, and if the latter, they must join the Partner Program by signing up and providing bank account and tax details – for those not in the United States, an account with online payment provider Stripe is needed, though in our region this is only available in Hong Kong, Malaysia and Singapore. Users pay US$5 a month to access paywalled content. The platform helps authors design and format their work as well as use tools to find and build an audience from among its claimed 170 million users. Fans can follow authors and authors can get in touch with them and send out newsletters and notifications. Authors are paid the same proportion of members' fees as the proportion of time readers spend there.

Patreon was launched in 2013 and, according to Crunchbase, has had six rounds of funding, the latest in 2020, totalling US$256.8 million. It provides a platform for a wide range of content creators, including musicians, artists, businesses and NGOs, but devotes one section to writers and journalists. It provides you with your own page and direct communication with your "patrons", who subscribe to your content at fixed monthly rates. You can sign up for three tiers of service, charges varying from 5 per cent of patron payments for the basic model to 12 per cent for the top one (plus payment processing fees in all cases). Patreon is a good platform for people with a variety of content to show.

Substack is much newer, having been founded in 2017, and has received US$17.4 million in one seed round and a Series A round, according to Crunchbase. It operates a newsletter service where audience members subscribe to a particular writer at whatever fee the writer wants to charge, with the company taking a

10 per cent cut and credit card costs. The site pays promising writers up front and recoups the outlay from reader payments; it does not require reimbursement if that fails. It claims it can provide a living wage and more: "Top writers on Substack make hundreds of thousands of dollars per year". This system obviously works better for those who already have a following, and its first big success was Bill Bishop, who had 30,000 followers for his previously free China blog, Sinocism. He reportedly earned a six-figure income after joining the new platform (Chang 2020). Substack took a tumble in early 2021 when it was criticised for its policy of paying writers who attracted a good audience even though they expressed distasteful views, and some writers quit the platform (Stenberg 17 March 2021).

Singapore-based Ghost, launched after a Kickstarter campaign in 2013, is a nonprofit developer of open-source technology for journalism that puts its products to use to provide space for content creators, from individuals to large teams, who in turn give Ghost an income. It offers four deal types for writers, from US$9, a month for a single staff user, to US$199, a month for business. Readers sign up as members, and they can log in, get newsletters and pay subscriptions.

The success of these platforms has attracted some big-time competition. A recent challenge has come from Twitter, which bought the newsletter platform Revue in early 2021 and was promising more attractive terms including charging writers just 5 per cent of whatever they earn. At the same time Facebook was planning to launch its own newsletter platform for independent writers in the United States.

Podcast hosts

Podcasts, though only recently becoming very popular, actually predate social media. Thus they started out being linked to via RSS web feeds, which meant they were hosted by sites all over the internet rather than accessed through a platform. In 2005 Apple made them findable via iTunes, bringing them into the mainstream and spurring the appearance of new hosting sites. In 2014 the US public radio smash hit Serial made podcasting famous, and two years later newly launched host Anchor.fm attracted a flood of users with its completely free podcasting production service, which can be done using smartphones. The enforced immobilisation caused by the coronavirus pandemic has fuelled podcast use.

However, the original aim was to build brands rather than make money, so revenue generation has lagged behind other forms. Agreeing on standards to measure the success of podcasts has proved difficult, putting off advertisers (Willens 4 June 2018), and paid podcasters like Luminary, Audible Channels and Stitcher Premium have performed poorly, according to one NiemanLab Report, whose author concludes: "[A]t this point, there's been very little evidence of a market that's just itching to pay for podcasts" (Benton 9 November 2020). Unlike the publishing platforms, podcast hosts (top places are held by music providers Spotify and Apple, which have three quarters of the market) don't do much to help producers make money. The latter customarily get their own sponsors, whom they promote on their shows, or their own ads or affiliates, or use any other way to make money, such as memberships and merchandise sales. Advertising has been difficult because it's hard to place – it can interrupt a podcast and kill tension – and hard to gauge for audience engagement. However, with the growing popularity of podcasts, the technology for analytics and for the insertion of ads into podcasts is becoming more sophisticated, and income has boomed (Bursztynsky 19 December 2019; McCarthy 28 January 2021).

The US market was predicted to be worth US$1 billion in 2021 (Radcliffe 8 December 2020). American podcaster Wondery, founded in 2016, attracted three funding rounds worth US$15 million (according to Crunchbase). It was reported at the end of 2020 to be valued at US$300 million and about to be bought out by Amazon, which already owned top podcaster Stitcher and audio book service Audible (Henry 3 December 2020). Apple was reported to be starting subscriptions in mid-2021 (Carman 9 June 2021).

Income direct from the audience

The most prized form of revenue is from your users. You don't have to share profits, you don't have pressure from outside to compromise on your content, and you can gauge from the payments how good a job you're doing. What's more, you get all your user data directly rather than having to rely on the tech giants for it so that you can do surveys and improve advertising.

As yet, though, only a minority of users are paying for news in this way, according to Reuters' 2020 survey of 40 countries. Just 20 per cent of respondents in the United States were doing so, and a mere 7 per cent in the UK (equal lowest with Croatia). In every country in Europe the figure was below 20 per cent with three exceptions: Norway, the top in the world with 42 per cent, Sweden at 27 per cent and Poland at 20 per cent. In Asia outside our region South Korea had 10 per cent and Japan only 8 per cent. So the figures for the five territories surveyed in our region stand up very well: in Hong Kong 29 per cent of respondents said they paid for news, in the Philippines 19 per cent, Malaysia 17 per cent, Taiwan 15 per cent and Singapore 14 per cent (Newman 2020). But those figures at least indicate there is room for expansion.

Paywalls

These are barriers that stop users from accessing part or all of your content unless they pay a fee to get access over a period of time – a subscription. This method was popular in the days of print, particularly for magazines and periodicals, and is also the way cable TV works. With algorithmic feedback (see pp. 92–93), paywalls can be adjusted and individualised, allowing many different configurations.

In the early days of digital media only the big business-and-finance news providers (*Wall Street Journal* (*WSJ*), Bloomberg and *Financial Times*), which sell the kind of content that makes money for their users, were able to operate complete paywalls. The only other kinds of outlet that could succeed were those with expert knowledge that could also help people make money (such as Taiwan's tech blog Stratechery) or provide specialist information on areas not open to the public (like China newsletters such as Sinocism). For almost everyone else this method was almost unthinkable: the word was that no one pays for news on the internet.

That began to change with the entry into the market in 2013 of The Information, a US outlet which charged high subscription rates for access to its prized expert tech coverage. Digital subscriptions started to take off more generally from around 2017, when social media was taking a bad rap for fake news and hate speech, advertising was being criticised for its low quality and ad blockers were appearing (Leslie 22 August 2019). The improvement of security measures and online payment methods helped. The coronavirus pandemic also increased subscriptions, with readers at home most of the time and not spending much money on other things. On the back of these changes people became willing to pay for quality journalism, bringing about a comeback for respected legacy media – by 2020 *The New York Times*, which had opened to subscriptions in 2011, had 4 million digital subscribers (though still allowed some access without payment) and *The Guardian* of Britain had turned its fortunes round with reader donations, which it then worked on turning into subscriptions, counting more than a million regular donors and subscribers at the end of 2020 while keeping all content available free. The challenge now is for new outlets to be able to inspire their readers enough to pay.

It's important to consider how to configure your paywall. A complete block is unlikely to work for a new outlet unless you have a very niche audience, so the usual choice is some kind of "metered" paywall. This allows a number of articles to be read free, after which the user is blocked unless payment is made. This means your content isn't off limits altogether and you can still rack up views and tempt new subscribers. A version of this is the "freemium" model, where "premium" content – either individual articles or sections – is paywalled and the rest is free. One clever Swedish outlet allows one hour of free reading of all content to maximise views before blocking it, a device that has boosted subscriptions (Southern 15 May 2019).

Today paywalls are customisable according to user data, so that different deals can be offered to potential subscribers, though this is only being done by large news outlets so far. Paywalls have been implemented in different ways by Malaysiakini (see pp. 160–165), The Malaysian Insight (see pp. 184–187), Frontier Myanmar (see pp. 131–135) and Coconuts – though, after much experimentation, the latter has taken the barrier down (see pp. 124–128). Others that have gone to subscription include Tech in Asia, e27 and DealStreetAsia, all based in Singapore and offering specialist information. Katadata of Indonesia set up a freemium model with its D-Insights featuring premium business content, though launching it just as the coronavirus hit in 2020 meant it was slow to get off the ground (see Chapter 8 pp. 3–7).

Paywalls have their problems. You may lose readers when you start one because some might decide they actually don't need your material enough to pay for it. So you must be careful to have or expect a dedicated core audience that is able and willing to spend. Then even the best audience can succumb to subscriber fatigue – many outlets are joining the paywall bandwagon and readers might be finding themselves over-burdened with payments, especially if their first need is for finance and tech outlets, which tend to be expensive. You may well be in competition for readers' money not only with media similar to your own but with big-time international publishers. The Hong Kong-based Initium did a clever bundling of its own subscription with one for *WSJ*, which was better value than the deal *WSJ* offered for itself alone (see p. 183), though that has now lapsed.

On the technical side, you risk your charged-for content getting out into the public domain and no longer being exclusive. People can sneak behind paywalls without detection by using on an "incognito" page where much of their data – cookies, search history, filled-in forms – is not saved, which means that sites with metered paywalls can't register the number of free views seen (Brownlee 31 July 2019). The Malaysian Insight's Jahabar Sadiq, who has implemented a paywall that blocks all content bar headlines and top sentences, was well aware that any subscriber can copy content and send it out free.

Publishers nonetheless have great hope for paywall income. The Reuters 2021 journalism predictions report found that more than three quarters of senior media personnel interviewed from round the world (though none from our region) planned to drive subscription revenues more than any other kind (Newman 2021).

Micropayments

"People keep wishing for micropayments. ('Just the one article, please! I'll pay for it!') But micropayments keep not panning out." That's how a mid-2019 NiemanLab article on Dutch micropayments news platform Blendle started (Schmidt 10 June 2019). Dubbed the "iTunes of journalism", this format had all the promise of Apple's music downloads, but it has gone the same way as iTunes itself – though while iTunes morphed into Apple Music, micropayments have all but disappeared. Yet there are some important exceptions.

First a look at Blendle. It started in 2014 with US$3.8 million in investment from *The New York Times*, *Nikkei* and German publisher Axel Springer, then got a further injection of US$4 million from two entrepreneurs, one Dutch and one Danish, in 2018. It worked by taking content from major media (first in the Netherlands, then in Germany and the United States) and providing access to that content for its users, who would pay in a small sum to cover a few reads. Then a fee, set by the publisher, would be deducted for each article read. The income was shared 70-30 between the original publisher and Blendle. However, Blendle guaranteed refunds, which too many readers took advantage of, and returns had to be limited. But it still wasn't enough. By 2019 Blendle had "hundreds of thousands" of pay-per-go users, but it still couldn't move into profit. The people who were keeping it afloat were its 60,000 core subscribers, who spent much more time on the site than the one-offs. The outlet said it would move to a subscription model (Schmidt 10 June 2019).

However, our region is home to the most successful micropayments platforms of all. In China, "super app" WeChat, or Weixin, was launched by tech giant Tencent in 2011 as a messaging system on the lines of WhatsApp, but expanded into not only video and audio calls but a Facebook-like social media platform. WeChat and its stable mate Weibo, a short-messaging system, benefit from the digital wallet WeChat Pay, which is connected to users' credit or debit cards and can be used online for small amounts sent between individuals or companies. The two platforms launched a tip facility in 2014 which became an important source of income for independent media (Li 10 January 2018; Zhang 2019). Overall, China's online payments are very sophisticated and allow for easy transfers of small sums. They do not work outside China, though Chinese companies like Tencent and Alibaba's Alipay are setting up in Southeast Asia alongside locally started payment systems. However, the market looks as if it will be too fragmented to provide a stable media income choice.

Some other outlets do offer the choice of one-off small payments. Cambodia's Sabay, growing out of a gaming company, developed its Sabay coins, priced at 100 riel each, just two-and-a-half US cents, which were distributed to internet cafés all over Cambodia for purchase on site. Hong Kong Free Press (see pp. 139–143) enables tipping via the Swedish micropayments platform Flattr, but this doesn't seem to be a major source of income.

Crowdfunding and donations

These payments have already been discussed under initial funding (see pp. 47–49), but they can work when needed for continuing funds.

There are better prospects when a highly regarded outlet is involved and comes through with the promised goods. Investigative outlets like the International Consortium of Investigative Journalists, famous for the Panama Papers investigation that revealed the secret stashes in Panama of many of the world's élite, run entirely on donations. In our region, Hong Kong has produced the most successful continuously crowdfunded outlets. With the mainstream media increasingly taken over by mainland Chinese interests, there has been a demand for independent news. The investigative outlet FactWire and news sites Hong Kong Free Press and Hong Kong Citizen News launched on crowdfunding (see pp. 135–139), and the first two have gone on to benefit from further exercises. All three also attract continuing donations from supporters. The Reporter has also survived on donations (see pp. 190–193), but other Taiwan outlets that have tried it have not: WeReport, a platform started in 2011 by academics to support individual journalists to do their own stories by putting their proposals up for donations, folded in 2020, as did Media Farmers and Vocus.

For a comprehensive treatment of how to raise funds from users, Google News Initiative's (GNI) Reader Revenue Playbook can be downloaded from the GNI site.

Grants and sponsorships

If "product thinking" is a good way to help you get your news business going commercially, the public service remit of media also makes it eligible for grants and sponsorships from a variety of organisations. These don't really constitute a regular income because they are usually one-offs and given for a purpose – from basic journalism training to instruction on covering development issues to safety training to new product support to business and technical advice to finding staff. But such payments can be an important revenue boost helping attain survival, and they can occasionally be long term, and so they are addressed in this chapter.

Getting grants and sponsorships isn't easy, and it helps to have experienced admin support or knowledgeable advice to negotiate the application processes.

Philanthropy

Academic researchers Matthew Nisbet et al. (2018), in a study for the Shorenstein Foundation at Harvard, found that private foundations had become an important source of nonprofit journalism funding in the United States, filling gaps left by the decline in trusted traditional commercial media, though not nearly compensating for that loss. Foundations are vehicles set up by wealthy individuals, families and companies who want to do social good. US research group Media Impact Funders shows that foundation support goes to media all over the world, often coming from US-based outfits, though a large amount goes to organisations involved in training, lobbying and so on rather than directly to media. Most goes to North America and Europe, but a good amount is being spent in our region, where the Ford Foundation, the Bill & Melinda Gates Foundation and Open Society Foundations (OSF), all US funds, are the most prominent non-government donors to media and journalism (Media Impact Funders n.d.).

The last is perhaps the most high-profile in supporting journalism. The tremendously wealthy OSF, a group of foundations set up by Hungarian-born anti-communist American financier and philanthropist George Soros in 1979, is, according to its website, "the largest private human rights funder in the world, working to build vibrant and inclusive democracies whose governments are accountable to their citizens." Journalism took up just 2.1 per cent of its global budget in 2020, but that's still a sizeable sum. It supports media freedom defenders, investigative journalism, independent media and diversity of voices. Recent regional recipients include the Cambodian Center for Independent Media (CCIM), which received US$15,000 for organisational support for two years in 2019, and the Independent

Mon News Agency of Myanmar, which received US$50,000 for "work on drug policy and legal framework" also in 2019 for two years. OSF also invests in Media Development Investment Fund (MDIF) in Asia (see pp. 42–44).

Soros gained fame when his currency market activities were blamed for triggering the 1997 Asian financial crisis, making him unpopular in the region, particularly in Malaysia, where the ringgit fell in value. This has led to criticism of his philanthropy, with Malaysiakini, which has received OSF funding and MDIF investment, accused of being backed by Soros. Malaysiakini emphasises that donor funding is accepted only on condition that there is no interference in its independent reporting; moreover, no grant can come to more than 10 per cent of the operation's total budget. In Singapore, New Naratif was denied registration ostensibly because it had a grant from an OSF branch (see pp. 169–174).

Individual philanthropists in our region have also supported media. Taiwan's The Reporter, an award-winning investigative outlet, got its first three years of funding from electronics magnate Tung Tzu-hsien, and he renewed his gift for another three years and is expected to renew it again. In Thailand, some of the country' biggest companies, including Charoen Pokphand, sponsor the investigative outlet Isranews Agency; Siam Cement sponsored not only Isra but art4d in its early days (see pp. 146–149 and pp. 107–109).

US tech giants

In their efforts to mollify media for lost ad revenue, Google and Facebook have set up their own foundation-like organisations.

Google News Initiative (GNI) started its Innovation Challenges programme with US$30 million in 2019. Its first Asia focus was on reader revenue and its 2019 and 2020 winners included Hong Kong Free Press (to set up on an open-source crowdfunding platform), Malaysiakini (for a reader rewards programme), Frontier Myanmar (for a membership scheme), Tech in Asia (also for membership) and The News Lens (for an online reader discussion mechanism). GNI also supports fact-checking (Katadata of Indonesia received funds in 2021) and a wide variety of technical and business training. The Facebook Journalism Project started in 2017 and focuses on training and help to use the platform to distribute content and make money, but it also hands out grants. It supported Splice Media's Lights On Fund, which donated US$5,000 to each of 56 regional media during the coronavirus pandemic (see Chapter 8 pp. 9–13). It also arranges long-term contracts for fact-checking, two beneficiaries of which are the Philippines' VERA Files (see pp. 206–210) and Rappler.

Overseas support

Governments of developed countries devote some of their budget to international aid, which is given either directly or through their official representation in the beneficiary country or, more commonly, via NGOs and international organisations. Often development aid has good governance as one of its goals and that covers press freedom, so journalism and media qualify for help through these channels, though support for outspoken news media isn't welcomed by the more controlling governments.

Government-supported foundations

One accessible but controversial source of support is a group of wealthy, mainly government-funded aid providers who sit in an uneasy space between official and foundation funding – perhaps they can be called quasi-government organisations.

The National Endowment for Democracy, the NED, has massive funds available for democratic development in the region. Founded in 1983, it calls itself on its website a "private, nonprofit foundation" that is "[f]unded largely by the U.S. Congress". It gives grants to "nongovernmental organizations, which may include civic organizations, associations, independent media, and other similar organizations" but not to "individuals, governmental bodies, or state-supported institutions such as public universities". One of the aims of its grant programme is to "[s]upport freedom of information and independent media", though other goals such the promotion of human rights and rule of law could also encompass journalism. Grant applications are taken on a quarterly basis.

According to its site, most of the NED's grants in our region go to non-media categories, but it does provide support for journalism in three countries. One is Myanmar (which it calls "Burma"), which received in total just over $1.1 million in 2019 (few details of recipients are given). "China" received over US$900,000 in the same year, though the categorisation is deceptive: more than half that figure went to the Berkeley-based China Digital Times, "an independent, bilingual media organization that brings uncensored news and online voices from China to the world", and another US$95,000 to the US watchdog Freedom Forum. But sums given to individual media in the region can be substantial. In 2019 the Philippines received nearly US$400,000, which went to the Philippine Center for Investigative Journalism, VERA Files, the Center for Media Freedom & Responsibility, the Mindanao Institute of Journalism and news site Rappler. The NED has, like OSF, gained a bad reputation among most of the governments of the region, who depict it as a tool of underhand US influence.

So too has The Asia Foundation (TAF), set up in the mid-1950s to support cultural activities in the region. Based in San Francisco, it has 18 offices in the Asia-Pacific including all Southeast Asian countries and China. It calls itself a "nonprofit international development organization" but has been said to have started out as a front for the CIA (see for instance Klein 2017). The list of TAF's donors includes many individuals and corporate entities, but it also receives funding from governments, among them the United States'. No individual contribution amounts are revealed, so it is included here as a government-linked organisation rather than an NGO. In the 1950s, it prioritised journalism training and support, and it has continued to help with media in Asia over the years but the focus today has moved to human rights issues such as empowering women, domestic violence and human trafficking.

Germany has six major development aid foundations, all linked to political parties, and they are allotted funds by the government. Established in the years since World War II to provide internal political education, they are officially independent nonprofits. The four original bodies are the Friedrich Ebert Foundation, connected to the Social Democrats; the Konrad Adenauer Foundation (KAF), connected to the Christian Democrats; the Friedrich Naumann Foundation (FNF), connected to the Free Democrats; and the Hanns Seidel Foundation, connected to the Christian Social Union. These organisations started getting foreign-aid funding in the 1960s, making them the main disbursers of German overseas development funds (Pinto-Duschinsky 1991). There have been two more recent additions: the Heinrich Böll Foundation, launched in the 1990s by the Green Party, and the Rosa Luxemburg Foundation (RLF), set up for the old East German state party. The foundations generally work individually.

The KAF has been running its Media Programme Asia since 1996. Among its projects are the Asia News Network (ANN), an agency started in 1999 which brings together one English-language news outlet from each country of East and Southeast Asia to facilitate the free exchange of their news. Another is the Konrad Adenauer Center for Journalism at Ateneo de Manila University, set up in 2000, which provides degree and non-degree programmes in journalism including distance-learning courses attracting working journalists from around the region (see p. 62). KAF also runs training sessions, workshops and conferences as well as local support activities such as helping set up the Club of Cambodian Journalists. The other German foundations don't have special media programmes but work on individual projects.

Overseas governments and international bodies

Some governments provide aid through their own dedicated outfits. One such is the Fojo Media Institute, a Swedish government agency that supports free and independent journalism, which has "capacity-building" projects in Myanmar, Vietnam, Cambodia and Laos and also gives grants to other bodies that carry out programmes that fit their goals. Other implementing organisations are close to their own governments and their allies, such as the Danish outfit International Media Support, whose Myanmar and Philippine programmes are funded by the official aid organisations of Denmark, Sweden and Norway, along with the Norwegian and Danish foreign ministries and the EU. Support also comes directly from government representative offices or their sub-organisations, which can give out grants and training for journalism. The US and British official representations in Myanmar were prominent in providing journalism courses in the run-up to the democratising of elections in the first decade of the 21st century.

Then there are national cultural bodies – the Alliance Française, the Goethe Institute, the British Council and so on – with art4d as an example of cooperation with several of these.

The United Nations is also a supporter of journalism in the region. UNESCO, whose remit includes the media, helped finance and organise Cambodian journalism training through the 1990s with backing mainly from the French and Danish governments, though it pulled out in 2000 after providing a new building for the Department of Media Communication at the Royal University of Phnom Penh to continue its work. The UN Development Programme also provided support in Cambodia when it organised a campaign in 2019 to encourage local media to develop sustainable business models. It provided accelerator funds for five small startups set up by young people, mostly women (UNDP 27 November 2019). Another supporter is the UN Democracy Fund (UNDEF), whose grant for "civil society organisations" includes journalism projects. The level of funding is major: US$100,000–US$300,000 per project, and each can take as long as two years. However, its list of grants doesn't include any given in Asia.

Journalism organisations also get involved. One that offers training is the International Center for Journalists (ICFJ), founded in the United States in 1984 by the then editor of the *Boston Globe* and his wife, and it covers most of the developing world with its training programmes. In this region, its website lists a traffic-accident coverage workshop for Southeast Asia, a country programme for Timor-Leste, a citizen-journalist multimedia news project for Malaysia (run by Malaysiakini), a reporting course for Vietnam, a (pre-coup) opportunity for Myanmar journalists to cover US mid-term elections and a partnership with China's Tsinghua University on its Global Business Journalism degree. ICFJ is itself the recipient of donations, listing them in its annual review, and works with the Knight Foundation on annual journalism awards and fellowships.

The Thomson Reuters Foundation, a branch of the international news agency, raises funding for its operations from the Norwegian and British governments and other foundations such as the Omidyar Network (one third of its income comes in this category) as well as from donations, including those given "in kind" – nearly 60 per cent of its income – and through commercial provision of training, which brings in less than 10 per cent. One of its regional projects was Myanmar Now, a news service based in Yangon that allows its content to be used by any other media free as long as acknowledgement is given. The foundation also trains and supports journalists: it has assisted Philippine reporters with election coverage and runs workshops on specific topics such as rural poverty and human trafficking, for which journalists are given financial support to attend. There is also a fellowship programme that sends regional journalists to the Reuters Institute for the Study of Journalism in Oxford. The foundation also has a range of guides and handbooks for coverage, downloadable free; they include oil and gas, international law, finance and business, ethics and many more. Another British media institution, the BBC, also carries out extensive media support in the developing countries of the region via its foundation arms.

Recipient media sometimes have multiple sources of aid-type support. Myanmar's Irrawaddy acknowledges on its site funding from a number of governmental sources – Canada, the Netherlands, Sweden, the US Agency for International Development (USAID) and the Norwegian Ministry of Foreign Affairs – and "international donors". Malaysiakini is also very transparent about its grants, citing the Canadian International Development Agency (CIDA), the Dutch Embassy in Malaysia and the German FNF, as well as a number of NGOs and ICFJ. Cambodia's CCIM, a support organisation for journalists that also runs its own radio stations, recently received funds from the OSF as noted above, but also acknowledges on its site, among others, the US International Republican Institute, the Delegation of the European Union in Cambodia, the British and Australian embassies, the Swedish International Development Agency (SIDA), the Deutsche Welle Academie (the training arm of the German international public broadcaster), UNESCO and the German RLF.

As already seen in some cases, funders also fund each other. Big foundations, governments and international organisations hand out grants to each other and to a plethora of NGOs to do field work. California-based media trainer Internews, which operates in 100 countries, lists on its site as funders 63 American and European foundations, 27 corporations and nonprofits, 45 government bodies and international organisations and 67 individuals. Some NGOs may get huge amounts of financing: US-based FHI360, whose main job is in fact health support in the United States and round the world, was given the task of running a USAID project for civil society and media in Myanmar that was financed to the tune of US$20 million for the first four years (2014–2018) and US$25 million for the next four years. It's unclear if the programme is still running.

This kind of overseas funding helps less-commercial and nonprofit media to survive, at least temporarily, and to fend off pressures from business and government. However, it has some disadvantages. The problem of being accused of foreign influence has been noted, and, since funders generally seek to support "independent" media, who may be critical of the authorities, cooperation often has to be carried out quietly. Research has shown that grants and similar funding may exert a subtle influence over the journalism it supports in other ways. British academics Martin Scott, Mel Bunce and Kate Wright (2019) found in a study of foundation-supported international nonprofit news that journalists often found themselves having to take on the admin work required to manage funding; also, they were steered away from regular news to cover distinctive stories with "impact" in certain key areas favoured by donors, testing the boundary between advocacy and professional practice (Scott, Bunce & Wright 2019). A more recent survey of US nonprofit media reported by NiemanLab similarly pointed out that foundations had an agenda, favouring projects that drove new technology or audience engagement or that required journalists to break the bounds of their routines when often the outlet just needed support for regular work (Hazard Owen & Benton 13 January 2020).

Information about grants, sponsorships and project funding can be found through ICFJ's IJNet, which has a very useful listing with forthcoming competitions, grants, courses, job vacancies and other opportunities for every region of the world. Its weekly newsletter is a must for this kind of news.

Sales

This may be counter-intuitive for journalists, for whom even advertising has a compromising nature, but there are circumstances where sales can fit in with your principles, routines, capabilities and bottom line.

The obvious product for journalists to sell is their own skills. They can provide reporting and editing or photography or graphics either as services on contract to other organisations, or as ready-processed content for paying customers. The latter may be an extension of sponsored advertising of the kind where you prepare special content for advertisers, but done for the client to use on their own site. Indonesian feminist outlet Magdalene set up Working Room, a centre with a pool of freelancers, to take paid editorial assignments, and it has become their main income driver (see pp. 156–160). Coconuts, meanwhile, offers "branded videos, production of sponsored original programming and commercial videos" on its own YouTube channel, its sites and Facebook pages. Others "sell" their experience or expertise. Alan Soon and Rishad Patel of Splice Media are seasoned professionals who offer consultancies in their outlet's subject matter – developing media startups in the region. They provide their services direct to media or to support organisations. In China, Fang Kecheng's News Lab is using the popular trend for "paid online knowledge" to make an income from talks by hired specialists (see Chapter 8 pp. 7–9).

Where media have developed out of other companies, or where other products have emerged from a media company, cross-funding can occur. Cambodia's Sabay grew out of an online game publishing outfit, the income from which supported the media platform for its first two years until it broke even. Indonesia's data specialist media use their skills to provide stories for their free sites and number-crunching for paying customers to give themselves an income (see Katadata, Chapter 8 pp. 3–7, Tirto, pp. 202–205 and Lokadata, pp. 153–156). Singapore-based Tech in Asia has, meanwhile, used its specialism to establish a job ads business for the regional tech industry. Its site claimed that in 2020 more than 22,000 vacancies were posted and drew 700,000-plus applications. Charges to employers range from US$29 for individual jobs to premium at US$69 a month for five ads to premium+ at US$690 a month for unlimited ads and top-level services.

It's even possible to sell goods and services directly. Way back when digital income was only beginning to develop, Kaye and Quinn (2010, 140) suggested "online shopping". They said news providers could sell goods and services on the basis of their strong qualities – "trust and attention-getting" – to give them "market power in the highly competitive e-commerce environment". They mention (143–144) *The New York Times*' Wine Club, which is still going strong today. Among others is *Reader's Digest*'s parent company's cookware and handyman brands sales (Radcliffe 27 February 2020). Thailand's art4d has set up an e-commerce service (see p. 109), and China's Chaping makes 70 per cent of its income from selling unique goods via a Taobao store (see p. 103). Such initiatives don't always work. The international Chinese long-form journalism site Initium, based in Hong Kong, copied an *NYT* high-class package tour initiative and offered quality visits to places of interest in China, but it took a lot of organising and didn't make much profit and so was dropped (see p. 183). Magdalene, meanwhile, tried to set up an online shop with its own product line but didn't have the capacity to make it work (see p. 158).

Events

Putting on events is a natural development for media startups. As Sirkkunen and Cook (2012, 106) found in their media business survey,

> Ticket sales and spin off revenue incomes from events are proving to be a lucrative diversification for many startups whose raison d'etre is editorial. The community building that can come from hosting events in real life spins off into the editorial and back again.

Events can range from informal coffee-shop sessions with journalists (done by The Reporter – see p. 192), discussion groups (New Naratif), social evenings with founders and senior staff (see Coconuts, p. 125), talks by experts, exhibitions and stalls at fairs (art4d – see p. 107) to major annual industry meet ups, which work especially well for tech and business outlets like Tech in Asia and DealStreetAsia.

The bottom dropped out of the events market when the coronavirus arrived in 2020, forcing social distancing, working from home and quarantine. Into the breach stepped online meeting facility Zoom, joined by many others as its potential became clear, and the world got used to virtual get-togethers. Seen at first as a temporary measure, online events soon established their own appeal: people could meet without leaving home and without dressing up – a lot cheaper and more convenient. There's not a lot of evidence to show how things have gone for news outlets that put on events, but one that has made good of the transition is Thailand's The Standard. It set up a new product, The Standard Economic Forum, which put on virtual talks by well-known speakers; these meet-ups sold far more tickets than they could have done at a real venue. Virtual events now make up 10 per cent of the outlet's revenue (see p. 198). Katadata of Indonesia also made this source of income into a new revenue driver (see Chapter 8 p. 6).

Mixing it up

Jeff Kaye and Stephen Quinn (2010, 72) cite a US media expert who studied new business models in 2008 as advising that new media should combine advertising, subscription, philanthropy and micropayments, the latter to allow impulse buying even though at the time they were very new – and he was calling for Skype to be used as the payment platform. Some parts of that call haven't happened, but the basics were correct enough. Research done on independent media in Latin America by the Knight Foundation and sponsored by the Omidyar Network in 2017 found that

> the online news startups mostly likely to become sustainable and profitable are those that combined multiple ways to bring in revenue, mixing advertising with crowdfunding, training, event planning and so on. Meanwhile, those dependent on just two or three sources of income are either struggling or stagnant.
>
> *(Pachico 20 July 2017)*

Indeed, most outlets interviewed for this book were following the same strategy: use every which way to bring in an income.

References

Benton, Joshua (9 November 2020). Can Spotify be the one to convince people to pay for podcasts? NiemanLab. Retrieved 2 December 2020 from https://www.niemanlab.org/2020/11/can-spotify-be-the-one-to-convince-people-to-pay-for-podcasts/

Bhattacharjee, Monojoy (26 February 2020). Programmatic accounts for 85% of US digital ad spending: IAB. What's New in Publishing. Retrieved 29 December 2020 from https://whatsnewinpublishing.com/programmatic-accounts-for-85-of-us-digital-ad-spending-iab/

Briggs, Mark (2012). *Entrepreneurial journalism: how to build what's next for news*. Los Angeles: Sage.

Browne, Ryan (21 January 2021). Google agrees to pay French publishers for news. *CNBC*. Retrieved 22 March 2021 from https://www.cnbc.com/2021/01/21/google-agrees-to-pay-french-publishers-for-news.html

Brownlee, Chip (31 July 2019). Google's new Chrome makes it easier to bypass newspaper paywalls. *Slate*. Retrieved 3 January 2021 from https://slate.com/technology/2019/07/google-chrome-update-incognito-mode-paywall-workaround.html

Bursztynsky, Jessica (19 December 2019). Spotify made huge investments in podcasts: here's how it plans to make them pay off. *CNBC*. Retrieved 9 February 2021 from https://www.cnbc.com/2020/12/19/how-spotify-plans-to-make-money-from-podcasts.html

Carman, Ashley (9 June 2021). Apple Podcasts says it'll launch in-app subscriptions globally on June 15th. *The Verge*. Retrieved 11 June 2021 from https://www.theverge.com/2021/6/9/22526186/apple-podcasts-in-app-subscription-launch

Chang, Clio (Winter 2020). The Substackerati. *Columbia Journalism Review*. Retrieved 1 January 2021 from https://www.cjr.org/special_report/substackerati.php

Choo, Bryan (6 January 2014.). How Singaporean bloggers can make money: Nuffnang vs GoogleAds vs other adnetworks. *TheSmartLocal*. Retrieved 28 December 2020 from https://thesmartlocal.com/read/singapore-blog-advertising-case-study/

Elliott, Deni, & Spence, Edward (2018). *Ethics for a digital era*. Hoboken, NJ: Wiley Blackwell.

eMarketer Editors (10 January 2019). In Europe, programmatic ad spending grows by double digits. *eMarketer*. Retrieved 29 December 2020 from https://www.emarketer.com/content/in-europe-programmatic-ad-spending-is-growing-by-double-digits

Faw, Larissa (25 November 2019). Programmatic ad spend to hit $147 billion by 2021. *MediaPost*. Retrieved 29 December 2020 from https://www.mediapost.com/publications/article/343745/programmatic-ad-spend-to-hit-147-billion-by-2021.html

Fischer, Sara (1 December 2020). Facebook News to launch in U.K. in January. *Axios*. Retrieved 1 January 2021 from https://www.axios.com/facebook-news-to-launch-in-uk-in-january-66ebb8b4-01dd-446c-8846-844c197f2808.html

Hazard Owen, Laura, & Benton, Joshua (13 January 2020). Foundation grants have strings attached and nonprofit journalists sometimes don't like being told what to do by them. NiemanLab. Retrieved 15 February 2021 from https://www.niemanlab.org/2020/01/foundation-grants-have-strings-attached-and-nonprofit-journalists-sometimes-dont-like-being-told-what-to-do-by-them/

He, Wei (23 November 2017). Toutiao grooms content creators. *China Daily*. Retrieved 1 January 2021 from https://www.chinadaily.com.cn/business/2017-11/23/content_34880992.htm

Henry, Charlotte (3 December 2020) It looks like Amazon, not Apple, is going to buy Wondery. MacObserver. Retrieved 6 December 2020 from https://www.macobserver.com/news/it-looks-like-amazon-not-apple-is-going-to-buy-wondery/

ICFJ (International Center for Journalists) (2017). The state of technology in global newsrooms. Retrieved 30 December 2020 from http://www.icfj.org/resources/first-ever-global-survey-news-tech-reveals-perilous-digital-skills-gap

ICFJ (2019). The state of technology in global newsrooms. Retrieved 30 December 2020 from http://www.icfj.org/resources/first-ever-global-survey-news-tech-reveals-perilous-digital-skills-gap

Jeffries, Adrianne (19 November 2020). Google to pull back benefit to news sites that adopted its preferred mobile technology. *The Markup*. Retrieved 31 December 2020 from https://themarkup.org/google-the-giant/2020/11/19/as-antitrust-pressure-mounts-google-to-pull-back-benefit-to-news-sites-that-adopted-its-preferred-mobile-technology

Kaye, Jeff, & Quinn, Stephen (2010). *Funding journalism in the digital age: business models, strategies and trends*. New York: Peter Lang.

Klein, Christina (2017). Cold War cosmopolitanism: the Asia Foundation and 1950s Korean Cinema. *Journal of Korean Studies*, 22/2, 281–316.

Leslie, Alex (2 August 2019). Subscription economy to get a real boost from advertising fiasco. *Disruptive.asia*. Retrieved 3 January 2021 from https://disruptive.asia/subscription-economy-boost-advertising-fiasco/?utm_source=mailpoet&utm_medium=email&utm_campaign=Weekly+26+August+2019

Li, Mia Shuang (10 January 2018). How WeChat became the prime news source in China. *Columbia Journalism Review* & Tow Center. Retrieved 13 February 2021 from https://www.cjr.org/tow_center/how-wechat-became-primary-news-source-china.php

Lim, Shawn (6 April 2021). Breaking up the Chinese walled gardens: what will the future of media in China look like? *The Drum*. Retrieved 16 April 2021 from https://www.thedrum.com/news/2021/04/06/breaking-up-the-chinese-walled-gardens-what-will-the-future-media-china-look

Mandese, Joe (19 January 2021). Time spent with ad-supported media hits all-time low, despite gains in total media use. *MediaPost*. Retrieved 9 February 2021 from https://

www.mediapost.com/publications/article/359711/time-spent-with-ad-supported-media-hits-all-time-l.html

McCarthy, John (28 January 2021). If you don't cast, you're last: inside big tech's podcasting goldrush. *The Drum*. Retrieved 9 February 2021 from https://www.thedrum.com/news/2021/01/28/if-you-don-t-cast-you-re-last-inside-big-tech-s-podcasting-goldrush

Meade, Amanda (16 February 2021). Google and Facebook: the landmark Australian law that will make them pay for news content. *Guardian*. Retrieved 23 March 2021 from https://www.theguardian.com/technology/2021/feb/16/google-and-facebook-the-landmark-australian-law-that-will-make-them-pay-for-news-content

Media Impact Funders (n.d.). Mapping the field of media and philanthropy: the latest data, networks and trends. Retrieved 14 February 2021 from https://mediaimpactfunders.org/

Moses, Lucia (7 June 2017). As Apple and Google take aim at ads, publishers tremble. *Digiday*. Retrieved 30 December 2020 from https://digiday.com/media/apple-google-take-aim-ads-publishers-tremble/

Newman, Nic (2020). Reuters Institute digital news report 2020. Reuters Institute for the Study of Journalism. Retrieved 18 July 2020 from http://www.digitalnewsreport.org/

Newman, Nic (2021). Journalism, media, technology trends and predictions 2021. Reuters Institute for the Study of Journalism & University of Oxford. Retrieved 16 April 2021 from https://reutersinstitute.politics.ox.ac.uk/journalism-media-and-technology-trends-and-predictions-2021

Nisbet, Matthew, Wihbey, John, Kristiansen, Silje, & Bajak, Aleszu (2018). Funding the news: foundations and nonprofit media. Shorenstein Centre on Media, Politics and Public Policy and Northeastern University's School of Journalism. Retrieved 19 June 2018 from https://shorensteincenter.org/funding-the-news-foundations-and-nonprofit-media/

Oremus, Will (25 September 2018). The temptation of Apple News. *Slate*. Retrieved 1 January 2021 from https://slate.com/technology/2018/09/apple-news-media-slate-ad-sales-no-money.html

Pachico, Elyssa (20 July 2017). Study offers tips on how to make independent news sites profitable. *IJNet*. Retrieved 27 December 2020 from https://ijnet.org/en/story/study-offers-tips-how-make-independent-news-sites-profitable

Parker, Ben (27 January 2021). How advertisers defund crisis journalism. The New Humanitarian. Retrieved 9 February 2021 from https://www.thenewhumanitarian.org/analysis/2021/01/27/brand-safety-ad-tech-crisis-news

Pinto-Duschinsky, M. (1991). Foreign political aid: the German political foundations and their US counterparts. *International Affairs*, 67/1, 33–63.

Radcliffe, Damian (27 February 2020). Why brand extensions are a great starting point for publishers interested in eCommerce. What's New in Publishing. Retrieved 16 February 2021 from https://whatsnewinpublishing.com/why-brand-extensions-are-a-great-starting-point-for-publishers-interested-in-ecommerce/

Radcliffe, Damian (8 December 2020). The state of podcasting in 9 charts. What's New in Publishing. Retrieved 16 February 2021 from https://whatsnewinpublishing.com/the-state-of-podcasting-in-9-charts/

Rubicon Project & Campaign Asia (2020). Programmatic ad buying in Asia: a closer look at programmatic ad buying trends and challenges across the region. Retrieved 29 December 2020 from https://rubiconproject.com/insights/research/programmatic-ad-buying-in-asia/

Schmidt, Christine (10 June 2019). Micropayments-for-news pioneer Blendle is pivoting from micropayments. *NiemanLab.* Retrieved 4 January 2021 from https://www.niemanlab.org/2019/06/micropayments-for-news-pioneer-blendle-is-pivoting-from-micropayments/

Scott, Martin, Bunce, Mel, & Wright, Kate (2019.) Foundation funding and the boundaries of journalism. *Journalism Studies*, 20/14, 2034–2052. DOI: 10.1080/1461670X.2018.1556321

Sirkkunen, Esa, & Cook, Clare (Eds.) (2012). *Chasing sustainability on the net.* Tampere: Juvenus. Retrieved 10 Aug 2016 from http://tampub.uta.fi/bitstream/handle/10024/66378/chasing_sustainability_on_the_net_2012.pdf?sequence=1

Smith, Steve (23 September 2019). Publishers look beyond the buy button to capitalize on affiliate revenue. *Folio.* Retrieved 29 December 2020 from https://www.foliomag.com/publishers-affiliate-revenue/

Southern, Lucinda (15 May 2019). Sweden's MittMedia increases subscriber conversion by 20% with a 'time wall'. *Digiday.* Retrieved 3 January 2021 from https://digiday.com/media/swedens-mittmedia-increases-subscriber-conversions-20-time-wall/

Statt, Nick (24 February 2021). Facebook will match Google's $1 billion news investment after Australia showdown. *The Verge.* Retrieved 22 March 2021 from https://www.theverge.com/2021/2/24/22299229/facebook-one-billion-investment-news-industry-australia-google-regulation

Stenberg, Mark (17 March 2021). Substack Pro leads to departures from platform, opportunities for competitors. *Adweek.* Retrieved 22 March 2021 from https://www.adweek.com/media/having-a-substack-feels-dirty-substack-pro-announcement-leads-to-departures-from-the-platform-opportunities-for-competitors/

Sutton, Kelsey (11 May 2018). 'We had no idea that it was coming': medium pulls the rug from under publications. *Columbia Journalism Review.* Retrieved 4 January 2021 from https://www.cjr.org/business_of_news/medium-publication.php

Uberti, David (6 June 2017). The digital advertising doomsday clock. *Columbia Journalism Review.* Retrieved 30 December 2020 from https://www.cjr.org/business_of_news/digital-advertising-google-ad-blocker-facebook.php

United Nations Development Programme (UNDP) (27 November 2019). UNDP business challenge winners. Retrieved 23 March 2021 from https://www.kh.undp.org/content/cambodia/en/home/library/undp-media-business-challenge-winner.html

Willens, Max (4 June 2018). Podcasting keeps inching toward measurement standard, but is reluctant to deal with the short-term pain. *Digiday.* Retrieved 24 March 2021 from https://digiday.com/media/podcasting-keeps-inching-toward-measurement-standard/

Willens, Max (25 February 2019). 'Hard to back out': publishers grow frustrated by the lack of revenue from Apple News. *Digiday.* Retrieved 1 January 2021 from https://digiday.com/media/hard-to-back-out-publishers-remain-frustrated-by-apple-news-monetization/

Williams, Rob (18 November 2020). How will publishers monetize their content on Instagram? *MediaPost.* Retrieved 331 December 2020 from https://www.mediapost.com/publications/article/357899/how-will-publishers-monetize-their-content-on-inst.html?edition=120483

Youde, Andrew (2017). The business of journalism. In Marsden, Paul (Ed.). *Entrepreneurial journalism: how to go it alone and launch your dream digital project.* London; New York: Routledge. 22–39.

Zhang, Shixin Ivy (2019). The business model of journalism start-ups in China. *Digital Journalism*, 7/5, 614–634. DOI: 10.1080/21670811.2018.1496025.

6
SUSTAINING AND SCALING YOUR ENTERPRISE, ETHICAL ISSUES

Introduction

Like any other business, a journalism enterprise needs strategies to maintain its initial successes and not only survive but expand, all the while continuing to serve the audience and staying true to its principles as far as possible.

Audience engagement

Whatever your form of income, sustaining your journalism startup will depend on having a valuable audience, that is, users who will either pay you themselves or provide a means to attract advertisers and other funders. Finding your audience is hard enough, but you can't stop there and must work hard to keep them coming back. That means keeping them engaged. This can be done by providing them with consistent quality content, encouraging them to read more and constantly checking back on what they are looking at to make sure you're on the right lines.

The goal is to build a loyal following that identifies with your outlet.

Quality content

"Most news entrepreneurs agree that publishing … great content is the best way to build an audience and then turn that audience into a community that adds value through sharing and engagement", says Mark Briggs in his book on entrepreneurial journalism (2012, 32). How to decide on type and source of content and get it distributed is discussed in Chapter 2, with a reminder to seek out the kind of stories you can go on getting. Hong Kong Citizen News's chief editor Daisy Li Yuet Wah tells how she readied a major investigative story to start the outlet with a bang, only to realise that that wasn't enough to keep it going.

DOI: 10.4324/9781315270432-6

HKCN's experienced leaders and young reporting team pulled through in the emergency and got a regular stream of stories coming in (see pp. 135–139). Hong Kong Free Press took an unpaid month to stock up on stories before launching (see pp. 139–143). From that experience founder Tom Grundy learned what many editors advise: invest in "evergreen" stories that can be kept for or reported during slow periods. These can be soft features or behind-the-news stories or interviews about topics that are not hot at the moment but of some topical interest. The main need, though, is to keep a reliable team working on stories that are gettable – that is, available to reporters within your resources – and cover what your readers want to know about.

Make an effort to encourage "recirculation" – keeping users on your site – by displaying links to your other stories. A study by The Lenfest Institute done on the Graham Media Group in the US found that readers were more likely to click on links in the following circumstances: when they were placed at the end of the page, when they included images, when they connected to related content rather than popular stories, and when they had simple and direct wording (Collier & Stroud 2018).

Using digital feedback to monitor and act on audience engagement

Digital measuring tools use code inserted on your site to tally information about your audience's behaviour. The resulting metrics can tell you how many people are looking at your content at any time, what age and gender they are, where they were referred from, which of your pages they look at and how long they stay there, how far they scroll down a page, whether they look further into your site and with whom they share your content. This data can be developed into analytics that can help you judge what engages your audience, that is, what attracts them and makes them stay longer. You can use it to glean pointers on how to fine-tune content to get readers to visit more often and keep them on your site longer. You can adjust topics, reporting style, writing and visuals as well as headlines, design, story positioning, tone of language, tags, etc.

Google Analytics is one of the most accessible and popular such tools, offering free and paid versions. It measures "core web vitals" – audience behaviour on your site – and lets you know trends, changes and anything else that keeps you up to date with how your content is being used, as well as giving you some idea of how you fit into the general picture. It also helps you optimise ads and identify readers likely to "convert" to paying for your content. Google's journalism support outfit Google News Initiative (GNI) also offers a number of free data tools – News Tagging Guide, News Consumer Insights and Realtime Content Insights – all with instructions on how to put them into practice. The GNI site shows how the Philippine news outlet Rappler used them to allow staff to monitor and set goals for their section's performance, to calculate which content and distribution platforms were best for readers, to improve the way their website worked and to optimise programmatic advertising. The result was a 20-per-cent year-on-year rise in average monthly readers, an 8-per-cent increase year on year in the number of articles read per visit and a 5-per-cent increase in ad revenue (Cornez & Hapal, n.d.). There are many analytics services based in the US – Chartbeat, Parse.ly (recently acquired by WordPress owner Automattic), comScore, Nielsen, Alexa and so on – and most have a free service as well as paid-for packages.

However, working out exactly which metrics to use to interpret your readers' level of engagement and how to act on the resulting information is still not straightforward. It involves not only complex figures but the opinions of stakeholders, business staff, journalists and users, as Amsterdam academic Balász Bodó (2019) points out in his study of news personalisation, so that it is done in different ways in different newsrooms. According to a 2019 IJNet article, the *Financial Times* defined engagement as "recency + frequency + volume" (that is, the more recent and more often the visits and the more time spent) while *The Wall Street Journal* focused on total numbers – monthly active users (MAU) – and *The Daily Telegraph* on subscriptions; *The New York Times* looked for people visiting at least twice a week and looking at three different topics (Hazard Owen 7 January 2019).

A new newsroom job has emerged to take on the task of corralling and analysing feedback and deciding how to act on it, that of engagement editor. Sweden- and Singapore-based academics Raul Ferrer-Conill and Edson C. Tandoc (2018) studied an international (but US-dominated) sample of these editors, whose job is, as they say, "bringing the voice of the audience into the newsroom". They found that, while there is a wealth of feedback data, that data is very technical in nature and only reveals user activity and behaviour, not really "the voice of the audience". Moreover, with the job of gauging the audience having moved from the business side to the newsroom, engagement editors were having a direct effect on editorial, pushing content choices to what had been popular or produced reaction rather than what the audience had to say. The authors warn that constantly acting upon audience feedback to adjust your content risks losing sight of your role – "decoupling journalism from its civic duty". Similar findings came from a study of African newsrooms (Moyo, Mare & Matsilele 2019).

Perhaps this perception was already filtering into the industry: the International Center for Journalists's 2019 global newsroom technology survey found that, in the two years since its predecessor report, use of all newsroom metrics had decreased except for one: "reach", which refers to the number of people who are exposed to a piece of content. So the simplest measure, page views, while used less than before, remained the most popular (ICFJ 2019).

Direct contact with your audience: social media, instant messaging, meetings and email newsletters

Media economist Robert Picard points out that being able to reach out directly to the audience allows digital journalists to create both short-term and long-term value by making their outlet important to their readers (Picard 2010, 57). Today there are many ways to contact your audience, but how best to do so?

Social media and instant messaging are at everyone's fingertips. The ICFJ's technology survey (ICFJ 2019) found that journalists were using these tools more than ever to engage audiences. More than 80 per cent used social media, especially Facebook, once a week or more, and more than 40 per cent used Twitter. However, instant messaging apps had overtaken the latter, particularly in Africa and Asia, with over 60 per cent of journalists in East and Southeast Asia using them. On any of these platforms your outlet can post new stories or livestream current reporting or remind readers of older but still relevant stories. Breaking news needs to be sent out immediately, but otherwise find a time of day when your audience is most likely to be looking – lunchtime, perhaps, or early evening after work or late at night when they have more free time for non-work and non-family activities. Tao Weihua of Chaping attracted his audience with a single WeChat posting at one minute to midnight every night (see pp. 115–118). Even more engaging are meetings with readers, replaced under COVID conditions with live online video sessions. These have been addressed in Chapter 5 because they provide a way to bring in some revenue, but the value of the contact alone is also high in terms of engagement.

Meanwhile, boring old email has made a comeback. Start building an address list early on by adding a box to your site's landing page or any page linked from social media or messaging to ask people to sign up with their name and email (don't forget to assure them that you will keep the data private). Notifications and newsletters can be sent out at any interval, from multiple times a day to once a week or even once a month, depending on your topic and your audience. They can be tweaked to address the receiver by name to make it seem more personal (though be sure the style of address is correct and appropriate). If your recipients open the newsletter, that's a sign of engagement, and they may take further action such as clicking on a link or joining an activity such as a panel discussion or even subscribing. A dedicated service like Mailchimp can help, and they usually have a free option to get started on. Reuters's 2021 journalism predictions report notes that that mainstream media have been finding email newsletters helpful to engagement, reducing "churn" (dropout rate) and helping bring new users on board. The trend has been for individual journalists or section groups to produce their own so that one outlet may have many newsletters – *The New York Times* was said to run 70 (Newman 2021). But even small startups can benefit from this form of contact with readers.

Devising a newsletter should be given careful thought. It can be a simple list of your day's or week's stories showing headlines and perhaps summaries along with links to the full story (which will have buttons to share on social media or pass on to friends) – a more personal way to communicate what goes out on social media. Myanmar's The Irrawaddy does this, with a story stub for each entry on its list and a quick link to the original. But it can be much more than that. Your list of stories can come with some extra information that isn't available to the public or background on how your journalists produced their pieces. Or it can come with a more personal touch – a founder or senior staff member may write about how they are coping with "working from home" during COVID or their struggles in getting their business off the ground. Singapore's Tech in Asia sends out a daily list with notes on current news but provides also a personal letter from one of the leading staff.

Specialist newsletters can bring readers news of what's going on in their field. Splice Media, whose audience is the digital media business itself, has two newsletters: Splice Slugs addresses media developments and Splice Frames provides news about design (see Chapter 8 pp. 9–13). Some outlets send out exclusive content. Hong Kong Citizen News distinguished itself from competitors with a newsletter containing original columns from four respected writers covering areas readers were interested in: local politics, international news, China news and business news. The writers donate their work and the missive is sent out every Sunday night when recipients have time to read.

Another way to keep in touch with your readers is through regular short questionnaires that relate to matters of the moment. Cilisos of Malaysia (see pp. 118–121) and Qdaily (see pp. 174–178) linked up such quizzes with marketing, providing not only a good way to get a response but to help with advertising and brand relations.

Making your audience into a community

The ultimate in engagement is an audience with a sense of belonging who are not only attentive readers willing to pay for content but who feel a personal connection to you and support you in difficult times. Many in our region have achieved that. HKCN's newsletter and its stand on democracy have brought it many followers and helped it raise donations. Hong Kong Free Press's coverage of the 2019 protests led to a tripling of its site traffic and brought more donations than ever before. New Naratif called for donations during the 2020 COVID crisis and quickly saw its supporters fill the funding gap (see pp. 169–174). In early 2021, Malaysiakini was fined the equivalent of about US$124,000 for contempt over reader posts, and its loyal audience donated more than half as much again within hours (see pp. 160–165). The Reporter of Taiwan runs on donations from its dedicated followers (see pp. 190–193), and New Naratif is on track to do the same.

These outlets have built up a sense of community by their principled stances and responsiveness to their audience. Before the coronavirus they also went out to meet their readers and set up events, though those now have gone online. Others have set up projects as a service to readers, such as Sabay's Enovel and Sabay Write, which provide opportunities for Cambodians to write fiction and get published; Sabay also does charity work (see pp. 178–181).

In recent years, going beyond subscription to nurture readers into members has become the favoured way to build engagement into a more formal format.

The Membership Puzzle Project (MPP) was founded by New York University professor Jay Rosen and the Dutch outlet De Correspondent (for this site's own problematic crowdfunding drive, see p. 48) in 2017 originally under NYU but moved in 2020 to Media Investment Development Fund (MDIF). MPP's site's "about us" page says membership goes beyond money: "There has to be a social contract between journalists and members. Working out what that contract should say is the core challenge." It closed operations in August 2021 but still publishes on its site a handbook describing methods for implementing a membership programme. One such method is developing a mindset for listening to readers so that you can act on what you hear, checking with digital feedback to see if you've got it right. Another is to have a mission the audience identifies with, and another is to make sure humans run your programme and not leave it up to automation. MPP's first Membership in News Fund, set up in 2018 and supported by Omidyar Network's Democracy Fund and Luminate, distributed $700,000 to 23 projects in 13 countries (most in north America and western Europe). In 2020 MDIF and MPP, supported by Luminate, reopened the fund with US$400,000 for projects outside the US and western Europe. Indonesia's respected *Tempo* was one of the winners.

Frontier Myanmar also had MPP help to develop its membership programme in the form of expertise and an admin team. Frontier founder Sonny Swe and his colleagues travelled to events round the world to publicise the outlet and get international support, while at home they sent out surveys to readers and potential readers and organised focus groups to discuss ideas. In response the outlet revamped its site but kept it free to view while offering extras to anyone who paid for membership. These are a fortnightly political insider briefing and "behind the scenes" emails and, for a larger fee, daily briefings and, most expensive of all, a Myanmar media monitoring service. Frontier could call on its loyal members to come up with more support to help it keep reporting after the early 2021 military coup (see pp. 131–135). In the Philippines, news site Rappler has its Rappler PLUS programme which, for a minimum of US$70 a year, offers exclusive content (investigative reporting, research, industry reports and e-books) and opportunities to attend the outlet's briefings, forums and workshops, as well as discounts in the Rappler shop. Coconuts, meanwhile, started a membership scheme in 2019, providing get-togethers in its various publishing locations and offering premium content and freebies, but had to abandon it during the coronavirus pandemic. It still offers memberships, however, to anyone who wants one, charging a minimum of US$5 a year to view the site without advertisements and other perks (see pp. 124–128).

Membership programmes take a lot of work to set up and run. They are effective with a core audience of dedicated supporters, but difficult to expand beyond the existing enthusiasts and, however much the media that run them would like them to, rarely provide enough income to keep the whole operation going. In Asia, diverse languages and cultures, high levels of media competition and, in some places, immature payment systems make subscriptions hard to run, let alone membership. If you have a special appeal, a membership programme that is organised without spending too much money and effort can bring you income, support, publicity and a loyal audience.

Expansion

You may not be the kind of go-getting entrepreneur who wants to make big profits (see p. 5), but if you're attracting both audience and income you will probably wan to grow your operation, gently at least. You will likely need more journalists to provide wider coverage, but you should also consider employing marketing and sales staff to improve distribution and earnings and, if you're building a bigger team, someone to deal with human resources. The tech side will likely be a contract job until the company is much larger. You may well also need a larger office space, though if you've cultivated the working-from-home solution in response to the coronavirus pandemic, you may be able to continue at least partly on those lines, keeping connections up through Slack or similar or just regular email and messaging.

As your company expands, it may become advisable to set up your support departments as independent units. A number of outlets studied here have hived off their own sales/marketing agencies that work not only for their own media but for outside customers – Malaysiakini has FG Media, in Indonesia IDN Media has its Creator Network, Coconuts has Grove and Taiwan's The News Lens acquired mobile ad tech company Ad2iction and market research firm TNLR. Frontier Myanmar is owned by Black Knight Media Group, which also runs a marketing agency that partly supports the magazine. Thai outlet art4d set up DesignNation, an e-commerce site to fund the journal, which the owner plans to build eventually into the main outlet. In China, Chaping also set up an e-commerce site for tech gadgets which today is run through WeChat and Taobao with direct links in stories on the site. TheSmartLocal of Singapore too does e-commerce and has its own deal-offering service, as well as units for data analytics, HR and project management technology. Indonesia's Katadata set up its Katadata Insight Center to provide research and analysis for paying customers.

Another way to expand is to create or acquire verticals – other sites run under the same company. The News Lens has done it all by acquisition, buying over the past couple of years a digital tech outlet, a site that covers new products, a sports site, another site with inspirational stories and a movie site. IDN Media has used both creation and acquisition. It started as a purely news site but has added others for young women and young mothers as well as one with recipes and a range of regional outlets. It has also purchased an e-sports site and a movie site. In other cases, the additions have all been home-made. In Thailand, The Standard launched an entertainment outlet for its younger audience, a separate site for its popular podcasts, another for business investors and another for events, while tech blog Blognone set up Brand Inside as a marketing site prior to its buyout as well as a tech job vacancy site, the latter also done by Singapore's Tech in Asia. Malaysiakini has its very popular KiniTV. TheSmartLocal has added a news outlet, a food blog and a site for women. In Cambodia, DAP News produces, besides its long-time radio station and news site, an entertainment magazine and an outlet for business, while Sabay has an internet TV channel, a news-in-brief app and website, a site for women and a video-on-demand service. Regional outlet Coconuts has set up separate sites for travel and food, and in 2020 purchased Thai lifestyle outlet BK Magazine and its fellow brands.

Ethical issues

The transition to digital communication not only brought with it all the old ethical problems of journalism, it exacerbated them and added new issues connected with making money. When faced with survival you may well ignore your principles and do something unethical to keep going, but even at less challenging times the temptation is there.

What's more, there's little in the way of instruction or help. If there are few enough texts about the business side of digital journalism, when it comes to the rights and wrongs of practice there is almost nothing. A study by Spanish academics Jesús Díaz-Campo and Francisco Segado-Boj (2015) found that most media codes of ethics had not changed to suit digital journalism, and those that had had mostly only added some words to the effect that the old standards still applied. The established quality media in the west have updated their own excellent ethics codes – Associated Press, Agence France Presse, Reuters, *The New York Times* and so on – many of which can be consulted online. But these organisations have journalism teams who don't need to worry about running the business, so issues arising from finances are little addressed. The Konrad Adenauer Foundation's *Entrepreneurial journalism handbook* (Nedeljkovic et al. 2014) still emphasises traditional ethical issues – honesty and transparency – and includes useful advice on using social media, but gives no help for dealing with business challenges.

Plagiarism

Finding quality content is key to your business success, but producing your own is expensive and time-consuming. With so much content easily available on the internet, many online media resort to plagiarism – using other people's work. This is done in many ways, from outright copying and claiming it as your own to posting others' stories on social media to putting content into a list of links on an aggregator. Are some forms of plagiarism more acceptable than others? Ethics scholars Deni Elliott and Edward Spence (2018, 65) ask important questions we need to ponder in the digital era: What is the difference between sharing and stealing? And between news aggregation and plagiarism? And how far can we control our original creations?

Aggregators point to their news lists as a public service that helps not only individual users but the news providers themselves by expanding their user network through links to the original stories. This claim has been at the heart of cases against Google News and Facebook in Europe and Australia, with both eventually agreeing to pay originators where seriously challenged (see pp. 31, 72). Some similar disputes have emerged in our region. Vietnam's Bao Moi aggregator faced a complaint from a powerful industry outlet and dealt with it by apologising and promising to include all original links in its story lists (Do 7 March 2013). ByteDance's aggregator Jinri Toutiao took Chinese online users by storm when it opened in 2012 because it provided them with personally targeted content completely free. It could do that because it took other people's material without payment and made its money from ads. In 2014 the company was sued by internet giant Sohu for copyright infringement because it was reformatting Sohu's content in a way that lost the links to the original. Toutiao responded that it was only providing links like Google News and filed a counter suit (Zhang 15 July 2014). Toutiao has faced several more copyright cases since, but changed its policy and started paying content providers (see p. 72).

For individual sites, the temptation to use other people's content to fill their newsfeeds is difficult to resist. The Vietnamese news channel Zing lost some big advertisers when it was accused of using unlicensed music (Do 7 March 2013). Chinese independent site Chaping came in for strong user criticism for using other people's work, and, though vindicated by a court decision, lost a great deal of business and had to work hard to get back the audience's trust (see p. 116). A check for copying is easily done through an online search, but when the original is rewritten it can be more difficult to prove.

One frequent target of plagiarisers is international news. Local sites want overseas coverage but are not able to afford their own correspondents or an agency feed, so find it easy to just copy and paste good stories or rewrite them to make them seem different. The theft becomes even less traceable when they are translated into another language. Qian Chen of the US's CNBC knew the language her work had been translated into and called out her plagiarisers in a follow-up article. She wrote:

> With nearly every news article I've written for CNBC.com, within a few hours of publishing, I could easily search certain keywords and find a Chinese-language doppelgänger online. Translated word-for-word by media companies in China and published without citing CNBC or my name, those articles often boasted millions of interactions and thousands of comments.

CNBC warned the copyright infringers, including Toutiao, and that particular article was taken down, but others were not (Chen 23 January 2018).

Many reasons are given for poaching other people's material. If it's a breaking story being covered by many outlets and your own can't cover it, then there seems little harm in reporting the piece of news in brief and attributing it to the source. But can you get away with taking a complete story from another outlet and republishing it as is? Many who do this say that attribution is enough, especially if there is a link to the original – and the story is getting a whole new audience, especially if it has been translated and even more so if it's in a country where the original is not available due to censorship. If you decide to rewrite the story to make it less traceable, then providing attribution and a link would be giving the game away. Quite a few sites take a story from another outlet and then do their own additional reporting, making it partly original. The honest thing to do is to contact the original source and ask for permission, but that not only takes time and effort and, possibly, payment, it means that a rejection will leave you unable to use that content and possibly any other from the same place. If you do need to grab other people's work, then a discussion needs to take place in your company about how to do it.

Biased and fake news

"While few working journalists and fewer scholars believe today that pure objectivity is possible, almost all would agree that hidden biases, covert manipulation, and disregard for factual truth are deeply unethical", say US academics Cecilia Friend and Jane B. Singer (2015, 54). Knowing these unethical practices exist is one thing, but dealing with them is difficult. Misinformation and disinformation – information that is incorrect or deliberately false and misleading – is common today and often backed by people who insist it is true.

Fake news is far from new but it blew into an epidemic in the west during the run-up to Britain's Brexit referendum in 2016 and Donald Trump's campaign for the US presidency the same year and during his four years in office. Media sprouted fact-checking departments but even when fake news was exposed its perpetrators continued to say it was true. The media don't always react the way you'd expect. In a case recounted by the *Columbia Journalism Review*, a video of Nancy Pelosi, speaker of the US House of Representatives and a Trump opponent, that had been slowed down to make her look drunk was shared thousands of times on social media. But even serious news outlets that decried the deed still showed the video in its manipulated form, reaping millions of clicks, and then they published more stories blaming social media for spreading the fake clip. *CJR* said that editors should have recognised it as fake news and not published it at all (Somaiya, 2019).

The fake news epidemic has deeply affected our part of the world, where the mass use of social media has given plenty of opportunity for powerful people to manipulate the truth for political purposes. Facebook, the most used platform, has a rigorous fact-checking process and pays partners in our region in Singapore, Hong Kong, Taiwan, the Philippines, Indonesia, Malaysia and Thailand, most of which are local media though the French news agency AFP features prominently. Facebook has at various times blocked the accounts of Myanmar's generals, both before and after their February 2021 coup, and of a key advisor to Philippine president Rodrigo Duterte.

ICFJ's 2019 survey of global newsrooms found managers more aware than ever of the threat of misinformation, with a third of the media surveyed actually having fact-checkers on staff. Online tools were being used by between a quarter and a half of newsrooms and by between a fifth and more than half of journalists, depending on the tool. The most used were Google Fact Check Tools and Facebook Fact Checker, but many others were popular: Google Image Search to reverse-check pictures and Google Earth Pro and Tin Eye to verify photos and videos; fact-checking websites like Factcheck.org and Politifact; Grammarly and Copyleaks to identify plagiarism; Storyful and Dataminr for social media verification; KnowNews for fake websites; Verification Handbook and similar sources; and Pipl for tracking content uploaders (ICFJ 2019).

Elliott and Spence (2018, 34) emphasise putting yourself above "self-interested or less-competent information givers" and maintaining high reporting standards. But however much of your own reporting you do, you will nearly always need to use other sites for story ideas, pointers to lines of enquiry and background, and you should ensure they are trustworthy. Friend and Singer (2015, 59) cite a checklist from an earlier work by Friend and others for evaluating online sites. In summary: look for the site's information about itself, and be particularly suspicious if there is none; make sure it is transparent about its information sources in the form of traceable acknowledgements or links; find out what the purpose of the site is, checking to see if it's promotional (such as a marketer's press release or a lobbyist's subtle campaign effort); look at its linked pages to ensure they are part of the original site; check the genuineness of the link by lopping off the end part of the URL and seeing if it goes back to the original site; look at the latest update to see if it is active; and use your critical thinking skills to make your own judgment – for instance, don't be led astray by slick and professional presentation.

Problems with advertising

Advertising can allow a media outlet to be independent of audience and business pressures, but it has always had its compromises. Advertisers prefer to deal with media that put out non-controversial or pro-establishment content, disadvantaging those with critical coverage – a phenomenon left-wing US academics Edward Herman and Noam Chomsky called "the advertising license to do business" way back in the 1980s (Herman & Chomsky 1988, 14–18). At that point this was an important difference because those that couldn't get advertising could be driven out of business. Today there are other ways to get income, but the general point remains true: outlets that do investigative or critical work are less attractive to commercial advertisers.

In hard times it could be tempting to soften or drop controversial content or to include subtle promotions for your advertisers. A NiemanLab report notes how easy it is to post positive reviews of affiliate items available through your site because your own income depends on sales (Hazard Owen 7 May 2019).

It's possible to try to second-guess programmatic ads though much harder, but the automated system into which thousands of ad tech companies have jumped has other problems. A survey of advertisers in Britain found that, among other things, the growing number of supply chains they had to deal with had become complex and opaque, that there was little standardisation of practices, and that fully 15 per cent of their spend could not be unaccounted for (ISBA 2020).

It's not surprising that the advertising system is open to outright fraud. Hoax stories put out during the 2016 US election campaign not only conned audiences but brought their creators a lot of ad money, in some cases as much as US$30,000 a month – making programmatic advertising a "noxious market" which needs to be made more transparent, according to University of Massachusetts researchers Joshua Braun and Jessica Eklund (2019). BuzzFeed reported a watchdog outfit's findings that many apparently thriving local news sites in North America were not real at all but complete fakes full of copied content whose only goal was to attract lucrative ads (Silverman 6 November 2019).

Paid content can also present ethical problems. A report by the respected Tow Center at New York's Columbia School of Journalism sees it as nothing more than financially supported public relations: where in the old days news media would publish press releases free to fill space, it says, they now make money out of doing pretty much the same thing (Sirrah 6 September 2019). The fact that some paid content looks much like editorial, especially if there is no mention that it is advertising, can make it very misleading, and can be used by people with the money to advertise.

A *Columbia Journalism Review* article describes the experience of a Reuters correspondent in Southeast Asia whose colleagues helped produce an investigative series on the Thai navy's role in the trafficking of Rohingya migrants from Myanmar for the seafood industry. These stories won a Pulitzer Prize. Later Reuters posted another article telling how the Thai navy was reforming to protect marine commerce and workers' rights – but this time the story was paid for by the country's ruling junta. Even though it was identified as such, the correspondent felt it gave a wrong message "because it gave space to a government to whitewash abuses on one of the same platforms on which they were exposed." In response, Reuters told *CJR* that the department that produced the advertising story worked independently of the company's journalists (Carroll 24 January 2019).

The main advice in dealing with all kinds of ethical issues is to build your reputation with transparency. Says entrepreneurial journalism specialist Mark Briggs:

> Unlike a news organization with a long history, a startup has no track record to establish its credibility. As a journalism entrepreneur, it's crucial to be open about the goals and standards of your site, especially if the funding for your startup is a new model that the audience might not understand.
> (Briggs 2012, 54–55)

This is where your mission statement comes in, a constant reminder of the standards you expect of yourself and your readers expect of you. There is often no legal punishment for ethical transgressions, but the implications can be far-reaching if your readers lose trust in you.

Conclusion

As the case studies in Chapter 7 show, there is no one-size-fits-all strategy to succeed in entrepreneurial journalism in our region. One reason is that every territory is very different in history, politics, development, culture and law, leading to very different business milieus for media. But also important is the fact that the digital space offers so many new routes and combinations of routes that there is huge diversity of business models even within territories.

Some major points can be drawn from the examination of all aspects of this kind of journalism and the experience of many who have tried it. Have some business nous on board – you might have enough yourself, but a journalism background may not be adequate. Early on, draft a mission statement that guides your principles and development, even if you change it later; put it on your "about us" page. Do your research before starting up to anticipate pitfalls. Think of your outlet as a product in business terms. Make a business plan whether or not you're going to apply for funding. Make sure you start on making an income as soon as you launch. Whatever your business model, finding and engaging an audience is key. For this you need to be able to produce consistent and well-presented quality content, and also to build contact with your users through digital feedback, newsletters, membership and so on to form a loyal community. Don't splash the cash but be prudent, even frugal. Build your company – team, culture, workspace and routines – to produce a steady and sustainable outlet that is open to adaptation and innovation.

References

Anh-Minh (7 March 2013). Stealing content in Vietnam is finally a real issue. Tech in Asia. Retrieved 26 June 2020 from https://www.techinasia.com/stealing-content-vietnam-finally-real-issue

Bodó, Balász (2019). Selling news to audiences: a qualitative inquiry into the emerging logics of algorithmic news personalization in European quality news media. *Digital Journalism*, 7/8, 1054–1075. DOI 10.1080/21670811.2019.1624185

Braun, Joshua A., & Eklund, Jessica L. (2019). Fake news, real money: ad tech platforms, profit-driven hoaxes, and the business of journalism. *Digital Journalism*. 7/1, 1–21. 10.1080/21670811.2018.1556314

Briggs, Mark (2012). *Entrepreneurial journalism: how to build what's next for news*. Los Angeles, CA: SAGE Publications.

Carroll, Joshua (24 January 2019). Reuters article highlights ethical issues with native advertising. *Columbia Journalism Review*. Retrieved 30 December 2020 from https://www.cjr.org/watchdog/reuters-article-thai-fishing-sponsored-content.php

Chen, Qian (23 January 2018). Plagiarism is rampant in China, and its media companies are raking in billions. *CNBC*. Retrieved 24 February 2021 from https://www.cnbc.com/2018/01/23/ip-plagiarism-is-rampant-in-china-and-media-companies-profit-from-it.html

Collier, Jessica, & Stroud, Natalie Jomini (2018). Using links to keep readers on new sites. Center for Media Engagement, Moody College of Communication, University of Texas at Austin. Retrieved 20 February 2021 from https://mediaengagement.org/wp-content/uploads/2018/09/Using-Links-to-Keep-Readers-on-News-Sites-1.pdf

Cornez, Valentin, & Hapal, Don Kevin (n.d.). Rappler empowered its news organization with better user data to achieve digital sustainability. Google News Initiative. Retrieved 28 April 2020 from https://newsinitiative.withgoogle.com/training/states/consumer_insights/pdfs/rappler-case-study.pdf

Díaz-Campo, Jesús, & Segado-Boj, Francisco (2015). Journalism ethics in a digital environment: how journalistic codes of ethics have been adapted to the Internet and ICTs in countries around the world. *Telematics and Informatics.* http://dx.doi.org/10.1016/j.tele.2015.03.004

Elliott, Deni, & Spence, Edward (2018). *Ethics for a digital era.* Hoboken, NJ: Wiley Blackwell.

Ferrer-Conill, Raul, & Tandoc, Edson C. Jr. (2018). The audience-oriented editor. *Digital Journalism.* DOI: 10.1080/21670811.2018.1440972

Friend, Cecilia, & Singer, Jane B. (2015). *Online journalism ethics.* Online edition. Abingdon, Oxon: Routledge.

Hazard Owen, Laura (7 January 2019). To retain subscribers, eliminate content no one reads. *IJNet.* Retrieved 21 February 2021 from https://ijnet.org/en/story/retain-subscribers-eliminate-content-no-one-reads

Hazard Owen, Laura (7 May 2019). Publishers love getting affiliate revenue from their reviews. So is it okay for Amazon to pay to get more of those reviews upfront? NiemanLab. Retrieved 29 December 2020 from https://www.niemanlab.org/2019/05/publishers-love-getting-affiliate-revenue-from-their-reviews-so-is-it-okay-for-amazon-to-pay-to-get-more-of-those-reviews-upfront/

Herman, Edward, & Chomsky, Noam (1988). *Manufacturing consent.* New York: Pantheon.

International Center for Journalists (ICFJ) (2019). The state of technology in global newsrooms. Retrieved 20 February 2021 from https://www.icfj.org/our-work/state-technology-global-newsrooms

Incorporated Society of British Advertisers (ISBA) (2020). ISBA programmatic supply chain transparency study: executive summary. Retrieved 30 December 2020 from https://www.isba.org.uk/media/2424/executive-summary-programmatic-supply-chain-transparency-study.pdf

Moyo, Dumisani, Mare, Admire, & Matsilele, Trust (2019). Analytics-driven journalism? Editorial metrics and the reconfiguration of online news production practices in African newsrooms. *Digital Journalism,* 7/4, 490–506. DOI: 10.1080/21670811.2018.1533788

Nedeljkovic, Marko, Petrovic, Milos, Zmijanac, Veroljub, & Spahr, Christian (2014). *Entrepreneurial journalism handbook.* Sofia: Konrad Adenauer Foundation. Retrieved 19 April 2020 from http://www.kas.de/wf/en/33.38746/

Newman, Nic (2021). Journalism, media, technology trends and predictions 2021. Reuters Institute for the Study of Journalism & University of Oxford. Retrieved 16 April 2021 from https://reutersinstitute.politics.ox.ac.uk/journalism-media-and-technology-trends-and-predictions-2021

Picard, Robert G. (2010). *Value creation and the future of news organizations: why and how journalism must change to remain relevant in the twenty-first century.* Lisbon: Formalpress/MediaXX1.

Silverman, Craig (6 November 2019). These hugely popular local news sites in the US and Canada are fake. *BuzzFeed.* Retrieved 29 December 2019 from https://www.buzzfeednews.com/article/craigsilverman/fake-local-news-sites-albany-edmonton

Sirrah, Ava (6 September 2019). Guide to native advertising. *Tow Center for Digital Journalism.* Retrieved 30 December 2020 from https://www.cjr.org/tow_center_reports/native-ads.php

Somaiya, Ravi (Fall 2019). The junk cycle. *Columbia Journalism Review*. Retrieved 18 April 2020 from https://www.cjr.org/special_report/facebook-video-pelosi-media.php?ct=t(Top_Stories_CJR_new_Jan_26_1_25_2017_COPY_02)

Zhang, Bolin (15 July 2014). Sohu vs Toutiao: Chinese mobile news app sued by news publishers for copyright infringement. The Center for Internet and Society, Stanford Law School. Retrieved 24 February 2021 from http://cyberlaw.stanford.edu/blog/2014/07/sohu-vs-toutiao-chinese-mobile-news-app-sued-news-publishers-copyright-infringement

7
CASE STUDIES

Introduction

The difficult conditions in mainland China, Hong Kong, Taiwan and Southeast Asia have not prevented the emergence of a large number of journalism start-ups in the region. The 30 case studies in this book are not exhaustive or comprehensive but demonstrate the many strands of the field in the digital age. Each unique in form, they range in business model from classic entrepreneurial outfits running on investment and advertising to frugal nonprofits supported by donations, and everything in between. They cover breaking news, alternative news, in-depth and investigative stories, data journalism and a variety of niches including business, technology, literature, light-hearted fare, women's issues, hyperlocal activities and professional matters. Courage, hard work and digital technology have allowed them to win loyal audiences, many poorly served by media in the past, especially the younger generation. The studies are based on interviews with people prominent in each outlet, and all have looked over the versions that appear here. The outlets are ordered alphabetically so that they are not pigeon-holed by country or type. Five studies that couldn't be accommodated on paper appear in Chapter 8 on the related website (www.routledge.com/9781138283091).

Case studies 107

THAILAND

art4d

art4d is a little long in the tooth for an entrepreneurial startup – it was founded in 1995. Besides, it clings to old technology, being basically a monthly print magazine. But right from the start, this journal for architects, designers and artists has focused on innovative ways to reach its audience, raise an income and build a niche media business.

Part of its success was just the luck of when it was set up: at that time the Thai economy was booming, especially the construction industry. "In those days," says editor-in-chief Pratarn Teeratada, "you could put a down payment on a condominium and sell the contract the next day for a profit". He and some colleagues at the firm Architect 49 saw an opportunity for a high-quality journal for people in the sector. "We chose to do a design magazine because we believed that there was some potential to get readers as well as advertising from sponsors, like kitchenware and imported furniture."

FIGURE 7.1 Pratarn Teeratada. Photo credit: Author.

Advertisers were indeed flush with cash and very willing to buy space in the magazine, but Pratarn didn't rest there. He saw that he could do much more to build the audience and attract financial backing. "We created a lot of activities such as workshops, talks, seminars, exhibitions," he says. People flocked to these events, resulting in sponsorships from the construction industry and partnerships with professional and cultural bodies. Within a year it was clear that there was good business potential. So when the financial crisis hit in 1997, art4d – which stands for "art for design" – was well cushioned to survive the deep recession. A little bit of downsizing was needed, such as cutting out the cost of freelance photographers, but they stayed on track. Today they are still going, though the digital revolution has forced changes, of which more later.

The initial idea of reaching out was to get the magazine's name known, but it brought many more benefits. The first event was a free talk given by the celebrated architect Dr Sumet Jumsai. It turned out to be a full house, and free copies of the then-new magazine were handed out. Soon art4d was collaborating with the Association of Siamese Architects to put on symposia large and small, and later got private sponsorship for events from the likes of the huge Siam Cement Group. The team also worked with foreign cultural organisations such as the Alliance Française,

Japan Foundation, British Council and Goethe Institute, which sponsored events and sent them on visits to see their countries' architectural monuments.

With all this going on, art4d expanded from one full-timer – Pratarn – with part-time help from design colleagues to five full-timers after the first year to a dozen in Year 2. Since then the team has ranged between 15 and 20 people as the economy has fluctuated. They all work out of their airy low-rise premises in a leafy sub-soi off Bangkok's Sukhumvit 26. The glossy mag with its arty photos became a place for young grads, many from the famous Faculty of Architecture at Silpakorn University, to get their first or second job and move on after a couple of years to study overseas, sometimes to return after their travels. This system works to keep art4d young and keen.

The magazine's enthusiasm is clearly sparked by its lively editor-in-chief, who has led the way now for 25 years. The key to his success, he says, is contacts. A graduate of the prestigious Chulalongkorn University's Faculty of Political Science, he can call on his classmates as well as architects, interior designers and graphic artists he got to know at and through Architect 49 and from professional get-togethers. He had support from volunteers when the magazine first started and today can find the right candidates for the ten architects a year needed for profile stories in the publication.

Circulation soared to 50,000 a month in the first decade of the new century but has seriously declined since to 10,000–15,000 a month recently. There are 2,000 to 3,000 subscribers or members, with about 100 new ones a month brought in by the busy marketing team. The outlet has stuck to print as the main platform because it suits its high-quality design photography, but advertising has decreased enormously, and the transition to online, which has been slow, was only taken up in earnest recently with the recognition that the market is changing.

Since digital is not the best platform for art4d, efforts to keep the audience engaged became the issue. Talk forums, design competitions and even group tours to visit buildings and tie in with sponsors' products were started to keep up interest, and sponsored events were covered in the magazine. They also started to work much more closely with advertisers. Says Pratarn,

> Before, they just placed their advertisements, and we only helped them to design the layout, or those that already had an agency sent the finished layout, and that was that – when the printing was finished, they just paid and the business was closed.
>
> But at the moment they don't just want to place their advertisement on our pages but want [us] to do more.

This could mean exhibitions, small seminars, business tours and just general support in selling their products.

So art4d has adopted another strategy: flexibility. "The thing is, the situation forced me to leave my roots to make it easier for the company to carry on", says Pratarn.

It has diversified into e-commerce with a business called DesignNation, whose main goal is to sell design products – "a marketplace for design", according to Pratarn. One feature was a weekly display of selected products at venues round the Thai capital, and the plan is to have annual DesignNation Expos. art4d owns the new business in partnership with Right Man, an events company, which has put up the capital needed. As art4d adapts to the new environment, Pratarn's plan is to transfer the whole operation lock, stock and barrel to DesignNation and run the print magazine as a small specialist business within it on a low budget. It will be more of a labour of love, where younger people can create content, as the new company takes over the commercial operation.

Pratarn is, with his usual enthusiasm, moving into more new ventures, nowadays with the emphasis on bringing good to the world. With some friends he established a social enterprise called Lucky Planet to bring attention to the deteriorating world environment and functioning via social media. He secured financial backing from a "very kind rich man", a Bangkok businessman. The organisation has set up small events at a fair just to the north of Bangkok to bring attention to what's happening in the environment. One was a "chef's table" where cooks had to serve things we might eat when the world is ending – such as cockroach protein bars and bees-wax chewing gum. "It's fun!" Pratarn says. He likens this activity to The Standard's (see pp. 196–200) events, combining social media and live happenings to reach out to readers.

Pratarn was planning to make Lucky Planet into a kind of social club for people who want to protect the environment and set up organic markets and much more but unfortunately his partner became very ill and the whole project had to be dropped. The COVID-19 epidemic also put a severe dampener on his activities, which have now become livestreaming events. It has also forced staff to work from home, though that's something he is thinking of making permanent. He is still pursuing DesignNation, which is now focusing on building a design festival for Bangkok, and, despite Lucky Planet's demise, is still full of ideas and hoping to "create a new social enterprise which could be scaled out to become a social media channel soon".

art4d is distinctly entrepreneurial, but, with all this activity going on, is Pratarn really a journalist? He has an interesting answer: "I always consider myself as a journalist, as a media person, because I feel it's a privilege to meet different people who have special talent." He goes on: "In the new world it's difficult to define people – you are a journalist? No, I'm a doctor! Even dentists might want to work for us, and it's ok." Anyone can be interested in organic markets and can make suitable content, he points out. "This is all new because of the disruption of the media business that forced us to do something not really to survive, but to make it as fun as it used to be." And art4d is still a design icon, now becoming well known to the younger generation through the design competitions it holds and its social media presence. "Many students comment on the page – like, every minute!" says Pratarn. Meanwhile, the architects and designers the magazine was originally aimed at are losing interest. Pratarn hopes that diversification will be the answer to regaining their attention.

THAILAND

Blognone

What started out as a hobby blog turned into Thailand's top tech news site – and then, instead of going it alone, got bought out by one of the country's most valuable leisure startups.

In 2004, before he had even finished his computer engineering degree at Bangkok's Kasetsart University, Isriya Paireepairit set up Blognone with fellow undergrad Wason Liwlompaisan. "At that time there were a few Thai tech magazines and newspapers that had websites, but the quality of the content was not what we wanted, so we just started one ourselves", says Isriya. After graduating, the two went on to get full-time jobs in IT, though Isriya also branched out into other fields – after getting a master's degree in information management at Sheffield University in Britain in 2008 he set up two companies, one of which was an online public policy think tank launched with another friend. He also wrote a regular tech column for one of the country's major newspapers, *Thai Rath*.

FIGURE 7.2   Isriya Paireepairit. Supplied by Isriya Paireepairit.

But they kept Blognone going. With Isriya making a name for himself and Wason having gone on to work as a programmer for a major IT company, the blog became the go-to site for Thais who wanted news about tech. Its potential started to show around 2010, when a regular reader from a big software firm asked to advertise. As more advertising started to roll in, Isriya decided to go full-time on the site, though very cautiously at first: "We didn't have an office, we didn't have anything, so we could keep it profitable with a very small amount of revenue." By 2012 they were earning enough to make it logical to register as a company and hire some staff.

Where to go next? "I investigated many, many other websites, such as Business Insider and Engadget … to see how I could create a first-rate business in online publication", says Isriya. "So, one thing that I found is, many companies have a lot of media outlets, maybe two or three websites for separate audiences. So I thought we should do the same thing."

He and Wason got together with two others, one of whom, Prommate Sirisukwattananont, had a background in journalism, and in 2016 set up marketing site Brand Inside. Prommate became its chief editor and a fourth partner, Khitichai Thangnitirat, took charge of sales. Like Blognone, the new outlet made its money from advertising. Blognone had started with simple banner ads, but moved later on to advertorials, setting up a team to make videos.

But where to go after that? They felt they had expanded as far as they could. Isriya talked to an adviser, a CEO who had taken his own company public more than 20 years before. That friend told him about the life cycle of a startup, from launch to IPO. Blognone and Brand Inside, he said, should go public, but were too small to do so. "So finally we [realised] we needed to merge with somebody to get bigger and go to the market", he says. Their initial idea was to look for an established media outlet, a TV station or newspaper. They put out feelers to see who was interested. No media came forward – Isriya thinks this was because of the 2013 auctioning off of digital TV licences, which had caused big losses for successful applicants because audiences moved to the internet.

But there were other interested parties. Two were not from any related sector. The third still wasn't from the same business but was a much better match. Wongnai Media, started in 2010 by US-educated entrepreneur Yod Chinsupakul, was inspired by the American online business directory Yelp. Wongnai, which means "insider", brought restaurant reviewing into the digital age in Thailand. According to Crunchbase, it had four rounds of funding from 2013, when it got an initial US$500,000 from the Japanese investor Recruit Strategic Partners, then two rounds with no amounts disclosed, to a 2016 non-equity injection from Google Launchpad Accelerator. Today it claims the largest restaurant database in the country – it has more than 300,000 on its list – and has expanded into beauty and travel. The Wongnai management team was young, the same age as the Blognoners. "I think we [had] a cultural fit more than other companies," says Isriya. But the deal was good too, though specifics have not been made public.

Since the 2017 takeover, Blognone and Brand Inside have continued to operate independently but in practice are subsidiaries of the bigger firm. "We share the same office as Wongnai, and the culture and the mindset", says Isriya. He and his team – totalling 25 now – are Wongnai employees and they get the same conditions and benefits as others in the company. Isriya also holds a position in Wongnai as head of its news content unit, and as such a role in management.

He feels it's really been worth it because he's got more resources. "One of the first things I did was to hire more people," he says. In fact, he expanded headcount for the two sites from 9 to 20 in the first year, with a focus on sales staff. By Year 2 he had doubled revenue. Blognone and Brand Inside make their money from advertising still, mostly advertorials done by their own staff, but an important contributor to increased income was a new sister site, Blognone Jobs, which has recruitment ads for the tech sector. The team have ventured into events as well, with an annual conference called Blognone Tomorrow focusing on Blognone's strength, enterprise IT.

The key to their longevity, according to Isriya, is their initial frugality at a time when the online media weren't yet popular. The landscape has changed now, of course, and online is mainstream. But also realising that Blognone wasn't going to make it on its own but had enough merit to attract a takeover allowed the company to follow a path many would reject because of the loss of independence it represented. For Blognone and Brand Inside, the move has proved a good one. They remain independent in their operations but have the support of a bigger company behind them.

THE PHILIPPINES

Bulatlat

One of the first online news outlets in the Philippines, Manila-based Bulatlat was founded in 2001 in the wake of the country's second "people power" revolution, which ousted the corrupt president Joseph Estrada. Its name is carefully chosen, but it has no equivalent in English: "bulatlat" refers to a search through a crammed container where you carefully remove all the objects inside until you find what you're looking for. Bulatlat's job, according to its site, is to "dig out facts buried by censorship and corruption and lay them out for public scrutiny, without fear or favor". An alternative nonprofit outfit, it uses its journalism to support civil society rather than make money. "It is our sense of advocacy to disseminate information to the public", says its associate editor Danilo Arao. "That's why many people believe in us."

FIGURE 7.3   Danilo Arao. Supplied by Danila Arao.

Yet even in the Philippines few readers of regular news know about Bulatlat. For one thing, says Arao, it's a small publication with limited resources and it has nothing like the reach of the high-profile for-profit startup Rappler. But the main reason is that it reaches a very different audience. "The people who support us are most especially from the marginal sectors of society – the striking workers, the farmers, the indigenous peoples", Arao says. "If you are poor and you come from remote areas, most probably you've heard of Bulatlat because we go there and we tell their stories, so that's how they learn about us."

Arao insists that Bulatlat isn't a business. It's registered as an NGO under the umbrella of its publisher, the Alipato Media Center, and is not concerned about the bottom line. "Rappler, it's an open secret, makes money, but in our case we don't", he says. With Bulatlat, the whole point is to do journalism that helps people. Yet despite its lack of commercial base, Bulatlat has survived for 20 years and is still going strong. It has a solid editorial team, a sophisticated website that is regularly replenished, a daily newsletter and updated social media. This must have taken at least a little business acumen.

The key to Bulatlat's ability to continue as a going concern, says Arao, is keeping costs down and relying on goodwill and – most of all – passion. Bulatlat takes its cue from Philippine national heroes Jose Rizal and Marcelo del Pilar, who produced the independence movement's newspaper *La Solidaridad* for several years in the late 19th century. Bulatlat's main saving is on staff salaries: it doesn't pay any. "If you look at journalism as a career, ... that would be unfair", says Arao. "But if you look at journalism as a commitment, I think it makes sense because we have people who are willing to do work out of their love for the profession." He notes that Rizal and del Pilar took no payment for their work and even put their own money into their newspaper.

Most who work at Bulatlat are lifelong activists. They are inspired by the outlet's philosophy and are keen to produce progressive journalism. They have other jobs – they freelance for other publications or run small businesses such as shops. Arao himself works full-time as an associate professor in the prestigious College of Mass Communication (CMC) at the University of the Philippines, where he has taught for nearly 20 years. The publication also gets free help in the form of unpaid student interns and pays little for web hosting because it bought the domain name Bulatlat.com way back when it started. The cost of the few regular outgoings – office rent and supplies, reporting expenses and equipment – is covered largely by donations from other journalists who are better off. Everybody who can do so chips in. Arao says he gives reporters lifts in his car and buys them meals.

One possible source of income could be ads, but Bulatlat rejects them on ethical grounds. Arao says,

> Our belief is that if, once we've solicited advertisements, there might be potential conflicts of interest if ever a company that advertised with us would be embroiled in a scandal, and we don't want to be put in that awkward situation.

Another bypassed potential earner is syndication. Because Bulatlat covers issues ignored by the mainstream media, it produces good, original stories that the major outlets often ask to republish. Bulatlat's policy is to allow them to do so free (it has some conditions – that the content not be changed, the story be credited to the original authors and a URL be provided). "We welcome that kind of arrangement", says Arao, because it brings publicity. Some see not charging as a mistake, saying, he goes on, "'these Bulatlat people are so stupid, why don't they grab the opportunity to earn money?'" But that would go completely against all that Bulatlat stands for. "From a business standpoint, we may be stupid, or, you know, not on a business footing, but it's not our intention to be on a business footing."

Bulatlat gets income from only two outside sources. One is donations from the public – you can give through the website. The other is one-off support for projects; it has received grants to produce two books and run a conference, and the providers involved have allowed it to put some of this money towards daily operations. This kind of funding comes from both Philippine and overseas donors (Arao isn't keen to identify them). The aim is in future to get more financial help from human rights and similar organisations that share Bulatlat's beliefs. The site is published mostly in English because it wants a non-Filipino-speaking, mainly international, audience to read its stories, including possible donors, though it does have some Filipino-language articles, including a column by Arao written for fellow alternative outlet Pinoy Weekly and cross-posted.

Bulatlat belongs to a group of like-minded nonprofit media and connected concerns called AlterMidya, "the people's alternative network". AlterMidya has its own site and acts as an umbrella for 8 radio stations, 9 news outlets (including Bulatlat and Pinoy Weekly), 14 multimedia operations and 5 representative institutions. Its elected chairperson is Luis V. Teodoro, former CMC dean. Rather than compete, members help each other cover non-mainstream stories. Arao says,

> For example, we are in Luzon and we need to send a reporter to another area that is very, very far from Manila and you need to take a plane to get there, and of course you need to buy food and other expenses every day to cover.
>
> So what we do in the alternative media is, we have very limited funding so we pool our resources together and we send only one of our reporters, and this particular reporter will be responsible for feeding the information to the other alternative media organisations.

If Bulatlat is very different from the for-profit Rappler, they have something in common: they are both highly critical of President Rodrigo Duterte and his government, for which they have both come in for some grief (for Rappler's woes, see pp. 46). In late 2018 and 2019, Bulatlat, along with two other AlterMidya members (one of them Pinoy Weekly) and AlterMidya itself, experienced a spate of distributed denial of service (DDoS) attacks, shutting down their sites. Bulatlat staff took heart from the fact that they were important enough to be targeted: "While we do not appeal to the audience of the government, we feel that the government is reading us, as well as the police and the military", says Arao. The four outlets fought back. With the assistance of a Swedish foundation that specialises in media forensics, they discovered that two particular ISPs had carried out the attacks. They filed a civil complaint in March 2019, after which the two companies, stating that they had no knowledge of or part in the attacks, declared that they supported press freedom and would prevent the same thing happening again. This led to the withdrawal of the case (Ellao 24 February 2020).

But things didn't end there. Arao was named among a group accused of conspiring against President Rodrigo Duterte in April 2019, though he says the charge was based on false information gathered by intelligence services (Santos 10 May 2019). Then in early 2020 AlterMidya and all its members were accused in the Senate of being a front for the underground Philippine Communist Party, a charge AlterMidya strenuously denies (AlterMidya 1 December 2020). Arao says the military has in the past accused Bulatlat of being a communist organisation. "We're not affiliated with any party", he emphasises, though he points out that PCP statements are reported appropriately in the interests of balance and fairness.

Bulatlat may be a sociopolitical activist media enterprise and not out to make a profit, but it has, through frugality and passion, developed a sustainable business model. "From what I've learned, as long as you have proper time management and you have very, very cooperative [colleagues], you don't get disappointed or disillusioned with what you're doing and in fact you derive satisfaction because you're making a difference", Arao says. "It may sound a bit corny or too idealistic. But that's how I was raised and that's how I've learned my journalism."

CHINA

Chaping

Tao Weihua finished his business administration degree at the University of Sydney in 2014, and, aware of the many new opportunities in China's growing tech market, headed back home to Hangzhou in eastern China. Things didn't work out. He tried to get work in big companies including Alibaba and NetEase, but nothing came up. So he joined a new company called Kaishiba, a consumer content directing platform, and took up one of its WeChat public accounts in 2015 to produce his own hobby outlet. He called it Chaping, meaning "bad reviews", and published articles poking fun at Chinese tech companies and did gadget write-ups. Its reference was to Google's then-motto

FIGURE 7.4 Mo Runhuo. Supplied by Mo Runhuo.

"Don't be evil" – "the very act of giving bad reviews helps prompt companies to correct their mistakes and to do better", explains Chaping's current branding and marketing director, Mo Runhuo.

Tao's distribution strategy was clever: he put out just one article a day, always at one minute to midnight. It was the right topic, the right strategy, the right tone, the right time and the right timing. The one-person "self-media" outlet caught the attention not only of a young audience but of the likes of Google and Apple, who started to cooperate with him on ads and new product launches. By 2018 Chaping had grown to be one of the top WeChat tech outlets in China with daily unique views up to half a million. They had half a dozen staff in their Hangzhou office churning out 100+ articles a day. Tao set up his own company, Hangzhou Muggle Network, named after the non-magical characters in Harry Potter – "because technology is the Muggle's magic", explains Mo – to run it and diversify the business into online gadget sales. By 2018 the company was reported to be turning over merchandise worth US$626,000 a year and was expected to expand that up to US$1.6 million (Zhao 23 May 2018). Tao was nominated as one of Forbes magazine's under-30 Asian media and marketing leaders.

Then came the big offer. Tencent, owner of WeChat, made Chaping the first independent WeChat media account to benefit from its Topic Fund, set up in late 2017 to support online content creators (Yu 28 May 2018). The total investment, also involving two other partners, was the equivalent of US$4.7 million. It should have been a moment for celebration.

FIGURE 7.5 Tao Weihua. Supplied by Mo Runhuo.

However, as soon as the payment was made known, the online world erupted with complaints from people who said Chaping had taken their work and rewritten it to make it difficult to recognise. A strong voice was internet critic San Biao Longmenzhen who wrote, according to SupChina, "Chaping built itself by plagiarizing others' original ideas; it has zero ability to create and all the capacity to copy and paste". Tencent, he said, was endorsing plagiarism when its avowed policy was to stop it (Yu 28 May 2018). The row even reached state media, with *People's Daily* condemning "article laundering". Soon after it was announced that the outlet was giving back the investment money (Jiang 28 May 2018).

Chaping got involved in two well-publicised plagiarism cases. A blogger took it to court in 2016 and showed how a Chaping piece closely resembled an article he had written earlier, but the court threw the case out for lack of evidence. Another blogger complained of similar plagiarism in 2017, but wrote articles criticising Chaping instead of seeking legal redress (Yu 28 May 2018). Indeed, China's copyright law doesn't ban outright the copying of published journalism, so it's very hard to succeed in a legal challenge. Chaping later apologised to the first complainant for using "similar phrases" and said articles should be sourced better and not be labelled as original when they are not (Deng 28 May 2018).

Mo Runhuo says San Biao's critique was "far away from the facts" and Chaping condemns copying. "No company can succeed by depending on plagiarism", he says. The explanation is that it wasn't done intentionally. "It's not easy for new media to police its content," Mo goes on. "Especially after expanding the company, it's not easy to oversee each person." The team were young – early 20s – with no journalism training and little idea of intellectual property rights. Mo points out that the court vindicated the outlet after all, but they still faced a severe and unexpected online onslaught – partly due, he suspects, to jealousy at the big investment they attracted. "I think in the environment of the internet, it's easy for the voice of criticism to start and get enlarged, and the voice of your defence is more likely to be drowned out." Still, the outcry had a serious effect on business, with advertisers and brand partners abandoning them.

Chaping may have made a mistake, but it rose to the challenge and quickly set about rehabilitating itself. The company mounted a public relations strategy which involved a series of articles explaining what happened and publicising their content. Mo says PR people at Alibaba told them they were doing it all wrong because they took a "strong attitude" to their critics. "But we were thinking, if we admit we lost, what would our followers think?" And it seemed to work. "Luckily our followers sided firmly with us", says Mo.

Then they set up a policy on using content. First, they put more effort into verification during the editing process. Second, they made sure that any information that came from elsewhere was clearly attributed. Third, they produced a new set of rules on how to respect copyright. The way they present their content now is to have as their site's main story an original in-depth article, and then secondary stories about tools and gadgets, with some more on e-commerce, and these can be sourced from the internet. Then they have two more leisurely "columns": one a "best of the day" roundup along with a funny picture, and the other discussing "major news", with commentaries on the big stories.

Audience figures have still not recovered – in 2020 main stories were tending to get 100,000 to 280,000 UVM (unique visitors a month), other stories 50,000 to 100,000 – but the drop is partly due to a late-2018 change in WeChat's public platform interface, where they show up in a timeline rather than by account name, requiring a different approach to catching eyeballs. Prior to that monthly uniques had been up to 320,000, though figures can still go that high for a juicy story – like one they did on search engine Baidu turning up a fake site as its top result for Deppon Logistics. The audience may be down, but it is loyal. Unlike competitors in the traditional media which only have readers, says Mo, his outlet has fans. "Chaping has a distinctive personal style so that fans can feel the vivid authors behind the articles", he goes on. "This personal style and distinction are mainly created by Chaping's language, which has strong emotional colour."

The business model is back to where it was before all the hoo-ha. Income is 30 per cent from ads and 70 per cent from e-commerce, but profits are exactly the reverse. They run an online store called Chaping Black Market in the form of a WeChat mini programme and Taobao store. Their own team of buyers scouts out gadgets that you can't get elsewhere and then they get their suppliers to source and price them, putting them up on the site in a position where users can buy while still reading the content. The intention is to combine technology and youth culture, and to this end Chaping cooperates with cool brands like Warrior shoes. The plan is eventually to develop new products of their own.

Things are well back on track for Chaping. With their new motto, "Debug the world", meaning to get rid of bad stuff and discover good, they are acknowledging the past and developing a better future. Their office in Hangzhou today has 100 staff – 20 in charge of content, 15 working on ads, 30 on e-commerce and the rest on developing new business. Many employees were actually early users of the site, including Mo, who's been there from almost the beginning.

Mo, having been through the rough and the smooth, has some good advice for entrepreneurial media startups.

One, never forget why you started. "Profit is important, but the most important thing is to find the common ground for your audience", he says. This is particularly so in the early stages "because you are passing on your values and finding the community where you are doing your media business". He thinks self-media are popular because many people share their values. "Only if the audience believe in what you put out can they be here with you together." Chaping's goal is to act for their audience in exposing unfair things. Then he says, speaking from bitter experience, you must have principles and run your business in a professional way. "Writing skill and core talent are both important", he emphasises. This is particularly so as you get bigger, when you need to develop team rules, teamwork and organisation.

And finally: choose a location which nurtures entrepreneurialism, like Hangzhou, home of Alibaba. The local government there is supportive of entrepreneurial efforts. It has been happy to ignore the reservations the older generation have for a negative name like "bad reviews" and support young people who have dreams and are willing to learn from their mistakes.

MALAYSIA

Cilisos

"Regardless of whether you're an adoring fan, a potential advertiser, a politician, a cyber trooper, or a toddler who managed to crawl up and reach the keyboard, we love hearing from [you]." This is how Cilisos calls on its readers to get in touch, displaying the tongue-in-cheek style that characterises its content. It actually calls itself a "non-news" site, and its "terms and conditions" section refers to its output as "fiction and semi-fiction". However, it goes on to say this is used "for the purposes of comment, criticism, parody, pointing out political and/or social injustice or any other purpose through which humanity is held up to the ridicule it frequently deserves".

FIGURE 7.6　Lau Chak Onn. Supplied by Lau Chak Onn.

Cilisos may be light-hearted, but it has serious intent. Rather than covering news – which many other Malaysian sites do very well already – it looks behind what's happening and tries to find something deeper. Case in point: in late July 2020 an article tackled allegations against the judge who had just found former prime minister Najib Razak guilty of corruption. Among the claims were that the judge was related to Najib's former promoter and later nemesis, Mahathir Mohamad, and that he supported the opposition DAP party. Cilisos showed the charges to be untrue (Noor 30 July 2020). While finding both a type and tone of content, Cilisos has also developed a good business model. It relies on sponsored content that is separate from but fits in with its own regular material, including its own special ingredient – a survey feature that serves both client and reader.

According to editor-in-chief Lau Chak Onn, the idea for Cilisos came from its funder and owner, Vincent Lee Fook Long, formerly chief executive of *The Star*, a popular newspaper belonging to the company of the former ruling coalition partner party, the Malaysian Chinese Association. Lee had visited the offices of the US outlet BuzzFeed and was keen to create something similar for Malaysia. He was introduced to Chak (as he is known), whose CV covered data and lifestyle journalism for a range of outlets including the Malaysian version of gadget news site Stuff, Esquire and German tech site Chip. Chak was not so keen on BuzzFeed, but, he says, "not consciously but sub-consciously I would have taken cues from John Oliver and from Cracked" – Oliver presents a critical-satirical TV programme in the US and Cracked is an American humour site. In 2014, Chak goes on, "we created Cilisos, which is what we saw as a bridge between delving deeper into topics and yet making it accessible to a wider audience". Hot and spicy content, in fact: Cilisos is the Malay spelling for chili sauce.

Lee provided the initial funding – Chak won't reveal the amount, "but it wasn't much, put it that way". It was enough for a year. People were bemused by what Chak calls Cilisos's "casual language". "Initially people, especially older people, were like, 'Your content is good, but then your language is so annoying!'" he says. But they soon got to like it. His parents and their friends started sharing it. "I think people recognised that we backed up what we said with real research", Chak goes on, even if they didn't always appreciate the memes.

Friends brought in their first advertiser, the major telco Maxis, and after that they had no trouble getting further top clients. "I think it was a very important step for us because by one blue-chip brand advertising with us that kind of made it look like, hey, it's okay to advertise with Cilisos because … their credibility won't make a mess of our campaign." They soon had Red Bull, Tiger Beer, Panasonic and Air Asia on board paying for sponsored content. Cilisos was the "freshest kid on the block", says Chak. "We were pretty unique in that space at that point in time."

Cilisos Media is one of a number of startup companies under the umbrella of Vincent Lee's investment vehicle Idea River Run (IRR). Lee is majority owner and Chak has a minority share. Two other founders have minority stakes – Lydia Kwan, Cilisos's sponsored-content editor, and UiHua Cheah, who left to become editor of AskLegal, a law information site, though he still works as consulting editor for Cilisos.

Cilisos has 17 staff: four reporters and one editor for each of its two sites (English and Bahasa Malaysia), three sales staff and a video team of five. Chak isn't really looking to expand. "To be honest with you, there is an active resistance to hiring more people because I prefer to work in small teams", he says. "And also I realise that the more people we hire, the more we [need to pay] and thus the more advertising pressure that we have, which might influence the quality of the content." IRR takes care of admin and HR for a fee. "I'm more than happy to pay them so that I don't have to worry about it", says Chak.

All of Cilisos's content is original, most of it from their own staff, an achievement explained by the fact that they only publish one article or video a day. That way they can produce well-rounded pieces and get them out properly to their audience. Chak says they have two commandments for every single story, whether regular or sponsored. The first is to add value and not just do what others are doing. "Either we highlight something that people did not observe or we feature something new or we make something easier to understand," he says. The second is that they never forget distribution. "We make sure that every piece of content is boosted on Facebook, [so that] it has the best chance of reaching as many people as possible", he goes on. "Because I believe that 50 bits of information that are transmitted are better than 100 bits of information that are not transmitted." Editorial posts are boosted on social media with the equivalent of US$12–34, and sponsored posts with ten times that much, with the aim of "seeding" the content to initial viewers. The Malay version also uses Facebook Instant Articles. Cilisos has URL optimisers that get headlines noticed, but is also registered with Google News, so when Cilisos has a unique take on a hot topic Google helps push it higher.

Cilisos staff provide most of the site's sponsored content themselves. "Basically the way we set ourselves apart from everybody else is that we keep the same values we have in our content and we try to carry that over to our sponsored content as well", says Chak. "Which is, we try to make it educational, we try to make it fun, and sometimes we try as best we can to make it data-driven as well because we do a lot of data-driven journalism." Cilisos has developed its own special tool – doing surveys for clients, something no one else has managed to copy. A company will sponsor an online SurveyMonkey questionnaire about a fun topic related to their business – for example, a cinema organisation on movies, a car ride company on friendliness – and Cilisos analyses the results and publishes them, often producing fun facts. This is not scientific research but for marketing purposes, Chak emphasises.

He believes Cilisos's strategy has contributed to its "pretty varied audience" of both liberals and conservatives, though weighing more towards the former and towards more educated, high-income people. With traffic driven through Facebook and Google, users are not the very young – the many platforms youngsters use make them divided and difficult to get to, Chak says – but the young middle-aged, late 20s to 40. What's interesting is that the audience has aged along with Cilisos. Chak says the site has about 400,000 UVM.

Technical matters and upkeep of the WordPress CMS are outsourced to a freelancer in East Malaysia whom Chak has never even met. He chose him because he was affordable, efficient and very reliable. "He's been 100 per cent trustworthy", he says. "Despite us not needing him often, he always responds within an hour." The arrangement suits them both. "We don't have that high technical requirements, so it works out both ways because he gets the regular stipend and not much work, and we get someone dependable for not much money." Chak is pleased that the technician has done some "hardening" of the site, that is, made it very safe, and there have been no major security problems.

Humour is key to Cilisos's raison d'être. The "about us" pages are full of jokey language, as noted above, such as a page giving recipes marks out of 22. They play elaborate April Fool's jokes. In 2019 they published a story saying they and three other outlets had set up an aggregator site called AmbikKau.com. Chak hates news aggregators. "They are the bane of journalism because they basically just re-appropriate content and don't actually send out reporters and don't add any value to articles", he says, making their money off the backs of genuine sites with very little work or expense. AmbikKau – it literally means "take yours", but also "it's a Malaysian version of 'up yours'," says Chak – was a fake site but Cilisos was filling it with content from the sites that had ripped off its own stories. "We were generating 90 articles a day with very little effort!" Chak says. AmbikKau had its first advertiser enquiry within a week, he laughs.

Chak sees the main problem for media not so much as press freedom but just trying to stay afloat. "The problem right now of why you are seeing more political content, why you're seeing more salacious content, is because media organisations are in survival mode", he says. "They're trying to do whatever it takes to survive, which means sometimes they have to take advertisers they don't want to take or they need to get page views they actually don't want to get." Chak has seen site traffic go down as people move away from text and towards video, and Cilisos has expanded its video team to keep up. They are experimenting with new formats, such as videos with text and no sound for people to watch on public transport, an idea they got from Al Jazeera's AJ+ platforms.

There are no big plans. "I think it's pointless to have a business plan, it's pointless when the media landscape is changing so quickly", says Chak. Cilisos is doing well enough for now. "I mean, I'm not driving a Ferrari", Chak says, but "I'm driving a Prius … a secondhand Prius."

CHINA

Ciwei Gongshe

Ye Tieqiao is a journalist's journalist. He took a bachelor's degree in the subject at Hunan University and followed up with a master's in the field at Peking University. In 2006, after graduating, he joined *China Youth Daily* and spent eight years working on in-depth stories and then moved up to become the *Daily*'s social media operations director. This combination of academic and practical experience gave Ye insights into how new platforms like super app WeChat and news aggregator Jinri Toutiao were radically changing the media equation from the traditional one-way channel (content producers to a mass audience) to an interactive one where what the producer wants to express has to be what the user wants to read.

FIGURE 7.7 Ye Tieqiao. Supplied by Ye Tieqiao.

So Ye decided to set up his own outlet to cover developments in the media. He thought it should be a kind of community and wanted to name it after a quirky animal. Having first considered wombats, he came up with Ciwei Gongshe – "Hedgehog Commune". Launched in 2014, it ran from a WeChat official account and covered everything to do with content, from print to video to audio to aggregators to virtual reality and augmented reality. His partner, Professor Shen Yang of Tsinghua University, put up funding totalling RMB300,000 (about US$46,000), though has since dropped out.

Ciwei got off to a good start with a bombshell interview. It was with a journalist who was part of the undercover reporting team who had become media stars after they did an exposé on unhygienic conditions at the Shanghai Husi meat processing plant. The team, from a local state-run TV station, had posed as workers to get jobs at the factory. They found that government inspectors had been tricked into thinking all was well when in fact staff were using out-of-date meat. The story had particular influence because Shanghai Husi is part of a US conglomerate and the products were being sold to high-profile chains like McDonald's both in China and overseas (Reuters 31 July 2014). Ciwei Gongshe's story about the journalist revealed how the investigation was done, and it went viral.

At this point, Ye was still working for *China Youth* and running Ciwei part-time as a "WeMedia" project under the auspices of a computer design studio. In 2016 he left his job to work on the new outlet full-time, registering it on his own. He had learned that covering media content alone wasn't profitable and was also politically risky, so he expanded the focus to include the major internet companies like short video apps TikTok and Kuaishou, audio outlets like Himalaya, gaming specialists such as Tencent and Netease and online literature companies like China Reading. Ciwei later received funding from Alibaba, though Ye did not disclose the amount.

Today the outlet has 33 employees, most of whom are "authors" (they are not allowed to have "reporters"). These staff are key to the outlet's operations. Ciwei takes on people who show exceptional talent, then pays them well, allows them to choose their field and set their own goals, and gives them long-term training and a growth plan. They produce one in-depth 3,500-character original article a week each. They are encouraged to go out to do their own reporting, even to distant provinces, rather than rely on online information and contacts. One story that made waves revealed that a rural women's collective in Shandong province that had been praised for posting content online had actually got their material by "laundering" other people's work (Bandurski 1 September 2018).

What makes the outlet a "commune" is its close interaction with the audience. Less time is spent on getting stories done and more is given to talking to readers after posting. "In traditional newsrooms, journalists finish their work after publishing their articles, but in Ciwei Gongshe the authors need to put a lot of energy into replying to comments and analysing the data thoroughly", said former deputy editor-in-chief Shi Can (who since being interviewed has left to join business magazine *Caijing*). With the updates WeChat has made to its public account interface, readers have to subscribe and authors can monitor and respond to comments. This both improves writer morale and increases user engagement. Authors have also set up about 50 WeChat groups which users can join to discuss particular issues and share articles. These can evolve into online communities themselves.

Ciwei Gongshe's formula has attracted a young (20–35 years old), well-educated and well-off audience from the top-tier cities – Beijing, Shanghai and Guangzhou. Interestingly, there are more women than men. It has continued to publish only on its WeChat public account, where it has 400,000 followers, but its articles are posted to most sharing platforms – the Twitter-like Weibo, where excerpts from long articles are posted to publicise them, as well as aggregator Jinri Toutiao, Quora-like Zhihu, multi-platform Sohu, streaming service Dayuhao and writers' platform Baijianhao.

The outlet's main income source – 60 per cent of the total – is native advertising. Content is written by its own journalists, a practice common on WeChat platforms, and it features as part of the regular content. Income also comes from events. One project charged journalism academics for a visit to learn more about the new social and aggregation platforms, and this was supposed to become the basis for future study tours but has had to be dropped for the time being because of the coronavirus pandemic. More profitable was the organisation of the annual Non-Fiction Writing Competition for three years, for which Ciwei received sponsorship of the equivalent of US$14,000 from Kuaishou and Alibaba's Ant Finance in separate years. This has also had to be discontinued.

Ye's heroes are China's nimble internet companies, particularly Jinri Toutiao and Alibaba. His plan was once to follow in their footsteps and build a versatile platform, but today he feels the priority is to do the right thing: "I now want to make a respected media outlet", he says.

SOUTHEAST ASIA AND HONG KONG

Coconuts

Coconuts has a unique profile. A network of sites covering the region – one each for Bangkok, Singapore, Jakarta, Hong Kong, Kuala Lumpur, Manila, Yangon and Bali – it puts out "fresh and juicy" hyperlocal news to each of its concurrent but separate audiences of hip young English-speaking professionals. No one else has tried anything like it, let alone succeeded. But when it comes to finding the right business model, Coconuts is no different from any other site. Its team has had to work hard to make things happen.

FIGURE 7.8 Byron Perry. Supplied by Byron Perry.

Byron Perry, an American journalist who had been working in the region for some years, launched Coconuts in Bangkok in 2011 with an injection of investment funding (no details of how much or who from have been publicised) that enabled the outlet to forget about income for the time being. "We were focused purely on growing our audience … as aggressively as possible", says Perry. People loved its quirky, humorous spin on local news. Within three years, Perry and his team could count a huge achievement: more than 4 million unique visitors a month (UVM).

Now they needed to start making some money.

They began in 2015 by selling advertising. Some was in the form of display ads but most was branded content. Originally called sponsored content but changed due to the preference of advertisers, it was produced in-house by Coconuts' marketing team – Perry is insistent that journalists don't get involved – and is clearly labelled as having a brand sponsor. It brought in a good income, and continues to do so today. But it wasn't enough. "That alone didn't take us to profitability", says Perry.

So in 2017 Coconuts started up another revenue earner: licensing and production. The minor side of this was the sale of text articles to big content aggregators Microsoft, Yahoo! and the Singaporean news app NewsLoop. That gave them "a little income stream", says Perry. The bigger operation was video. Coconuts TV, "our video channel focused on the weird and wondrous untold stories of Asia", as the site says, releases its work on YouTube and has made productions for Netflix, Malaysian-based iflix, MTV Asia and MediaCorp of Singapore. By 2019, income from this source had equalled that from advertising. Coconuts was on track to break even.

The next step turned out to be more tortuous than expected. In 2018, despite audience numbers falling from that original high, Coconuts decided to set up a paywall as the basis of a regular income stream. "The great thing about subscription revenue is that it recurs", says Perry. "Every year, every dollar that you earn should return the next year, minus the churn rate." The outlet decided to go one step further and set it up as a membership programme. The added value that made subscription into membership of Coco+ resided in two main attractions.

One was freebies. Members received a tote bag on signing up and more giveaways later, plus discounts on food, travel and entertainment. Coconuts got most of these perks through partners and advertisers without cost. The other was events. The cornerstone of these was the "Coconuts Colloquiums", held in the cities of publication. The site described them thus: "Fuse one part powwow (some call this a 'panel'), one part mixer-mingler thingy, booze for miles, and the sparkly magic of entertainment-meets-insight. Hopefully, you'll leave our sessions a little bit more enlightened and a lot more inebriated." Topics ranged from press freedom in Malaysia to the LGBTQ experience in Singapore to women leaders in the Philippines, and in Bangkok and Hong Kong they even discussed the subscription business itself. Other events included launch celebrations and anniversary parties. Going out to meet its "Coconauts" in Bali, Bangkok, Hong Kong, Jakarta, Kuala Lumpur, Manila, Singapore and Yangon proved "invaluable" for the outlet, said Perry at the time: "Every single event has gone great and, whether it's 40 or 80 people that showed up, all of them are leaving as brand evangelists and are excited about Coconuts".

In preparation for the membership scheme they drastically reduced content – from a huge 2,000 stories a month to fewer than 1,000 – to improve quality. "Previously we would do a lot more stuff that was high-volume, get-it-out-fast, don't worry about doing any original reporting", says Perry. "But with our drive towards subscriptions we have to provide information and context and a voice that you can't get elsewhere, and so we're putting more resources into that." The emphasis moved to Coconuts' own reporting.

Then began a process of experimentation with the paywall.

The first effort was a metered type. Readers could view up to 15 items a month free but after that had to pay for membership. Perry expected a backlash and a decrease in traffic, but there was no drop in visitors at all, and many signed up straight away. With the confidence that engendered, the team fiddled with the number of free stories, reducing it to ten a month and at one point only five. Then they decided to move to a freemium model, walling off premium content for members while keeping the rest available without payment. That had a big downside: their journalists were unhappy with it. "Our writers and our editors didn't like having the stuff that they spent the most time on be fully blocked", says Perry. He didn't like it much himself because of the decisions that had to be made on which content should be premium and which free. "A lot of our stuff is in between – it may be sourced from social media but there's a lot of original reporting", he goes on.

So in 2019 it was all-change again, this time to a hybrid model, a combination of everything that had gone before. All content was free, but some articles were designated premium, though not marked as much. For these articles, users could read up to five a month and then would have to subscribe before reading more. That worked somewhat better. Coconuts could post newsy stories quickly to bring in traffic and at the same time open up their original stories to some extent. With the premium stories not labelled, readers were not aware of that until they hit the limit. "We don't want to aggressively block people from reading our content", Perry said at the time. They also didn't want to force people to use free backdoor routes, such as incognito windows. With the subscription costing only US$5 a month, it wasn't worth it.

Membership remained small – Perry won't give out numbers but the goal was only 1 per cent of readers anyway – and contributed only a tiny amount to revenue, but adding it to the multi-pronged business model produced some pleasant results. "One thing that's been awesome to see is that, starting the paywall, focusing less on viral content, focusing more on quality content, we've seen our audience grow," Perry said. To bring more members on board a set of newsletters was added – one for each location and one each for top trending stories, TV, travel and food (the latter two sites are verticals, run separately from the rest since 2018).

In 2020, however, the coronavirus changed everything yet again. First, with advertising "hammered", as the announcement put it, the site lifted the paywall for pandemic coverage, while mounting a campaign for more people to become members or sign up as patrons. By September, though, the team had given up. In the changed world where live events were no longer possible, they removed the paywall altogether. "In this climate, we want Coconuts stories to be free and accessible for all", the site announced. "The paywall by nature blocked people from reading our stories, limiting access for those who didn't pay and limiting the reach of Coconuts. Our traffic has grown by about 10 per cent so far in 2020, but we will be able to reach even more readers and make a bigger impact without the paywall." Coco+ remained in place as before, but was no longer connected to content, members paying "any amount" starting from US$5 a year.

Meanwhile, the outlet went into expansion mode. A new vertical, Grove, the Coconuts brand studio, was set up to offer creative services both for Coconuts and for other clients. In August 2020, Coconuts TV formed a partnership with US private equity firm Raven Capital Management to produce a series of pilot programmes on Asian topics. In September the company bought out BK Magazine, a Bangkok lifestyle outlet, and other Thai brands from Asia City Media Group. Coconuts could now tout a combined audience of 2 million UVM on average for branded and display ads and offer 360-degree campaigns across digital, print, video and events.

Coconuts is a truly international company, registered in Bangkok, Singapore and Hong Kong. It is supported by private angel investors in the US and Hong Kong who have put in several funding rounds either as loans or in return for an equity share, though Perry is not willing to reveal their identities or investment details. He himself has a share of the company too.

Coconuts has a strong commitment to ethical journalism. That may seem a tall claim when it still puts out "processed" content from other sites, but that is changing, Perry says, with 80 per cent of content original to some extent. One very strong principle is that journalists do not get involved in advertising – in other words, Coconuts is respecting the "church and state" split. "Nobody on our editorial team is involved with our sales or branded content whatsoever," says Perry. "That's really important to me." Editors do not attend sales meetings even though their expertise could help. Transparency is another value. Commercial content is clearly marked as such, and advertising policies are stated on the website.

Coconuts long relied on Facebook to filter traffic to it, though it has never used Instant Articles. "We always knew it was important to maintain the audience on our own property, our website", says Perry. When the site hit its high of 4.2 million UVM in 2015–2016, fully 50 per cent of visitors came via Facebook. However, the lead position has been taken over by Google search, which is now responsible for 35 per cent of referrals, while Facebook counts for only 17 per cent. The sheer volume of content coming out of Coconuts – even after cutting down their output – means that they pop up on Google search with little effort needed for SEO.

The Coconuts site uses WordPress, which is supported by one in-house technical lead, who, with the help of a small outsourced team in Vietnam, oversaw the implementation of the paywall as well as a site redesign in 2017 that brought more consistency to the eight hyperlocal pages and added a single home page, making Coconuts more of a single regional brand. But local news for each location is "still our core DNA", says Perry. The outfit is run by 50 staff in total, 20 having come from Asia City. The journalists cover news by phone from their offices and go out to report their own stories, mostly "evergreens", or timeless pieces, that stay fresh for a long time.

One thing Byron Perry would change about the way he developed his multi-focused site would be to concentrate from the start on income generation rather than go all out to get unique visitors. "I wish from the beginning I had focused on monetisation", he says. Making audience revenue the main income stream is still the goal, he goes on, and he hopes that more outlets push for that option so that more audiences will become willing to pay. Coconuts may have had to adjust its business model more than once, but its advantage is in its special appeal – "the sense of humour, the conversational style and the unique voice" Perry describes it. This combination, he goes on, is "what separates us from our competitors the most and that's what I think all of the audience that love us love about us most."

CAMBODIA

DAP News

In 2008, the sensitive frontier between Cambodia and Thailand erupted in a conflict largely provoked by Thai political infighting. The focus was the area round the majestic Preah Vihear temple, high on the Dangrek escarpment on Cambodia's northern border with its neighbour. This ancient holy site had been judged by the International Court of Justice in 1962 as belonging to Cambodia in a victory still treasured by the Khmer people. The renewed clashes that broke out in October 2008 caused national concern, and every Cambodian wanted to know what was going on. News coverage was available in a range of newspapers and broadcasters but always lagged events.

FIGURE 7.9 Soy Sophea and Soy Rithy. Photo credit: Author.

In early 2009, a pioneering breaking-news website started to provide a much speedier service. DAP News – dap-news.com – had been set up the year before by *Deum Ampil*, a weekly newspaper established in 2006, and hit its stride at a time when 3G and smartphones were taking off. People rapidly took to its fast, convenient and trustworthy coverage of the major issues of the day, particularly Preah Vihear. Its current editor-in-chief, Soy Sophea, remembers that they got a million hits for some news stories, and there were so many visitors at times that the site froze.

DAP's good reputation remains today, but its own story has been one of very changing fortunes entwined with Cambodian politics and the country's cut-throat media business.

The man behind both the newspaper and online outlet is Sophea's older brother, Soy Sopheap (Sophea's shortcut to remember the name difference is that he is "minus p" and his sibling is "plus p"), Cambodia's most prominent journalist.

Sopheap's career goes back to the early 1990s, a time when the media were wild and free under the new democracy. He received journalism training from a number of international providers – many foreign-funded programmes were available at that time – and worked for, among others, the Japanese news agency Kyodo. He was firmly in the opposition camp, co-founding an outspoken newspaper, *Moneaksekar Khmer*, that was highly critical of the government. Then in in the early 2000s Sopheap stunned everybody by moving across the political divide to a government-supporting TV station, where he became a news superstar and got close to Prime Minister Hun Sen. To this day he remains a stalwart of the pro-government media, working now for Bayon, the TV station belonging to the PM's daughter.

Deum Ampil means "tamarind tree", and this refers to the trees under which journalists gathered to eat breakfast at open-air cafés outside the then National Assembly (though today both ministry and food stalls have moved). It was a small paper, but in 2008, according to Sophea, Minister of Information Khieu Kanharith suggested that it should expand, and it went into partnership that year with a local property company, Heng Development.

This led to the setting up in 2009 of the Deum Ampil Media Center, a nonprofit that housed the news operation but also trained budding journalists, who now had few opportunities to learn because most international news aid programmes had ended. Sophea, who had worked at *Deum Ampil* from the start though initially part-time (like many Cambodian journalists, he was running several jobs), had followed his brother into the profession. He too had been trained on internationally supported programmes and worked for diverse media, so he was in a position to teach. The Center took trainees on for a year, giving them transport costs and food but no pay. Sophea says he and another couple of trainers who worked with him trained more than 50 journalists, who now work all over the Cambodian media. Two other initiatives came out of the new partnership. One was a monthly magazine called *Morakot* (Emerald) and the other their own radio station, for which they got a broadcasting licence for FM 93.75 Mhz in 2009.

Their biggest new operation, of course, was the digital news outlet, which was inspired by Sopheap's experience at Kyodo. It didn't have an easy takeoff. The first challenge was just getting people to go online at a time when digital was so new. DAP took a novel step, according to Sophea: celebrities were invited for interviews for the magazine and on the radio and would discuss the internet and social media, and then in turn would be asked to write about DAP on their own blogs. This move brought many newcomers to the digital world. At the same time, the outlet carved itself a political niche for following the prime minister, who at that point hadn't discovered how to communicate via social media. "We tried to focus on what Hun Sen said, what he talked about, and then we briefed our readers", says Sophea. Business took off and the outlet was doing well.

Then in 2010 came the first big letdown. The property company partner not only pulled out, but launched a competing online news outlet. Soon after, *Morakot* had to shut down and even the newspaper stopped publishing for a while. However, DAP News wasn't in too bad a position overall because it had already established itself and had developed a strong income stream from banner ads at a time when there were no better choices for advertisers. It started up a new magazine, *Looking Today*, an entertainment outlet targeting younger people than those who read DAP News. In both 2011 and 2012, the DAP News Centre won the national Best News Website Award. But a bigger blow came in 2015 when a partnership to open up a new site called Fresh News, which produced the first mobile news app in Cambodia, came apart due to a personal fallout, with DAP cut out of what became the preferred government news outlet and a thriving competing business.

"DAP was at its lowest point", says Soy Rithy, Sopheap's son and today DAP's chief marketing officer. It hasn't really recovered. No new long-term partner or investor has appeared, and meanwhile the online media market has filled up with new sites, often more entertainment-oriented and reader-friendly and fronted by clever business brains (see, for example, Sabay and KhmerLoad, pp. 178–181 and 149–53), while the legacy media have also established themselves in digital form. The DAP operation is still run by the Soy family – Sopheap is director-general, Sophea editor-in-chief and a third brother is CEO, while two more brothers head finance and admin, with Rithy as CMO, and it's run out of a family member's home which has been mortgaged to help pay for the operation. Even Soy Sopheap's income from his job at Bayon goes to support the outfit.

Banner advertising is still DAP's main source of operating income. While newer media may have moved to impression-based deals, DAP still works with time-defined packages – one banner ad is priced at US$800 a month – which means advertisements stay up for longer. In 2018 the name Deum Ampil Media Center was dropped and replaced by DAP Advertising Co. Ltd., a registered company, which contains the DAP website, *Looking Today*, the newspaper and the radio station. The reason, according to Rithy, was that new rules required advertisers to pay Value Added Tax and they had to be billed for it, but the Center, as a nonprofit, didn't pay tax.

Today the news operation has about 90 staff, 25 of whom are in Phnom Penh and the rest stringers in the provinces. Untrained, unpaid journalists are still hired even for permanent positions, according to Rithy, "because of the financial situation", but they are given training and expenses. They can work for other outlets too, and can also earn commission if they introduce advertisers. It's not an ideal situation, but it's necessary in current circumstances and the training provides a service to society, says Sophea. DAP has content-sharing partnerships with local outlets including Sabay and for international news with Xinhua, Kyodo and Japan Today. The news website continues to be lively, covering news and social affairs. A news app has been created but isn't as popular as Fresh News's, though the website is more popular than its rival's, according to Rithy. *Looking Today* has proved a success, and is now represented by a bright and lively website, while the radio station continues under the management of a partner. A new business site has also been launched, DAP Business, on the strength of CEO Soy Vichet's connections.

The Soys see their main advantage as being their professionalism and credibility, attracting readers who are well-educated middle-aged people, including government officials. The newspaper has been suspended again as a regular publication, nowadays appearing only once every month or so with a print run of about 1,000 copies sent to officials "to remind them" of its existence, says Rithy. But the paper will not be forgotten. Rithy thinks print might come back into fashion when people get tired of the "many Facebook pages and websites that publish and livestream crime news, traffic accidents, celebrities' news and clickbait".

The outlet is still seen to be pro-government – a survey done by a local NGO found it had nearly the lowest level of perceived independence (CCIM 2017) – but in a milieu where non-pro-government media are at risk and today hardly survive it's the obvious option. Sophea notes that both government and opposition criticise DAP for being biased, but company policy is always to get multiple sides of a story. They will find an NGO or an activist for comment on a story about the government, for instance. "Let people judge who we are", he says. "We're not saying we're pro-government or pro-opposition or pro-NGO. But from the stories we have run, you can judge."

From being a news pioneer to braving the ensuing cutthroat media market has taken a toll, but DAP is determined to go on. Soy Sophea remembers how Information Minister Kanharith once told them that the media was a battlefield, and you cannot rest for long. "If you don't fight, you are lost", he says. "We remind ourselves of that every day when we are driving home or back at home." And with the Soy Sopheap "brand name" behind them, they believe they cannot fail.

MYANMAR

Frontier Myanmar

Frontier Myanmar, an in-depth and investigative magazine, opened in 2015 in print format – it had an online presence, but print was its main platform. That wasn't so surprising given Myanmar's late start on the digital transition, but it also had a lot to do with its founder's beginnings as a printer and then newspaper publisher, and to the fact that he missed out on the internet's openings when he was in prison for eight and a half years on charges of breaking censorship rules. Frontier gathered a good following for its strong political reporting, but it moved

FIGURE 7.10 Sonny Swe. Supplied by Sonny Swe.

boldly on to a new entrepreneurial frontier. It established a business model that brought in direct income from its appreciative audience: membership. Then the bad times came. The military ousted the popular elected government in early 2021, a situation compounded by the unfettered spread of COVID-19. One of Frontier's editors was jailed and its staff were hit by the pandemic. Later in the year it was forced to shut down its print, website and social media operations. But its solid membership meant that it could keep going with its prized newsletter while waiting for better times.

To go back to the beginning, Sonny Swe, the founder concerned, started his printing career on his return to Myanmar after studying in the US in the 1990s, when the military junta of the time was practising heavy censorship. His most high-profile job was putting out a newspaper in Mandalay. Then in 2000, he took up an opportunity to co-found a weekly newspaper, *The Myanmar Times*. Published in Myanmar and English, it soon became popular among news-starved readers and was in profit after just six months. "I was a little spoiled making money so quickly", says Sonny Swe.

However, he himself was not there for long: he was jailed in 2004 on censorship charges that had more to do with the purge of the political faction his father, a general in military security, belonged to.

His enthusiasm for the newspaper business increased during the time he spent inside, and when he was released in 2013 he headed straight to the *Myanmar Times* newsroom before even going home. "Because in prison you have to keep your hope alive", he says. "And the way I survived was to keep my hope that one day I was going to reunite with my colleagues, my co-workers, and I was going to manage *Myanmar Times* again."

However, when he got back to the paper, much had changed. In 2012 censorship had been lifted, and the market was now replete with new publications as well as returning exile media outlets. Also he had been left behind in the tech stakes. "I didn't even know how to send an SMS on a smartphone because I couldn't find the 'send' button", he remembers. Meanwhile, the ownership of *Myanmar Times* was changing too, leaving him on the outside. He left the paper and next joined online site Mizzima, but that proved short-lived

So in 2015, the year of Myanmar's first fully free elections in 25 years and the promise of democracy, he set out on his own and launched Frontier Myanmar. A weekly magazine in English, it came out in print and made its money from newsstand sales and subscriptions (20 per cent) and print advertising (80 per cent). Content was posted online as a secondary matter. Building a media outlet was difficult enough in the now-crowded market, especially given the competition from subsidised government publications, but there was worse on the horizon – what Sonny Swe calls the "digital tsunami". Smartphones only became available in Myanmar in 2010, and at first that didn't seem to change things because of lack of connectivity, but they took off with the arrival of affordable 3G networks in 2014. By 2017, the effect was painfully evident: advertisers were abandoning print but didn't yet trust digital. The bottom fell out of the whole ad market.

Sonny Swe's next move was a clever one: he restructured Frontier to add a new income source. With a partner from Singapore, he set up Black Knight Media as the overall company owning Frontier and hived off the magazine's ad sales department to form a separate marketing and communications agency under the same umbrella, also called Black Knight. Its profits would all go into supporting the magazine. The agency started out small by doing translations and providing fixers for foreign media, but ad and marketing custom soon picked up. "We decided to offer more services to advertisers rather than just banner ads on print pages," says the head of Black Knight agency, Khin Thandar Htay. It moved into branding and branded content and took a leading role in educating customers in the new ways of online, developing into an all-round agency. It was spectacularly successful. "In 2½ years we increased revenue 250 per cent", says Thandar.

However, it was still not enough to support Frontier Myanmar. Frontier had built a very high-profile audience comprising foreign residents – diplomats, NGO workers and so on – and educated local professionals, and had established an excellent track record. Brooten, McElhone and Venkiteswaran (2019, 35–36) call it "one of the most respected journalism outfits in Myanmar, with a reputation for tackling taboo topics". One of its stories, for example, exposed corruption on the Karen State Highway construction, causing the World Bank to stop financing the project. "We don't do promotions, restaurant reviews, movie reviews, only serious reporting, stories that have an impact and change society", says Sonny Swe. But this content isn't the kind that's suited to making big money.

In 2018, the magazine was in deep trouble. With funds running low, all salaries, including Sonny Swe's, were cut, and at one point payment was delayed in three consecutive months. "Sleepless nights!" he remembers. Frontier was almost at the point of shutting down. Convinced that it could still make it, the publisher reached out. Invited as a speaker to international media conferences like those put on by the UK and Canadian governments ("Defend Media Freedom"), the International Press Institute and Splice Beta (see Chapter 8 pp. 9–13), he started meeting other media business people from around the world – so many, in fact, that he found himself giving out 500 name cards a month. He soon came across people who were keen to help. Thus in 2019 Frontier Myanmar moved to a new model – 60–70 per cent commercial and 30–40 per cent funded by donors, allowing most staff salaries to be restored. Donations were to be only a stopgap measure, Sonny Swe hoped at that point, and in the meantime the publication would "basically regroup and reinforce and take on a different mindset."

That new mindset was memberships, and many of the donations that came in were designed to support the transition. Frontier had already been considering a paywall in 2018 when Sonny Swe attended the Global Investigative Journalism Network conference in Seoul, and he remembers that when he got there all people were talking about was memberships. He was impressed and decided to give it a try when he got home. However, he quickly realised it wasn't going to work in the circumstances at the time in Myanmar. "We started crunching the numbers", he says. "It wasn't reasonable at all, right? We were dreaming, dreaming, dreaming." He was ready to give up, but then his contacts came through. Luminate, the arm of Omidyar Network that deals with media, helped him link up with the Membership Puzzle Project, an outfit set up by New York University professor Jay Rosen and the Netherlands-based online journalism platform De Correspondent and at that time run by the Media Development Investment Fund (MDIF). It supplied advice and support for membership programmes.

But serious financial help was needed to carry it out. With Splice Media hired as consultant (Sonny Swe met Splice's Alan Soon and Rishad Patel at a WAN-IFRA conference), Frontier made an application to the Google News Initiative (GNI) Challenge – and won. It received a grant of US$100,000 in 2019. Then Denmark's International Media Support (IMS) offered funding to staff the project. Meanwhile, money for the commercial side of the business came from Luminate, and then MDIF stepped up with training for the finance department. What's more, Sonny Swe got moral support from several highly experienced regional journalists who became not only advisers but friends: former *Bangkok Post* editor-in-chief Pichai Chuensuksuwadi (who now sits on Frontier's board), CEO of social news network Rappler in the Philippines Maria Ressa, and Malaysiakini's Steven Gan and Premesh Chandran (see pp. 160–165).

There are many ways to run paywall and membership programmes. Frontier had decided that regular content would remain free and payment would be voluntary, something Google approved of. The grants from GNI and IMS went towards carrying out surveys and focus group research. Staff sent out questionnaires and called people in according to their professions, and then used the feedback to hone the details. They finally put into effect three tiers of membership, all emphasising being part of the Frontier community. The cheapest costs US$80 a year and gives digital access to content before the print version is issued (Frontier is still in theory print-led), a 50-per-cent discount on the print edition and access to monthly events. The second tier, at US$150, adds Frontier's daily briefing, and the most expensive, at $250 a year, adds a daily monitor of the Myanmar media.

As all this was going on, Sonny Swe, the former technophobe, embraced all that new tech has to offer. He oversaw the upgrading of the website, its CMS changed from Drupal to WordPress to take advantage of the latter's e-commerce plug-ins (choosing from among WooCommerce, Stripe and Pico), and the company is using MailChimp, SurveyMonkey and the Notion project-management app. "New things are coming out every month and keeping up with these and repackaging content can make money", he says. He borrowed a data team to make a start on data journalism, producing a series of stories on Chinese money in Myanmar. Podcasts had been going since 2017, and online TV was planned, though not imminently due to lack of expertise. Frontier was already increasing its income by taking all forms of advertising – not only display but also native, sponsored and branded. The latter, Frontier's own stories done by its own journalists but paid for by a brand, were the most lucrative.

As the transition got under way, Sonny Swe travelled all over the region in 2019 giving talks about Frontier's moves and became the international face of the membership business model. The scheme was launched on 1 February 2020, not a moment too soon because other revenue streams became threatened as the COVID-19 outbreak spread. The print version was temporarily dropped, a renewed membership campaign was started and the outlet got emergency funding from Google and other supporters. In July, with the November elections on the horizon, a staff revamp took place, with some long-time employees leaving and ten new people recruited, including an in-house data journalism team. Frontier was far from out of the woods, with the coronavirus spreading relatively late in Myanmar, but having a membership programme at least provided a solid revenue base to hold on to.

The military coup was a blow to the whole media industry in Myanmar, with physical distribution channels closed and the internet often blocked. Membership was all that kept Frontier going – it now had about 10,000 members, of whom 800 were paying. What was encouraging was the attention the online site was getting. "We are seeing a huge growth digitally", says Sonny Swe. "Audience engagement is well beyond our expectations." The coup faced huge opposition, with protesters fighting back in the streets. Frontier's journalists joined many others in braving the dangerous conditions as well as risking arrest to report on the situation and supply the original, in-depth, analytical content its members appreciated.

HONG KONG

Hong Kong Citizen News

Not all startups are launched by hungry young entrepreneurs clamouring to get experience and learn from their mistakes. Hong Kong Citizen News's founders come from the other end of the spectrum. They are some of the biggest names in local journalism, veterans at the top of their game who have earned respect for their work and their contribution. That background ensured an outpouring of support from people who knew and trusted them, giving them a boost when they started in 2017 and staying with them as they developed. Four years later, with a reader-driven revenue model building, HKCN doubled down by taking on board a whole award-winning team of China reporters who had resigned from a

FIGURE 7.11 Daisy Li Yuet Wah. Supplied by Daisy Li Yuet Wah.

local cable TV station. The audience welcomed the move. "Support from readers was overwhelming", says chief editor Daisy Li Yuet Wah, with subscriptions doubling within two months.

Li, who worked for many years for quality paper *Ming Pao* and later with outspoken Next Media in Hong Kong and Taiwan, recounts how it all came about. "We started with a couple of us talking about the idea, and then it grew into a bigger group", says Li. "Then we asked around the core members, 'Who is willing to go further?'" Finally, ten people signed up as company founders. Among them are the other two besides Li who actually run HKCN. One is Chris Yeung Kin Hing, long-time reporter and columnist with two respected newspapers, *South China Morning Post* and *Hong Kong Economic Journal*, who is in charge of local commentary. The other is Keung Kwok Yuen, controversially sacked as *Ming Pao* managing editor in 2016, who deals with China and international news. Other founders include Mak Yin Ting, formerly of government broadcaster RTHK; Kevin Lau Chun To, once *Ming Pao* chief editor and the victim of a vicious knife attack in 2014 which put him in hospital for months; and Joseph Chan Man, a journalism professor at the Chinese University of Hong Kong. Yeung, Li and Mak are former chairs of the Hong Kong Journalists Association.

The outlet's core values, says Li, are: "Uphold press freedom in Hong Kong, uphold one country two systems [the arrangement by which Hong Kong has its own government], freedom of the press, independent judiciary and full democracy". With these commitments they didn't want to register as a for-profit company, but Hong Kong doesn't have a nonprofit option. Li says,

> Since we weren't aiming at making a profit, and we knew that we didn't have the ability to make a profit anyway, we took some time to ask a lawyer to come up with Articles of Association to make us look like a social enterprise.

Civic Journalists Ltd. was registered as a company limited by guarantee in the names of the founders. Any money they make has to go back into the company and the founders can't take any out, while their maximum liability would be just HK$100 (less than US$13) each.

Such was the confidence in HKCN's founders it had no trouble attracting funding even before it started. A pre-launch crowdfunding drive through Fringebacker, the local platform used by Hong Kong Free Press (see pp. 139–143) and investigative outlet Factwire, raised the equivalent of US$346,000. Then there were some big donations. Three anonymous benefactors gave a total of the equivalent of US$256,500. A further US$77,000 came from a reward fund set up by Kevin Lau's University of Hong Kong classmates to find his attacker – a job the police had done, so they agreed to give the sum to HKCN. Additionally, two donors gave around US$13,000 each, and a couple of supporters in the US handed over Hong Kong stocks that were sold for about US$18,000. Li emphasises that the donors are not investors, but people mostly even older than themselves who liked the outlet's sincerity, even though it didn't even have much of a business plan.

The funds gave Li and her team a comfy nest egg to start out when they launched in January 2017 with a small team of young journalists doing the reporting. But getting a new outlet going was much more difficult than they expected. They had prepared an in-depth feature about the unpopular then-outgoing chief executive, Leung Chun Ying, who had received an unexplained large payoff from the sale of a company he owned (they later won an award for this story). Li had thought this would be enough to get them started, but she was wrong. "We ran it for two days", she says, "and then on the third day, oh my god! I don't have any stories at all! And on the fourth day, so what can I publish? On the fifth day there were still no substantial good stories." For the whole first month she was scared witless that the enterprise wouldn't be able to take off. But they got through it. "Gradually we picked up the momentum", she says. "We used trial and error and we got to know that the team, despite not being that experienced, … can dig out good stories."

Li herself was surprised by the outlet's success, which she considers "a miracle". One of the keys has been keeping a tight rein on expenditure. Li puts this down to her years of experience running Next's *Apple Daily* Taiwan operation. "I was managing the biggest online website in Taiwan. I had a very big team. So somehow I know what's needed, and what's a luxury, in our view." One luxury they have saved on is the salaries of the three founders who run the day-to-day operations, who get much less than they did in their old jobs. Also they found an office at a low rent in an unfashionable former industrial district. But the special ingredient is that they get a lot of free support.

Three of the founders and one other journalist, a long-time China beat reporter, work free to provide content for a weekly newsletter, and this has become the basis of their business model. Li reasoned that a paywall wouldn't work because there isn't enough content to tempt readers behind it, and ads can't produce enough revenue on a nonprofit site, so this exclusive newsletter, containing four high-quality analytical articles of at least 2,000 characters each and sent out by email every Sunday evening, is what subscribers get for their money. All the original Fringebacker donors got automatic subs for a year, as have all donors since, but anyone else joining has had to pay the equivalent of US$13 a month. With HKCN's readers being older and having the wherewithal to pay, subscription was the logical way to go for regular income.

Other methods have much less promise. Li says they didn't want to follow up on crowdfunding because Factwire's second exercise produced a much lower amount than the first, indicating a loss of interest among supporters. They don't want to rely on donors either, preferring to build a business relationship by making them subscribers to the newsletter service. They have signed up for programmatic advertising with Google and Facebook, but without in-house expertise to do all the background work the income is "trivial", says Li. And they can't seek funding from overseas "because we know it's sensitive here in Hong Kong", she says. "Once we go that route, we will have a lot of attacks." Indeed, HKCN has been criticised by the mainland Chinese media as a "yellow" – pro-democracy – outlet, with Chris Yeung being named in particular, as well as the HKJA (Zhao, Li & Ling 18 August 2019).

Li points out that though they are doing good journalism, they do have a point of view, just not as outspoken as democracy supporters now-defunct *Apple Daily* and online outlet Stand News. "We have our own stance, but what we want to give the impression of to the public is that we are more focused on professional journalism. When we criticise something, we put evidence first." One of their models is Taiwan's WeReport, an NGO which gathered funding for stories to be done (though it has now closed). "This is part of our aim, if we can survive and have ample financial support … to allocate a certain portion to support journalists or civic journalists", says Li. "They [would] pitch the stories to us and then we allocate the money to help them to finish their stories."

HKCN has had a lot of help with the tech side of things. While they have paid a professional developer to set up the site and logo, regular tech support has come from an old Next colleague of Li's who left to set up his own company. They pay him a monthly retainer at "mates' rates" and his team look after the system and servers as well as security issues. Another friend who has his own data company acts as an external partner on a pro bono basis and helps to develop the content management system as well as support data news stories. He has also helped with search engine optimisation, SEO, which Li has come to rely on for referral since Facebook changed its algorithms to downgrade news sharing. He has produced a system to scan stories and pick out keywords and also link photos to search, saving a lot of manual effort. An effort by a programmer colleague to produce an app didn't work out and was dropped in 2019.

The small reporting team is run by managing editor Maisy Lo Man Sze, formerly of *Ming Pao* and *Next Magazine*, and consists of four reporters, several student interns and a photographer. Li says that this is far from enough because they have to cover daily news as well as work on investigative and in-depth stories. Interns tell her they are worked much harder at HKCN than their classmates in other news companies. But the team has produced some excellent followups to their first blockbuster on C.Y. Leung. One they are particularly proud of is an analysis of Hospital Authority data that peered behind the PR screen to show that the most densely populated district, which also had a high proportion of elderly people, had the lowest hospital funding allocation.

In late 2020, iCable sacked 40 journalists ostensibly due to the economic impact of the coronavirus epidemic. Many suspected the move was politically motivated, and Szeto Yuen and his ten-strong China reporting team resigned in sympathy. They had a loyal audience but had no particular plans. Li, a contemporary of Szeto's, suggested they should explore setting up their own outlet, as HKCN had done. "The more we discussed it, the more we felt there was a synergy between the two teams", Li says. A merger would save the former iCable group the trouble of setting up a company and bank accounts (getting the latter in Hong Kong has become more and more difficult), and for HKCN it would be a chance to cover China, which they didn't have the capacity to do on their own.

It was a bit of a gamble: combining teams would require a bigger office and a better studio to make video than their old makeshift facility. But they went ahead and announced the arrangement in January 2021, at the same time asking subscribers to sign up for a whole year (US$156) or more to help fund the expansion. With readers taking up the request, they hired a full-time COO to take on the task of overseeing and expanding subscriptions to develop an audience-driven revenue model. With money matters sorted, the main problem now is the shrinking space for freedom of expression in Hong Kong following the sudden imposition by Beijing in mid-2020 of the severe National Security Law.

Li is still surprised that it all worked out. "If you'd asked me when we started, how confident are you that you can do it, I would've said no, I don't know, we have to try", she says. "Now if you ask me how confident are you that you can do it? I say, 100 per cent confident."

HONG KONG

Hong Kong Free Press

The received knowledge is that crowdfunding is good to launch a media outlet with, but it's not sustainable. The belief is that even if people support you when you start out (and that's a big "if") they will see their donation as a one-off and you will need to use the initial funds to carry you over until you can find a more regular source of income. Tom Grundy's Hong Kong Free Press has certainly given the lie to that idea, with supporters not only standing by his outlet when it started in 2015 but actually giving more each year. Five years on they were still providing 86 per cent of income. But HKFP might be an exception that proves the rule: few others seem to have made it work.

FIGURE 7.12 Tom Grundy. Photo credit: Author.

What's its secret? One is that Hong Kong is a prosperous community where people are able to pay for media. Two is language: although most Hong Kongers speak Cantonese, a fair proportion don't have any Chinese at all – expats and returnees from overseas – and many locals have good English anyway, so there is a demand for media in that tongue. And three is timing: the two main local English-language papers – *South China Morning Post* and *Standard* – and terrestrial TV stations – TVB and ATV – have been taken over by mainland Chinese owners and have been losing their paying audiences and advertisers as discontent with Beijing's mishandling of Hong Kong grew.

It was the Umbrella Movement of 2014 that inspired Grundy, a teacher and freelance journalist from Britain who had started up a blog some years before. In 2015 he set out to raise some money to do something a bit bigger – his plan was to set up a Huffington Post-type of outlet with a team of writers. It was a chicken-and-egg situation, Grundy recalls: how do you build a product to raise money without raising money first? The answer in this case was by putting in a great deal of effort. While calling for support on local crowdfunding site Fringebacker, he set up a website with a countdown holding page which he and his team worked on for a month in a frenzy of gathering content. Their work wasn't even displayed at the time, so there was nothing to show donors what the new outlet would be like. Grundy himself took no salary at first and saved more money through the donation of a free office by a veteran journalist. He worked all hours, sometimes staying overnight in the disabled toilet to avoid the Arctic air-conditioning. It was "chaos", he remembers.

But the amount that rolled in went way over the initial target – he had asked for the equivalent of just under US$20,000, but ended up with more than US$77,000 – revealing the pent-up demand for a different approach to news. A number of new Chinese sites giving space to the pro-democracy movement had appeared, but nothing in English. Grundy had himself covered the protests on Twitter, and now stepped into the news vacuum with HKFP, with an emphasis on even-handed coverage. "There's no need to take a strong editorial stance on things, just report the facts", said Grundy, though he acknowledged that the site's readers tend to be pro-democracy.

Grundy had no business background but faced few problems in setting up because there was no competition. His plan was to go the normal route and seek out diverse income streams. He was able to attract some advertising, but it was tough and HKFP's budget couldn't stretch to a marketing person. So he put out a crowdfunding call for a second time in 2016. This time he was more ambitious – asking for the equivalent of a quarter of a million US dollars. However, the amount raised came to only a little more than the first round. This second fundraiser had perhaps come too quickly after the first and was extended, building up the total, after which rounds were done annually. According to the 2019 annual report, income from donations of all types went from US$136,000 in 2016 to US$227,000 in 2017 and US$316,000 in 2018. Then, when things seemed finally to be flagging, HKFP's strong coverage of the mounting protests of the second half of 2019 tripled traffic to the site and took donations to a new high of US$333,000. With a 2020 site relaunch on WordPress's Newspack platform, the outlet expanded and quadrupled its original reporting from 4 to 16 features a month and in January 2021 reported that monthly net income from regular supporters – "patrons" – alone stood at just under US$22,200.

Grundy parted ways with Fringebacker in 2016, working out his own fundraising mechanism to save the 5 per cent fee and not to have to follow its rules, and in 2019 HKFP won a US$78,400 award from the Google News Initiative to design a crowdfunding platform that could be used by any small media outlet (the product, NewsStream, is due to début in 2021). With things going well, in early 2020 HKFP took a month's break to refresh and emerged with a changed team, an upgraded website, and a new lease of life – and a whole new source of news in the coronavirus pandemic, where Hong Kong was one of the first to be hit, followed by the renewed protests and the mid-year clampdown by Beijing.

Grundy has been amazed at the generosity HKFP has been shown, calling it "a news outlet powered by kindness". Two authors donated book proceeds, people sent in winning lottery tickets, two couples donated their cash wedding gifts, and he got HK$500 (US$64) notes thrust at him at public events ("a nightmare for accounting"). Once a western lady approached him after an HKFP event at which local activist Joshua Wong spoke and gave Grundy an envelope. She said, he recalls, "Oh I've put the address on here and a stamp because I didn't know if I would see you – you can recycle the stamp, maybe, you … can put that on something else, sorry about that". She left and when he opened the envelope there was a cheque for the equivalent of more than US$19,000. In his 2018 TEDx talk, Grundy called this kind of donation "an alarming sort of reverse mugging". But he's very happy to be mugged in this way.

If HKFP has failed to diversify its income sources, the support it gets in the form of small donations both through crowdfunding and through direct payments from its "patrons" not only has been a near-miracle in entrepreneurial journalism terms but has given the outlet control over what it does. "It means we are not reliant on any one big donor", says Grundy. "If someone gets upset with us, it's fine if they cancel their donation or whatever. We have no shareholders, we're answerable to nobody and everybody – ultimately only answerable to ourselves." With media not permitted to register as nonprofits with the local tax authorities, HKFP has structured itself as company limited by guarantee with a HK$1 deposit and all surplus revenue ploughed back into the operation. In 2019, according to its annual report, it "went through a legal examination to be recognised as the equivalent of a US charity". In March 2020 it produced a well-thought-out and comprehensive code of ethics that would make a good template for any other media startup.

The increasingly enthusiastic support has given the outlet the means to pay staff decent salaries, provide them with health insurance and give them maternity/paternity leave. It has also meant that, since losing their free office, they can afford an airy space in a co-working area, rented at a discount, and have moved on from their kind volunteer tech supporter to a paid-for web team via NewsPack WordPress VIP and paid legal support ("if it were not for people giving us the legal help when we've got into … hairy situations, we wouldn't have dodged so many bullets").

Most importantly the reliable income has allowed HKFP to pursue high journalism standards. Early on there was an effort to grab readers' attention with clickbaity content or re-writes from the local Chinese press. "Now we are focusing more on quality features and getting scoops and exclusives and networking and getting ourselves out there", Grundy said. "Acting a bit more like a more quality, respectable newsroom rather than [relying on] stack-it-high, cheap sort of quantity over quality." One of HKFP's top scoops came in 2018 when it was the first to publish the news that *Financial Times* correspondent Victor Mallet, a Briton, had been denied a working visa just for being the person who introduced at a Foreign Correspondents Club luncheon a speaker who was an advocate of independence for Hong Kong. The story had repercussions for months, causing embarrassment to the unpopular Hong Kong chief executive, Carrie Lam Cheng Yuet Ngor. "I'm very proud we broke that story", said Grundy.

HKFP has also changed the way the territory's officials deal with online media. Local law had long required newspapers and broadcasters to register, which made them subject to many rules but at the same time gave them access to government press conferences and the chance to ask questions of officials. Online media were not required to register, but also could not register even if they wanted to, and so were not permitted to attend these events. Grundy mounted a campaign to get digital-only media on to the official list and was successful in doing so in 2017 – though the government office in charge of registration still insists on knowing who the "printer" is and requires a printout of the home page every Monday sent in by post.

HKFP seems to have found its stride and is not keen to change. Grundy is suspicious of technology fads such as chatbots and blockchain. Social media companies put on a lot of pressure to take up new tech tweaks favoured by their algorithms, but these require a lot of resources, he says. He even hates that new media darling, podcasting. "The number of people who've told me to do podcasts!" he exclaims. "Podcasts are already a niche within a niche in Hong Kong … and it's an even smaller number of people who consume news in English." Grundy sees the written word as far better for HKFP's kind of journalism. "[O]bviously the most important and searchable and indexable way of telling these stories is through text", he says. "You can search text. You can't search video … So it's part of our duty to write the first draft of history … in text." That's not to say that pics and videos don't appear on their site, most via mobile phones, though they hired a professional photographer during the 2019 protests.

HKFP is not completely alone in making a success of crowdfunding. After HKFP's debut, watchdog site Factwire, published mainly in Chinese by a group of respected investigative journalists, did even better, raising more than US$608,000 in just three months. Hong Kong Citizen News followed suit with a crowdfunding exercise in 2017, receiving US$346,000, though it abandoned the method when it found direct donations more promising (see above). It seems Hong Kong is the only place in the region, and possibly the world, where crowdfunding has become a long-term form of revenue, and perhaps because of its particular historical circumstances as pro-democratic views become overwhelmed by pro-Beijing forces.

HKFP's principles are stated on its site: "We seek to amplify the voices of the voiceless, not the powerful, and will monitor the status of Hong Kong's core values and freedoms. The HKFP team is fully committed to reporting the facts, without fear, favour or interference." Grundy points out that the site covers pro-government people and always puts the government's view into its stories, but acknowledges it doesn't have the resources to provide a comprehensive news package as bigger newsrooms do. In mid-2020, the new Beijing-imposed National Security Law seemed to spell trouble for those giving a voice to the pro-democracy movement. HKFP, however, was still carrying on as normal, though it put aside US$192,300 in a legal defence fund.

INDONESIA

IDN Media

In Indonesia, where most new media are run commercially, one group stands out for having achieved the entrepreneurial dream: successful launch, multiple investments from some of the biggest names in the region, and quick but careful expansion. IDN Media started in 2014 with just two people – Winston Utomo and William Utomo, brothers who had done their degrees in the US. They began the operation out of a bedroom when Winston was working for Google in Singapore. Today, with Winston CEO and William COO, IDN (which stands for "Indonesia")

FIGURE 7.13 Winston Utomo. Supplied by Winston Utomo.

has ten companies and multiple offices with 500 team members – and 60 million-plus unique visitors a month. Many of these users are valuable millennial and Gen Z audiences, with more and more of them coming from outside the capital Jakarta and beyond the main island Java. What's more, they are providing much of the content IDN'S platforms display.

One reason for IDN's success is that it has segmented its product for specific audiences, both in terms of the outlets themselves and of the content within each one. Its first company in 2014 was IDN Times, originally a news-in-brief site which quickly turned into a kind of BuzzFeed-style take on international and local news. It's still their flagship, but the Utomos have since set up new ventures aimed at specific markets: in 2016 came Popbela, focusing on young women, and recipe site Yummy; in 2018 Popmama for "millennial mamas"; and in 2019 they opened geek culture site Duniaku.com. That year they also acquired e-sports site GGWP.ID and in 2020 movie company IDN Pictures. (Not all their new products have worked out: IDN TV didn't take off and its parts were split between

IDN Times and Yummy.) The company has also formed other offshoots to help with production and business: the IDN Creative digital agency opened in 2015 and the IDN Creator Network for marketing in 2017.

The conversion of some of their massive audience into content providers has been an important factor in IDN's progress. "What makes us different is we are not purely a media company but a media platform company", says Winston Utomo. "So 40 to 50 percent of our content is being generated by our community and readers." This is not unusual among Indonesian media – indeed, many others are trying this – but Utomo says IDN Times has much more UGC than others and takes it to greater lengths. He says this makes the outlet "more like a mixture between Facebook and Toutiao" (the latter referring to the major Chinese aggregator). This approach solves the biggest problem for content, he goes on: relevancy. "If we create content via our in-house journalists, yes, the content can be good, but the question is, can the content be relevant? So how we try to address this problem is by having everyone write for themselves."

This is part of the reason IDN Times has started to pursue a hyperlocal strategy, producing individual sites for everyone in Indonesia, from Aceh to Papua. By mid-2020 there were eleven regional sites, five covering Java, three covering Sumatra and one each covering Bali, Sulawesi and Kalimantan. "The fact is this: 90 per cent of people do not live in Jakarta, but 90 percent of content is about Jakarta", says Utomo.

> People who live in Jakarta often take things for granted. They think that, "We are Indonesians". However, they are just a minority, right? I have been to many cities … and they are very different in the way they consume content and so on.

Locals not only know about what's going on in their area but are also most interested in it, providing the relevancy that is so important to the site. For example, the people who know best about the food culture in Palembang are the people who live there, Utomo says, referring to the south Sumatran capital. IDN Times plans to open sites for all 34 of Indonesia's provinces eventually.

A little financial incentivisation helps encourage the submission of good content. IDN offers small payments to UGC producers to share content with friends and update it frequently to get more views. "The more people read them, the more money they will have", says Utomo. Content providers usually have full-time jobs and do their IDN work for pin money. For some, though, it has become an important source of both income and recognition. Utomo tells of a person with a disability who had suffered bullying and now turned her life round, writing about 80 articles a month; seeing her work trending online gave a huge boost to her confidence. Another youngster who contributes a similar number of stories a month didn't have the chance to go to university but saved up her IDN earnings to open her own business, a photocopy shop. Utomo sees the US$100–200 people can earn each month from IDN as particularly important in the smaller cities and regions, where few media opportunities exist.

Word of the UGC process is only spread organically, that is, by social media and from person to person, and no money has been spent on advertising it. The fact is, they don't really want too much user material because of the difficulty in controlling quality. At the moment, the company has an algorithmic process to provide a template, check spelling and remove plagiarism, but a team of editors is still needed to check facts, edit content and eliminate bias. Utomo would like to minimise the manual role in the process: "the challenge is to improve our machine ... because we can automate much of this stuff". But it will still be curated by IDN's strong and experienced in-house editorial team. With better AI, a strong system and brilliant journalists, he says, the company can become a regional content creation powerhouse. He is firm that it must be "in a controlled environment ... where we know the facts, we verify the facts, we check the quality, there is no bias and so on". This is where IDN Times differs from Facebook and Toutiao, he says, because "we have some media responsibility". The Utomos plan to use the same strategy for their other outlets.

From 2018 until the last closing in 2020, the company has been profitable, which is a rare achievement for a technology firm. Nine-tenths of IDN's income comes from online advertising, another 5 per cent from non-digital ads (offline, events and so on) and the last smidgeon from platform revenue – the Utomos hope to expand the latter significantly in the future.

IDN Media has had four rounds of investment. The first was a seed round in 2015 from Willson Cuaca's Singapore-based East Ventures, and this was followed by Series A, B and C rounds up to 2019, with East Ventures participating in all exercises along with Indonesian conglomerate GDP Venture, US media specialist North Base Media, Thai corporation Charoen Pokphand's True Digital, Japan's LINE, and Hong Kong-based Central Exchange among others. IDN refuses to reveal the amounts involved, but Utomo does say that he and his brother still own a majority share in the company.

He thinks that what has inspired confidence in investors is the commitment the two of them have to IDN. It's their first venture and they are in it for the long haul, he says, and are not looking to cash out or become serial entrepreneurs. "What I believe is, someone who has everything to lose, that person or those people will have more chance to be more successful, right?" he says. "And for us, this is our only thing. We put everything that we have, our heart and our capital and everything, into this business. So that's what they maybe see in us, the founders."

Then they are extremely careful with their money. "Since day one, because we've had to face bankruptcy so many times, we know the feeling of not having money", Utomo goes on. So from Series B, they focused on revenue. "If we can make a profit, that gives us proof that we can actually turn this into a sustainable and healthy business", he says. "If we can make it a very healthy and sustainable business, with a good cash flow, then we can do so many things." In these circumstances, their investors have left them pretty much alone to make decisions, "which is a privilege for us".

Neither brother had any journalism experience before setting up IDN, but Winston had his stint with Google in Singapore for a couple of years and William, now COO, had experience in investment, so they brought other useful skills into play. They have also imbued the company with their strong commitment to diversity and equality. The website sets out these principles very clearly: "[W]e have 8 values that we believe in [at] IDN Media: gender equality, unity in different races and ethnicities, unity in different religions, unity in different worldviews, anti-sexual harassment, anti-bullying, anti-stereotyping, and redefining beauty".

These considerations take in recruitment too:

> [W]e don't hire people based on a certain label. We hire individuals. Because none of their background matters. Great attitude, strong work ethic, and passion matter. Not their race, religion, gender, background, sexual orientation, character, or worldview … We want IDN Media to become not only the biggest company in the region but also the best workplace.

The two brothers also appreciate their staff, now numbering 500 – they call them "Timmys," which comes from the Indonesian "tim" meaning "team":

> We are blessed to be surrounded by so many kind-hearted, brilliant, positive, and passionate Timmys … [T]hey all are exemplary individuals who possess a common goal, which is to make positive impacts in today's world. They are the reasons why IDN Media could become what it is today.

The way forward now is to build the sites they have set up to fulfil their plan to cover the whole of Indonesia. All the IDN outlets have their own apps already, but the eventual goal is to have a "super app" through which all can be accessed. The way to do that, says Utomo, "is to create the best media platform in the region with powerful technology, a strong team, and solid culture".

THAILAND

Isranews Agency

It is surprising enough to find an investigative journalism outfit thriving in Thailand in these difficult times for the media, but the Isranews Agency is an unusual setup in almost every sense. Formed under the umbrella of the country's top journalism bodies and named after a celebrated Thai journalist who spent years in jail, it started out with funding from a democracy-linked government health fund but, having lost that, struck out to find new big-business backers who agree not to interfere in its work. This being a temporary measure, the search for a new business model is on.

FIGURE 7.14 Prasong Lertrattanawisute. Photo credit: Author.

Isranews's story goes back to 2008, when the Thai Journalists Association (TJA) and the Press Council of Thailand (formed in 1997 to monitor and regulate the media) each put in Baht 100,000 (about US$3,200) to create a journalism training body called the Thai Press Development Foundation. At the same time, under the TPDF they formed the Isra Institute, whose remit was mainly to cover national reform issues, including public policy, which had come into the spotlight after the 2006 ousting by the military of elected prime minister Thaksin Shinawatra.

The Institute was successor to another reporting effort founded three years earlier, also by the TJA and the Press Council, called the Issara News Center, a pilot project designed to focus on peace journalism in reporting the flaring conflict in the country's Muslim south. This programme had been funded through the TJA by the Thai Health Promotion Foundation. ThaiHealth, as it is known, was set up in 2001 by an act of Parliament to combat smoking, drinking and obesity and financed through a direct levy on tobacco and alcohol based on excise taxes. ThaiHealth also funded the TPDF and the Institute as part of its remit.

In 2011 veteran journalist Prasong Lertrattanawisute was appointed head of the Isra Institute. A former head of the TJA, he had been editor of the mainstream daily paper *Matichon* and also of the main business daily, *Prachachat Business*. In these roles he had become famous for his investigative stories, among them one that revealed a deputy prime minister's false declaration of assets (the deputy PM subsequently lost his job) and another even bigger story that exposed then-PM Thaksin's hiding of his wealth by transferring assets to his family and employees to make it seem as if he complied with the terms of his office (Thaksin was later indicted on corruption charges) (Bloomberg Business Week 2 July 2001). When Prasong took over, the Institute was doing more training than reporting, and he revived the latter role to cover the south and public policy.

At the same time, he created the Isranews Agency with the express purpose of taking on investigative and in-depth coverage to publish on its own website and social media. Working out of the TJA's headquarters in a spacious low-rise building on crown land in the Bangkok district of Samsen, it's named after famed pioneer investigative reporter Isra (also spelt Issara) Amantakul (1921–1969), the TJA's first president, who was charged with being a communist in 1958 and spent nearly six years in jail.

The unit, still under the ThaiHealth-funded Institute, produced some notable revelations about corruption in high places. A story about massive tax avoidance by high-level officials got those officials sacked. Another story revealed that members of Parliament were hiring their own families as consultants. Thus the Isranews Agency became the go-to outlet for whistleblowers when they wanted their stories told. One of these stories seems to have got Isranews into trouble: it revealed that the elderly father of Prime Minister Prayuth Chan-ocha had sold land to one of Thailand's richest tycoons – it was already known that the high-priced sale had taken place, but not to whom. That exposé seems to have been the trigger behind an investigation into ThaiHealth, particularly its funding of the TPDF.

ThaiHealth was set up by an act of Parliament in 2001 to encourage healthy lifestyles. Its funding came from a 2-per-cent surcharge on alcohol and tobacco taxes, giving it a huge revenue – its income rose from US$58 million in 2003 to US$132 million in 2017. Its remit was to support diverse partners to address growing lifestyle health issues (Ponguttta et al. 2019). That was interpreted as including journalism training, and the *Bangkok Post* reported at the time of the 2015 misspending charge that the TPDF had received some Baht 96 million (about US$3 million) over the previous eight years (Jikkham & Thip-Osod 21 October 2015). Now the rules were changed to ensure that funding was only given for relevant projects and nothing else.

Ever-resourceful, Prasong moved quickly and brought on board some rather unexpected supporters in the form of Thailand's biggest business concerns, including Charoen Phokphand and Siam Commercial Bank. The operation had to downsize – they now have seven reporters instead of the 20 they had before – but today it is stable and puts out a regular stream of good stories. At Prasong's initiative, the Institute receives funds from, besides CP and SCB, Siam Cement Group, Kasikorn Bank, Ch. Karnchang Construction, Bangchak Petroleum, Thai Oil and Chevron, as well as the Thai Energy Foundation. Income from these sources totals Baht 8.9 million (about US$287,500) a year, partly in payment for banner advertising and partly in donations. The Isranews Agency gets just under half of that total.

Doesn't this commercial backing compromise the agency's investigations? "No", Prasong says, firmly. "There is no condition that we can't report anything," he explains. "And no one dares to ask us not to report because they know what Isra is like". But they are still careful in how they go about their investigative work. The key to steering clear of deep trouble is how they present the story, Prasong goes on. "We don't make it with colourful headlines, but show the facts. We make it soft but intense with accurate information."

They still face legal challenges. In 2017 one of their reporters was charged with trespass for entering the apartment of a figure close to the national police chief while doing a story on the latter's property. The TJA complained of non-compliance in the conduct of the investigation, and Isra launched a campaign through their website to help fight the case, raising Baht 200,000 (nearly US$6,500). The charge was eventually dropped. Two cases involving the news agency remain outstanding, one a defamation suit brought against Prasong by an employee at the Thai oil and gas company who was revealed in a story to be corrupt, and the other brought by police claiming Isra staff had given false evidence after witnessing a clash between high-ranking police officials. Prasong takes it all in his stride. "It's normal for media that you get charged with defamation", he says.

But while Prasong would like to produce Watergate-type stories all the time, the reality is that with only seven journalists each is expected to do two to three stories a day, and big investigations are difficult to carry out. So their aim is to seek out stories behind the news. "We try to get a different angle from the mainstream media, and report a series", he says. Typical of this is their coverage of the tragic death in 2018 of Thai businessman Vichai Srivaddhanaprabha, owner of English football club Leicester City, when his helicopter crashed leaving the football ground. While the local press just translated stories from international news, Isra reporters found a quite different story: the late tycoon's collection of Buddha images that had cost him Baht 3–4 billion (US$100–130 million).

Even though the audience is not massive – Isra has about 200,000 likes on Facebook and its stories tend to get around 20,000 views – Prasong knows that those who follow the site are real enthusiasts. Their generosity in the trespass case proved that. He wishes that enthusiasm would blossom into continuing support. He is not really happy with the current business model – they have some advertising income from the banner ads of their corporate supporters and about Baht 7,000 (about US$225) a month from Google AdSense, but this is not enough to survive without the donations.

Prasong would like to do more fundraising and most of all put up a paywall. "In the long term we would like to rely on readers," he says. Malaysiakini's Prem Chandran and Steven Gan are his heroes (see below). But the time is not ripe for subscriptions: "Thai people think the news is free, and they don't like to pay". He sighs as he points out that this as illogical given the huge donations to temples and hospitals. If he could get more money, Prasong says, he would get in some in-house tech support to make the website more sophisticated – at present that work is done outside. But for now, Isra is lucky enough to have a good income to survive on.

CAMBODIA

Khmerload

What upsets In Vichet is that Facebook and Google hog the profits from the ads they place alongside other people's content, taking as much as 80 percent of the digital advertising market. "They get the lion's share", says the CEO of the Cambodian entertainment news site Khmerload. "We're fighting for the remains of the pie." This "distributed content" setup may have been what took early media startups like the celebrated millennial-attracting BuzzFeed into the big time, but the business model,

FIGURE 7.15 In Vichet. Photo credit: Author.

Vichet says, is "not quite hot any more". He has been doing his due diligence and has come up with a better one, and he is preparing to make it happen. His plan is to build a "super-content" app which will generate more value for his company.

When you visit a regular website, Vichet says, you don't leave much information on the site itself but you do leave many details with the search engine or social media that got you there. Those platforms collect your data and use it to send you ads you'll be interested in. This is efficient and lucrative for both the advertisers and the platforms, but not for the media outlet. Khmerload uses Facebook Instant Articles, which distributes and monetises content, but the advantages are on the platform's side. The content provider receives only generalised information about users, has little control over advertising and gets just a small cut of ad revenue. Facebook, Google and Amazon have all grown rich through their control of user data.

Meanwhile, Vichet goes on, apps collect users' data themselves, allowing the app owner to target ads and cutting search and social from the process. Vichet cites the Chinese outlet ByteDance, whose Jinri Toutiao news app and Douyin/TikTok short video app have made it perhaps the most valuable media-tech company in the world. "Each user registers with some information, so it means that they have all the data of those users, so they can do advertising targeting, right? Based on the interest, based on the age or sex or things like that", says Vichet. He points also to the Japanese news app SmartNews, founded in 2012 and valued recently at more than US$1 billion. The lesson Vichet has derived from this due diligence is to move away from distributed content, stay ad-focused and get hold of more first-party user info. Development of the app is under way, with the technical side well advanced already. However, the next stage is going to be more difficult. "The best way is to push … more mobile readers to use our own app, and that requires a lot of effort, especially a lot of capital." That's where his next big ideas come in.

There are two main thrusts to his plan.

The first key to getting people to take up the app is content, says Vichet, and his approach is to hire a huge stable of writers. He refers to Grab, the Southeast Asian ride company. "They have tens of thousands of tuktuk drivers in Cambodia [who] are … basically their staff," he says. "They are making money for Grab." In the same way, he goes on, people who sell through Amazon and Alibaba's Taobao are making money for those companies, while Facebook's 2-billion-plus users do the same. "That's the beauty of the platform," he goes on. "You make everyone work for you!"

Vichet knows that his current editorial staff – 25 in Cambodia and 20 more in Myanmar (they run a similar site there called Myanmarload) – won't be able to provide enough content. He also knows that poorly paid contributors won't do a good job. So he is going to attract "thousands" of new writers by paying them well. Which poses a chicken-and-egg situation: "In order to make good money for writers the platform has to be big, but in order for the platform to be big, to get a lot of traffic from users, you need to have a lot of writers," he says. "So it will be like this … We will pay content producers first, we will pay a lot of money to get them to write stuff like that."

The second key to success is a content recommendation algorithm. This, Vichet says, is how Facebook makes itself so addictive. He laughs as he thinks of how journalists tend to consider only the media element in attracting eyeballs when tech and biz people have plenty of other ways to keep users coming back. "They do a lot of experiments to make the platform better, incrementally better day by day," he says. "That's why they can get people to come back and use their app, and become addicted to the app." Khmerload is already making recommendations to readers, but the information they have on them is as yet not very detailed. The app, he hopes, will change that. "So people who want to advertise, say, travel, they don't need to advertise to all the people using our app, they just target those who like reading about travelling, things like that."

Khmerload, founded in 2011, has done very well for itself already. Like most Cambodian online media, it gets its main income from banner advertising, but, with its audience of enthusiastic millennials (it has nearly 20 million followers on Facebook and boasts nearly 9 million monthly users and 54 million monthly pageviews), it has no shortage of advertisers. Investors are also enthusiastic. In 2017, the parent company, Mediaload, received US$200,000 from Silicon Valley-based 500 Startups, the first time a Cambodian company had received funding from a US-affiliated venture capital outfit.

In 2019 came a bigger investment, this time US$5 million, from locally (Phnom Penh) based, Belt Road Capital Management, but this was for the umbrella company, Groupin, and mainly for its e-commerce operation. Groupin, owned by Vichet and two of his brothers and his sister, contains Mediaload (Khmerload and Myanmarload) and Little Fashion, an online retail portal started in 2010 that is run by his sister and shares its premises with the digital outlet. With the app development in mind, Mediaload set out to find "a good strategic investment" of "a couple of million" and in October 2020 it came through: an undisclosed Series A sum from the Thai telecoms corporation True, part of the Charoen Phokphand empire (Sainul 2 October 2020).

Khmerload – short for "Khmer Download" – goes back to Vichet's days posting his own content via social media, especially on Reddit in the US, where he had studied. He became interested in monetising his output. He rang up the then-top Cambodian digital news outlet, DAP News (see pp. 128–131), and, posing as a potential customer, asked for their ad rates. Hearing that they were selling spots for as much as US$1,500, he says, "I thought, OK, there's an opportunity!" DAP was publishing political news, but Vichet decided he would go for entertainment and lifestyle, and that he would be the first in Cambodia to distribute via Facebook.

He started out in a frugal manner, roping in his brothers to help him create and upload content, often sensational stuff, with the goal of becoming the most visited website. They did well, but soon realised that a high hit rate alone was not enough to attract advertisers. This is where they learned a lesson. "We had to put ourselves in line with the standards of journalism so that people see us as serious media so that we can get more advertising revenue", he says. They hired an editor to work on their output – at first just by proofreading but later to take full charge of content – and this improved their brand. "We learned over time, we learned", says Vichet, though he acknowledges that, given they don't do investigative or political journalism, "we don't need to be very strict with the rules".

Nonetheless, Vichet still had to work hard to get advertisers' attention. "I tried to sell the banner advertising by myself. I went to many friends, many shops, and at that time, you know, they weren't quite familiar with digital advertising", he says. "So it was actually hard to sell to them." However, once the concept became familiar and the site became well known, people started to get on board, even if he did have difficulty changing the mindset of advertisers from insisting on fixed banners paid for by time to accepting packages based on number of impressions ("I cannot see my ad!" they would complain, and he told them, "Refresh!"). This effort was assisted by constant tweaking of the website to make it more attractive to users, something many other media in Cambodia don't even try to do. Today Khmerload is one of the top go-to sites for advertisers and they are so sought after that they don't even have a team working on ad sales, though investors are pushing them to set one up.

Vichet started out with a degree in management from Cambodia's National Institute for Management and another in foreign languages from the Institute of Foreign Languages at the Royal University of Phnom Penh (RUPP), where he taught for a while. Then he won a scholarship to take a master's in economics in the US; later he started, but didn't finish, a PhD in the same subject at the University of Michigan, returning to Cambodia to set up Khmerload instead. That academic background was good preparation for the media startup business, but the firm's success is also due to the two talented and well-qualified brothers who have joined him in the firm.

Vichet puts the real inspiration for the company down to older brother In Mean, an internet pioneer who ran the first internet café in Cambodia in 1997 when digital was very new. Mean had his own website way back in 1999 and also ran a chat server, but it was too early to make money in Cambodia from the internet business. Another brother, In Vichea, won a Fulbright Scholarship to pursue a PhD in curriculum design in the US. He is now COO and is "an attention-to-detail guy", according to Vichet, and keeps things in line. Their younger brother, In Visal, has a degree in IT from RUPP, and went on to study coding and is now a leading member of the IT community as well as company CTO. Thus Khmerload has, in one family, most of the skills and experience needed to start up a media outlet.

Except for actual media skills. Indeed, one of the main criticisms levelled at them is that they still don't do "real journalism". There is something to that charge, as the lack of strictness on standards suggests. For a start, they don't hire journalists to work on content. Paid professionals are too expensive and expect to put out only about ten articles a month, says Vichet, when at Khmerload they need to be finishing two or three a day. So who do they hire instead? Novelists, writers, scriptwriters, he says, "because they can write much better, more attractively". For another thing, Vichet admits that they translate content from other sites, particularly overseas ones, without permission or payment, but says this is normal in Cambodia, and they at least credit the sources and provide a link to the original. Vichet defends what Khmerload is doing. "People dismissed us, like, your content is not serious, it's not serious journalism", he says. "But for me, I said, okay, entertainment is … part of life, you know, [journalism is] not just to inform people, educate people, but people need to be entertained as well, so I believe in that."

The company has always had ambitions to expand internationally. Khmerload is registered in Singapore partly because the plan was to spread around the rest of Southeast Asia, though initially that hasn't proved very fruitful. Although Myanmarload, launched in 2016 and now a registered media outlet in Yangon with its own office there, continues to operate well, efforts to set up elsewhere since have been thwarted. In Vietnam the brand attracted a million followers, but the competition was fierce and, with money already spent on setting up in Yangon, they decided it was too costly to keep going.

A test run in Indonesia brought them 350,000 followers, but again the market was highly competitive, and in this case they realised they weren't prepared for the sensitivity of topics, particularly religion, which got them inundated with comments questioning their content. They felt this meant that they would need a full local setup there too, which they weren't prepared to go for. Under consideration for the future are Bangladesh and Nepal.

The new investment will help get the expansion plan back on track. Vichet rues the fact that, while Singaporean companies are considered to be international and can easily raise millions in investment, anyone from one of the poorer countries of the region is deemed only suited to working in that country alone. "I'm on a mission to prove that Cambodian entrepreneurs can scale overseas, we can do well in the region as well", he says.

INDONESIA

Lokadata

Didi Nugrahadi is one of the legends of Indonesian entrepreneurial journalism, but he isn't a journalist. Well known as one of the founders of the Detik.com news site in 1998 – the original respected Detik newspaper had been shut down by the Suharto government in 1994 – he is an accountant by profession. After leaving Detik in 2005, he helped found a digital agency, a social media consultancy, a primary school and a social media analytics site. Then in 2013 he moved back into the media by setting up Beritagar.com, a news aggregator that used advanced machine learning technology. With the Indonesian digital market becoming very competitive, just two years later Beritagar.com was swept up into the takeover wave. It was bought up by one of the big players in the Indonesian startup sector, GDP Venture, the internet investment arm of the massive Djarum Group.

FIGURE 7.16 Didi Nugrahadi. Supplied by Didi Nugrahadi.

What happened after that didn't quite turn out as expected.

When Beritagar.com started out, says Didi, the idea was to avoid relying on advertising and to build a business model based on data. It was the first media site in Indonesia to use AI and Natural Language Processing (NLP) to mine and process material from many of the country's small media and to target audiences with personalised content. The brain behind the system was computer scientist Jim Geovedi, known as the man who developed NLP for Bahasa Indonesia; an old friend of Didi's, he became the company's research director. Beritagar.com journalists would also use the information gathered by machine learning to write articles and give context to investigative stories. Meanwhile the data itself was being built up into a massive resource to provide services to paying clients. "We were not the first in data-driven journalism", Didi acknowledges, but the outlet was definitely the front runner in archiving data: "We were focused on the development of a data library, a data warehouse".

By 2015 Didi was beginning to realise that Beritagar.com needed a lot more investment to cover the costs of storing all the data and paying the staff to process it. He happened to meet "the GDP guy" at an event, and the latter was impressed with the outlet's setup. Things happened quickly from there. Financial details of the GDP takeover deal have not been made public, but Beritagar.com was bought out – and then immediately merged with another aggregator recently bought by GDP, Lintas.me, with most Lintas staff joining those from Beritagar.com. The new company was named Beritagar.id – just a slight difference from the old name, giving it a more Indonesian feel – and it was held under GDP subsidiary Lintas Cipta Media, or LCM, with GDP shareholder Herman Kwok as CEO and Didi as COO. Geovedi left before the takeover, though he did train Beritagar.com's developers first.

GDP Venture's umbrella includes some big names in the Indonesian internet world – among them e-commerce site BliBli and B2B outfit MCM Group – but it also owns some other well-known media. One is Kurio, a smart news app that grew out of Lintas.me. Another is Kaskus, the top online community forum, and a third is Daily Social, a tech blog. GDP has also invested in many other companies including IDN Media (see above) and Kumparan, a social media outlet started by other former Detik people. All the GDP components were located in different offices and did not meet up except at management meetings, according to Didi, though Beritagar.id was developing AI for the other outlets to use.

The most important part of the Beritagar deal, says Didi, was that GDP would leave the outlet to its own devices. The new bosses were true to their word. "They never, never push us to write some certain articles for the[ir] sake", he said in 2019. "Independence is the most important thing for Beritagar.id as a media company." The big bonus was the availability of new resources. "We hired some people, we bought technology, we bought products to do some AI developments", Didi said. New storage capacity was added as the data-mining operation was built up to take in more than 300 Indonesian media listed with the official Dewan Pers (Press Council).

Beritagar.id's bots were soon crawling some 15,000 articles a day. (Although there were no agreements with the outlets being searched, there were always back links to the original articles, Didi says.) The resulting data was cleaned, classified, clustered and summarised for the outlet's journalists to produce stories from. They were only publishing about 15 stories a day – very few compared with the hundreds posted by most of Indonesia's news sites – but they continued the old outlet's well-researched data-driven journalism, some of it investigative. These stories were very carefully designed to appeal to the site's mature audience of mostly 25–45-year-olds.

The same year as the GDP takeover, a new company was formed under Beritagar.id to deal with the company's data operations. Called Lokadata.id, it added to the daily media trawl paid-for data from reliable public sources, expanding the archive and increasing data services to provide business intelligence for clients. Nonetheless, Beritagar.id was finding it difficult to fund its rather costly AI system and journalism on income from data alone and started running sponsored content to bring in more cash. By 2019 this paid content, produced by a marketing team separately from editorial and clearly labelled, was contributing 40 per cent of the outlet's revenue, though Didi was hoping to reduce that share as data income built up.

However, another big change was ahead. In October 2019 there were press reports that 17 Beritagar.id editorial staff had been dismissed and rumours that the outlet would close (Agung 27 December 2019). Then came the official announcement from CEO Herman Kwok: in December Beritagar.id would be folded in to Lokadata.id, the merged outlet doing both data journalism and business analysis (Wahyudi 21 October 2019). When the time came, the company announced that the merger was a "rebranding" of the two under the Lokadata.id name. "The main purpose of the rebranding of Beritagar.id to Lokadata.id was just to focus on our product", says Didi. This involved an emphasis on data-driven business and economic articles, strengthening Lokadata.id's credentials as a business site, though it also continued other kinds of coverage.

Lokadata.id has 80 staff, 14 of them journalists who are producing regular, business and data journalism on its free-to-view site, which attracts a heathy 18 million UVM. The bots are crawling more sources than ever to expand the data warehouse, bringing in 70 per cent of the company's income in 2020 from selling services such as baseline data, market insights, stakeholder mapping, policy analysis, content analysis and sustainability reports, all illustrated with graphics and visuals. In 2020 the coronavirus epidemic caused Lokadata.id to struggle but it still reached break-even point. Sponsored content still supplied the other 30 per cent of revenue, and Didi was hoping to see that drop to 20 per cent in 2021, which would put him within sight of achieving his initial goal of relying totally on data for revenue. But he plans eventually to diversify income sources by monetising the main site, plans as yet undecided.

Thinking about advice to give budding entrepreneurs, Didi counselled not starting out with the idea that all will be well – "Don't ever think [you're going to be] successful!" You should focus on the business model, he says, "because without a revenue model, nothing". But that's a hard thing to do.

INDONESIA

Magdalene

When three highly experienced Indonesian women journalists decided they had had enough of working for other people and wanted to set up their own outlet at the end of the first decade of the 21st century, their inspiration came from the likes of Huffington Post, Slate and Daily Beast, all new and successful American digital startups. They didn't have much idea about what to cover, but the advice they got was that, having little financial backing, they'd do best to focus on a niche market. Looking round for audiences that weren't being served well by other media, they realised that one huge population wasn't getting good value: women.

FIGURE 7.17 Hera Diani. Supplied by Hera Diani.

It wasn't that there were no outlets for Indonesian women – indeed, there were many, such as Female, Femina and many more. But many were very commercial. "We found the mainstream media on women's issues were not very fulfilling – you know, too lightweight, focusing too much on fashion or lifestyle or sex", says Hera Diani, one of the three. "They did not cover the rich and diverse experience and representation of women." Those that did were

FIGURE 7.18 Devi Asmarani. Supplied by Hera Diani.

at the other extreme – serious journals, "very academic and heavy". Not that they disapproved of either type, but what they could see was a "middle ground" that wasn't being addressed, a place where women's issues that weren't being brought up in the mainstream media could be discussed in the kind of language regular readers could understand.

In 2013 they launched Magdalene to fill the gap. It took its name from the biblical figure Mary Magdalene, the friend of Jesus whose controversial image has made her a feminist icon. They described it as "a slanted guide to women and issues". Diani took on the job of managing editor and another founder, Devi Asmarani, became editor-in-chief, though in practice took over the business side; the third founder dropped out. At first they published only in English, the language they had used most in their two decades of journalism at local and international news outlets, but, with elections coming up in 2014 their readers liked the political stories they were publishing and pressed them to go bilingual to reach more people. Today 90 per cent of Magdalene's content is in Bahasa Indonesia, though it still has an English page for local non-Indonesians and overseas readers.

The site repudiates the commercial media's promotion of the kind of body image where "women have to be thin and [have] fair skin and straight hair", as Diani puts it – one of its 2020 articles defines "body goals" as "when you don't feel dizzy with your big arms [and] your stomach folds when you sit or pose to make you look 'thin'". It also covers a wide range of intellectual matters like spirituality and sisterhood as well as lighter fare such as TV and film reviews, profiles of "wo/men we love" and health advice. But Magdalene's overall aim, says Diani, is "to be a progressive media [site] to present progressive ideas … or to create a more progressive society".

Thus, she goes on, "we present issues with gender perspective and give a platform to marginalised people to voice their concerns". That sometimes takes it into the realm of "things considered taboo by conservative Indonesians, like LGBT issues, and then religion, or lack thereof" – in fact, they have found that the most-read topics are sexuality and religion. The site's "about us" page sums it up: "Magdalene is the manifestation of our vision of online media that offers fresh perspectives that transcend gender and cultural boundaries. We host the voices of feminist, pluralist, and progressive groups, or anyone who is not afraid to be different."

There was definitely a demand for this kind of content. Diani says a story about the persecution of women who stopped wearing the hijab, the headcovering required by Islam, proved to be one of their most popular. "So there are a lot of discussions people can relate to", she goes on. However, the sensitive nature of the content has attracted criticism from diverse directions. "Of course, there are people who disagree … and condemn us, saying this is like a kafir media, it's blasphemous," she says. "We have also been attacked by the leftists, like left feminists, radical feminists. They call us liberal feminists, and say that we are Islam apologists, that we side too much with religious people."

The reprisals have been nasty. In May 2020 Magdalene faced DDoS (Distributed Denial of Service) attacks that caused the website to malfunction for several hours every day for about two weeks. Its journalists and contributors have also faced doxxing and morphing, that is, having their identities and personal data revealed in public and their pictures tampered with, Diani says. One reporter's face was morphed into a naked body and distributed on porn sites. The staff have been called "sluts" on Twitter, and been told to "shut up and shut down the website".

Unsurprisingly, it's been difficult to find a business model. "I mean, in the US you have feminism in magazines or media, in Europe as well, but here it's totally new and we're not seen as commercial", says Diani. Making things more difficult was the fact that the founders were business neophytes. "[It was] very difficult because we have a journalism mindset, and it's very new, running a business", she goes on. "It's still very much a learning process for us." Besides, they didn't want to go the obvious route for a media outlet founded on principles, that is, to seek grant funding. "[W]e want it to become a profitable media company, not a foundation … or depending too much on grants and so on." They'd like to have funding from VCs or big media but it hasn't happened yet. "Maybe because we're too niche, or the focus on gender perspectives and feminism makes it difficult to attract bigger traction in terms of audience and advertisers", says Diani.

Although they didn't plan it that way, Working Room, a unit they originally set up to provide training sessions and courses such as writing workshops for media and NGOs, became their main income driver. It has developed into an agency. Run by a separate team from the magazine, it has a pool of writers, translators and designers who can be pulled in to work on contract projects for other companies. So successful has it been that the editors are thinking of hiving it off as an independent entity in the long term.

They have not neglected other sources of income. One is advertising. They do native, programmatic, banner and affiliate (except for cigarettes and skin whiteners, which are banned). Another is events, mainly serious gatherings such as seminars and discussions, but these led to something new: a standup comedy night, which came about through trying to address religion in a humorous way. It was their first live podcast and it was a success: they expected 150 guests and 200 showed up. Another initiative they started was the Magdalene Shop, planned to sell "cool merchandise" both via the site and at events, but it hasn't reached its full potential.

In 2018 business received a boost from the US-based Media Development Investment Fund (MDIF) (see p. 44). An initial grant – MDIF didn't think Magdalene was ready for investment – was given to kick-start the outlet. It paid for the setting up of their office and allowed the two founders to put in full-time hours instead of part-time, as they had been doing up to that point. It also helped hire a business manager to improve their income flows and a community engagement manager to keep in touch with readers and organise events. MDIF also gave technical advice to improve the website, provided training workshops and sent Magdalene staff to seminars with other media companies in the region. Diani sees this "angel" help as crucial to the growth of the outlet.

In early 2021, however, Magdalene was struggling. The coronavirus epidemic had hit business hard, with live events becoming impossible, though they moved into the virtual world with webinars like everybody else. The situation worsened with the ending of MDIF's grant in December 2020. The outlet received a new grant from the Australian Department of Foreign Affairs & Trade, but it was only for six months. What they have done is focus on Working Room contracts, but that has taken a lot of staff time, leaving the shop with no one to run it.

The full-time team has remained small. Diani and Asmarani edit content, and they have two reporters as well as a digital media specialist and a sales person. They also have part-timers working on finance (one the originally MDIF-funded business manager), IT, design, graphic design and illustration, as well as two columnists and one reporter on piecework. There are also a dozen freelancers who don't get paid but are happy for their copy to appear in Magdalene because it's the only outlet that can accommodate their writing. The site actually invites anyone to contribute and provides guidelines for doing so. Magdalene also produces videos and does podcasts in collaboration with KBR Radio, which provides studio space. About 40,000 people listen, mostly via Spotify. This doesn't bring in an income, but they create special podcasts for sponsors, including international NGOS and government institutions.

The team have been getting content distributed through the usual means – search and social media – but organically rather than paid for. Twitter, more popular in Indonesia than elsewhere in the region, has proved the most successful of these platforms. They have also organically developed an influencer group of about ten people, all with hundreds of thousands of followers, and have caught the eye of celebrities, one of whom is Mona Eltahawy, the Egyptian feminist and writer. Diani doesn't know how these prominent people found Magdalene, but they have in turn brought more readers to the site.

The outlet counts 500,000 page views a month – not a great figure for populous Indonesia, but high for a specialist publication. Readers are mostly in the 18–34 age bracket, though the editors were surprised to learn they had some fans as young as 13. Also unexpected was the finding that men have consistently taken a 20–30-per-cent audience share. This may include some LGBTQ followers, Diani says, but there are many straight men as well.

Their topic area has, since they started, become more and more covered in commercial media. One of the major digital outlets actually copied one of their articles, she says, and two big players, Tirto.id (see pp. 202–205) and Kumparan, are now featuring feminist content. The US outlet VICE, which has an office in Indonesia, published a video on sexual assault in universities that it made in collaboration with Tirto.id and *The Jakarta Post*. But the other outlets are mainly interested in big issues like sexual harassment or sexual violence, Diani says, and they lack sensitivity when dealing with minority groups. "I spoke with the transgender community for example, and they said that they no longer want to be interviewed by media other than Magdalene because [those media] don't know how to handle the reporting appropriately", she says. "They still use the names that they used before they became transgender. It's small things like that. And then they're still not very careful and sometimes out them."

Indeed, the Magdalene team sees the mainstream as partly to blame for misperceptions. One of its hits with followers was an Instagram campaign called #WTF Media that publicised sexism and misogyny in the media. "It's still very patriarchal in the media", says Diani. "They still objectify and sexualise women and they're still very much homophobic." Magdalene is still very much ahead of the game, perhaps even ahead of its time.

MALAYSIA

Malaysiakini

No study of entrepreneurial journalism in our region would be complete without looking at Malaysiakini. As one of the longest surviving online startups, and a profitable one as well, it certainly seems to have cracked the business model conundrum and proved that digital media can be sustainable. Launched in 1999 by two former journalists, Steven Gan and Premesh Chandran, it has never involved big-time finances, but it has done more than establish itself as an alternative read: it is now by far the most popular online news outlet in Malaysia according to Reuters's digital news report (Newman 2020). Its huge public support was demonstrated in early 2021 when the outlet was fined the equivalent of nearly US$124,000 for reader comments deemed to be in contempt of court; a call for donations brought in more than that sum in just five hours.

FIGURE 7.19   Steven Gan. Supplied by Steven Gan.

It's true that the overall situation in Malaysia has been a help to the development of media. The country's long-term conservative coalition government, set in place at the first general election in 1959, was still part of a vibrant political scene, and finally in 2018 an opposition group of parties was voted into power, though that government was overturned in less than two years. Also Malaysia has a strong news culture, and the long-time domination by the ruling coalition's media produced a demand for independent voices. As for business, Malaysia's economy is a free-market one and its people are relatively wealthy and educated. And good

FIGURE 7.20   Premesh Chandran. Supplied by Premesh Chandran.

timing was a factor: when Malaysiakini launched, the internet was just starting and the government was not only allowing digital media to set up freely without the registration required of traditional media but promising no censorship.

Still, many other online outlets appeared at the same time and didn't survive, and indeed there was no easy path for Malaysiakini. It faced not only financial difficulties but political and legal ones, from a police raid on its offices in 2004 to a number of troublesome court cases – editor-in-chief Gan, though himself cleared in the contempt case, still faced an investigation into sedition charges over comments he made after the outlet's conviction. Much of what Malaysiakini has achieved has not been a given but can be put down to the way its two founders set it up and ran it. With more than 20 years to look back on, Gan and Chandran can see clearly the strategies that have got the outlet where it is today.

One is that they separated the editorial and business sides in the traditional way. Perhaps this wasn't surprising given their newspaper backgrounds, but they point out that journalists who start up digital media tend to double up as editor-in-chief and CEO. "From the get-go we decided that one should look after editorial and the other one should look after business", says Gan. Chandran fitted the latter job, Gan goes on, because "despite the fact that he's a journalist, he is great with numbers". The two keep their jobs very distinct. "I don't get involved in editorial activities", says Chandran. "I think having a 100-per-cent focus on business is important." Gan remembers times when he wanted to take on extra staff and Chandran refused on the grounds that there wasn't enough money. "And that's great!" Gan says. "Because I think you need someone to say, … you need to look at the numbers. If you cannot afford it, you cannot afford it, and … it is important to have someone to tell you that."

Which leads to the second point: Malaysiakini's careful approach to spending. Gan says the operation is "prudent and frugal", Chandran calls it "tight and economical". One area for parsimony is salaries at the upper levels. Gan goes on:

> We do pay market rates for our lower ranking staff, but for the senior staff, because they've been in journalism for a while, they know exactly what Malaysiakini is … all about, and a lot of them want to join Malaysiakini because they want to contribute to make Malaysia a better society. So it's a mission.

Today the outfit lists more than 100 people working for the news site and company subsidiaries KiniTV, a video news platform, and FG Media, a digital ad agency. That's still not a large staff for an operation putting out daily news in four languages – Chinese, Bahasa Malaysia, Tamil and English.

Another important factor in the business model has been diversifying revenue sources. They started out with advertising alone but soon realised that that was never going to bring in enough to cover costs. This led to a decision to drive revenue from readers, and they put a paywall in place way back in 2003. "We went against the grain by getting subscribers very early on", says Chandran.

This is something a journalist probably wouldn't have considered, he believes. "As an editor you want to maximise your readership and your impact, so you wouldn't think about reducing your audience in order to get subscribers." It was a good move. Even though at the time credit cards and digital payments were little developed, people were so keen to get access that they paid by cheque or brought in cash. With hindsight, though, Chandran thinks Malaysiakini could have done more to get subscriber numbers up. "We could have done better in terms of marketing … our subscription", he says. "Reaching out to [readers] and having better … payment methods, improving our technology. There were a lot of little innovations that we could have done to get things right."

Malaysiakini has come in for some criticism for putting the paywall up on only the Chinese and English sites, leaving the other versions free. But the founders point out that, though the policy seems discriminatory, it provides the right combination for the outfit. "Number one, we are actually earning some money from our subscribers, from those two websites", Gan says, "and at the same time we are able to get enough traffic to Malaysiakini so that at least we are able to tell advertisers that we are big enough for them to advertise."

Indeed, the paywall could never support the whole operation, so advertising was kept up and actually overtook subscriptions. Even though Malaysiakini had a good lot of subscribers (the actual number is a company secret), it was getting only about 20–30 per cent of its revenue from them. Until recently, as much as 40 per cent of income came from programmatic advertising, which has a special advantage says Gan:

> I think a lot of advertisers are uneasy about advertising in Malaysiakini per se, but they can go to Google and if their ads happen to appear in Malaysiakini they can tell whoever is complaining to them …, look, it's not our fault, it's the machine that's doing it.

The other 30 per cent of income came from direct ad sales, for which FG Media provides support (the same subsidiary also did for-profit events and took on work from outside customers). In 2020, however, the coronavirus epidemic caused advertising to plummet. "Malaysiakini was forced to adapt quickly", says Chandran. The strategy was to double down the effort on subscriptions, and this led to a very good 40-per-cent increase. In 2020, subs and ads contributed a similar proportion of Malaysiakini's income.

Behind many of Malaysiakini's business decisions has been a partnership with Media Development Investment Fund (MDIF) started in 2002 (it was then called Media Development Loan Fund) (see pp. 42–44). Unlike a regular venture capitalist, MDIF provides not only money but all kinds of training and support to help business move forward. The Fund took a 29-per-cent share of Malaysiakini's equity (no figure has been published for the amount paid, but Chandran calls it "a small investment") and a place on its board for the MDIF head, at first Sasa Vucinic on an informal basis and later Harlan Mandel, who is now officially the third member alongside the two founders. Malaysiakini has MDIF to thank for suggesting and supporting the paywall, but its staff also helped out with guidance and advice on all kinds of business strategy. "They have played a very critical role", says Chandran. "They came in at a critical time, where we were just growing, and we needed that extra boost, an investment to move us further along."

Again unlike most investors, MDIF wasn't looking for a quick and profitable exit and today it maintains its investment and Mandel's place on the board. Quarterly strategy meetings with MDIF staff still play an important role for Malaysiakini. The Fund's supporters "form an external governance mechanism", says Chandran. MDIF has full access to company accounts so that they can express concerns on, say, grants Malaysiakini is applying for. The fund's worldwide media investments give its staff valuable experience to pass on to Malaysiakini, but it also works the other way: MDIF sends Chandran, Gan and others from the site to train media in the region, especially in support of its (now defunct) Myanmar Media Program. Malaysiakini staff also do training at home and round the region through the Kini Academy, a for-profit company in which Malaysiakini has a 60 per cent share.

One regular source of support for Malaysiakini has been grants – indeed, their setup funding included US$100,000 from the Southeast Asian Press Alliance (SEAPA) (the rest came from Chandran, Gan and some supporters). It has also received help from, among others, the German party foundations (for election coverage), as well as from the Canadian government development body and the International Center for Journalists. One grant that did well was from the US National Endowment for Democracy, which gave them US$35,000 to start KiniTV, according to NED's website. Today, Gan says, this little "guerrilla outfit" is challenging big-timers like satellite broadcaster Astro.

However, the fact that such monies come from western sources, including George Soros, the Hungarian-American financier whose hedge fund dealings triggered the 1997 Asian Financial Crisis, has led to accusations that Malaysiakini is US-financed. The founders respond that the grants are small, are mostly for short-term nonprofit projects and never make up more than 10 per cent of total income. Gan points out that grants allow them to take on activities that help the company without taking from the newsroom budget: "We are able to be raise additional money in order to make our content better so that we can do our job better in that sense."

If good business practices are behind Malaysiakini's success, there would be no business at all without the independent, professional journalism that attracts its many readers. Its "about us" section features a "frequently asked question" about the perception of Malaysiakini as "anti-establishment", to which it responds that "the media should play a role to report on current affairs in such a way that it both informs the public of key political debates as well as holds those in power accountable". It goes on: "Malaysiakini is often the first media to expose wrongdoings, corruption and abuses of human rights [and] will do so, regardless of political party or personality involved."

Certainly that stand has been the foundation of its popularity. Gan points out that most companies work hardest to attract advertisers. In Malaysiakini's case, "our focus is always on connecting with our readers, with our subscribers", he says.

> Most of our effort is basically with them rather than spending time on wining and dining with the advertisers. I think there are a lot of websites [that] put up great content, but they forget about the fact that they need to do outreach work.

Although for many years most of the site has been paywalled, Malaysiakini has made it free to all during all elections since 2004, the first poll after subscriptions started. In 2018 it moved with the times and opened up a little more, allowing non-subscribers to read ten free articles per month. This has given a huge boost to readership.

The audience is not passive. When Malaysiakini launched, the internet was giving Malaysians their first chances to express themselves openly – something the mainstream media had not done. Gan can't see why they hadn't, given that many reader contributions were very well-written. "When we were first set up", he says, "our most vibrant section was actually the letters page, you know, the people writing to us". Today the audience are still very much part of the outlet. In 2019, Malaysiakini won a Google News Initiative grant to build a "Kini community" by designing a reward system and loyalty programme to encourage greater interaction with readers. Malaysiakini's announcement of the win quoted Chandran as saying, "We strongly believe a more engaged readership is key to supporting an independent and credible media" (Malaysiakini 27 March 2019).

Readers are welcome to pop in to Malaysiakini's Petaling Jaya offices and chat to the staff. They are also ready to give back. "[A]t the time you need their support, you must be willing to ask them for help", Gan says. "A lot of them, apart from subscribing to Malaysiakini, they want to do more, so in that sense you give them the chance to do it." He cites their 2013 Buy-a-Brick campaign to raise money for the new office building. Today at the back there is a wall with 1,000 bricks with donors' names on: they brought in US$500,000. The generous response to the call to cover the contempt fine shows that that sentiment continues.

As for the technical side of things, since Malaysiakini launched during the early stages of the internet when connections were done via 56k modems, the outfit has kept up with developments. "Because we started off in 1999, which was before WordPress existed, or before most of the current technology existed, we've always been building our own technology", says Chandran. "So we've always had … a strong tech department that builds our own tech." Malaysiakini had its own operating system back in 2002, as well as its own customer relations database. The tech team today has seven staff in total to manage a suite of technologies they built themselves, including Newscraft (content management system), Newslight (subscription system), Newscrowd (Kini Community), Newsmetrics (data dashboard) and Newsdeck (monitoring).

Another Malaysiakini attribute that has contributed to its success is its willingness to experiment. "Most things are trial and error, so we ... trialled things out", says Chandran. "Some worked, some didn't work, but, you know, that's expected in business." On their website is a list of "inactive products", including a prepaid subscription card from the days when payments were difficult, as well as a mobile app, a publisher called Kinibooks, a citizen journalism training programme, a database for the 2004 and 2008 elections and a nonprofit civil society capacity-building outfit. Some have just run their course, others have morphed into new entities, and some have failed. Among the latter is KiniBiz, a subscriber-only business news service in which Malaysiakini had a half share. This ran into competition from market leader The Edge, which in turn opened its own news outlet to challenge Malaysiakini. The match ended in stalemate and both media dropped their new enterprise and stuck with their old specialities.

The opposition win in the 2018 election was good news for Malaysiakini, which may well itself have helped encourage voters to change the old order. The resulting government, Gan said, respected press freedom, and he felt the time was right to work on forming a Media Council that would make the sector self-governing. With the overthrow of that government by the establishment coalition in 2020 such ambitions have had to go on hold. But Malaysiakini can pride itself on not only being a media outlet that has broadened the political arena in Malaysia with independent and quality journalism, but has done so while being a successful business.

SOUTHEAST ASIA

Mekong Review

Some things about the Mekong Review go completely against the grain for a modern media startup. No. 1: even though it was founded in 2015, well into the digital age, its main platform is print. It does have a website, but it comes out quarterly on paper and gets delivered to cafés, shops and homes. No. 2: it doesn't have a business model to speak of. Since it was started on a journalistic impulse, such concerns have largely gone by the board.

FIGURE 7.21 Minh Bui Jones. Supplied by Minh Bui Jones.

Nevertheless, the outlet has a lot going for it. It appeals to a literary-minded audience who are willing to pay for it. It attracts quality contributions from journalists, who appreciate it as a place they can publish material other publications won't take – and they get paid. And, perhaps key, it has an enthusiastic boss with a wealth of journalism experience who puts in the hard work and loves doing it. Mekong Review may not be a huge commercial success, but it serves a niche audience with quality content. Its path has been up and down. It actually turned a small profit within a couple of years, but in 2019 came to the brink of closure. Its survival into the second decade of the 21st century testifies to the continuing interest in it and the staying power of its founder.

That founder, who is also its owner and editor, is Minh Bui Jones. Born in Vietnam and raised in Adelaide, he started in journalism in the 1980s when he worked for the student newspaper as an undergrad at the University of Adelaide. He also did graveyard shifts at the college radio station and got a job as a TV producer with the government-run SBS channel. Then he moved to academic journalism as associate editor of the *Australian Quarterly*, a political science journal, and edited an Asian cultural publication called *Amida*. A trip to New York weeks after 9/11 inspired him to help found the magazine The Diplomat, later bought out by James Pach (see Chapter 8 pp. 13–16). Bui Jones moved to Thailand and worked briefly as news editor for Asia Times Online, then went on to Cambodia, from where he edited *American Review*, a foreign policy journal which was put out by the University of Sydney. He also took on the job of ASEAN editor for Knowledge@ Wharton, the ezine of Wharton Business School in the US.

Mekong Review emerged from that long career in journalism. The timing of its launch had two background circumstances. One was that Bui Jones and his family were about to head back to Sydney from Cambodia and he didn't want to leave Asia behind. The other was the prompting from several people who had seen him start up *The Diplomat* who suggested he launch an outlet to replace *Far Eastern Economic Review* and *Asiaweek*, the two long-time regional affairs print weeklies that had gone out of business in the 2000s. Bui Jones turned down the opportunities, feeling those publications were of their time and not suited to the new circumstances. He was looking to do something different.

Inspiration came from an assignment he did for Wharton. He had pitched a story to his editors about the bad behaviour of Chinese visitors in Chiang Mai, something covered heavily in mainstream news. When he got to the northeastern Thai city, though, he was surprised to find the reports didn't reflect the situation. "I actually thought the Chinese tourists were quite charming, quite well-behaved", he said.

> And, you know, I saw something in them that I hadn't seen for a long time, and that was this love for travelling. We in the west had become quite jaded because we'd been doing it for so long. Here were people who had been saving for 10 and more years for their first overseas trip.

He wrote the piece as agreed, but knew he had a better story that didn't fit what his employer would want. He wondered how many good ideas like this didn't get aired.

There must be a lot of journalists like myself who have these observational stories or these offcuts, so to speak, that would never see the light of day, that the papers in the capital cities of our respective countries would never publish because it wasn't part of their mental map of Asia.

He added, "I thought, wouldn't it be great if there was a publication that understands how we operate as journalists and could publish them?"

The opportunity came days later, when, still in Phnom Penh, Bui Jones was taking his son to a violin lesson and bumped into three friends who were setting up a literary festival at Kampot on Cambodia's coast. Would he compère one of the sessions?, they asked. He agreed. Then he realised this would be the perfect place to launch a new publication, even though the event was only three weeks off. "I threw myself into it, gathered a team together overnight and then I hit the ground running", he says. "And we made it!" The first issue of Mekong Review came out at the festival on 7 November 2015.

Bui Jones didn't have time to plan ahead. "In that helter-skelter period I didn't think about, you know, the life of the magazine or how long it would last, and I didn't quite know the frequency of the magazine, or its coverage or its scope." People liked it, though, and enough money came in to fund a second issue. The content mainly covered Cambodia, where people rarely buy publications at newsstands, and Bui Jones needed a novel way of getting it out. He noted that readers were more likely to pick up something to look at while relaxing over a coffee. "A lot of the cafés in Phnom Penh would sell magazines", he says. "So I would go and ask the café owners whether they would stock the magazine, and quite a few of them were happy to."

Word got around and people in Vietnam and Thailand asked to buy it, so he followed the same pattern in those places. For the first three years Bui Jones delivered the copies himself or got family, friends and friends-of-friends to help by, for instance, picking them up at a bus station drop-off and taking them to a café, with the occasional bundle going astray. Gradually the publication's distribution extended to bookshops and to Myanmar, Malaysia and Singapore. By 2020, Mekong Review's print run was 2,000 copies and they were being sent out to retail outlets and subscribers across Southeast Asia as well as Hong Kong and the US, with most issues selling more than 70 per cent of copies, some even selling out. The 2020 coronavirus pandemic hit the delivery model, however, with shops closing and distributors going into hibernation, forcing a cut in the print run to 1,500.

Bui Jones feels he chose the right moment to launch the publication. "I think magazine timing, if you don't have a lot of money, or any money, is the only asset you have really", he says. He had seen his old outlet, *American Review*, fail because it had come too early, going out of business before US politics became controversial under Donald Trump. What was wanted in 2015, he saw, was a good old-fashioned print publication. "I felt very strongly at the time that a lot of people who read a lot, like myself, were fed up with the internet", he says.

> We were, I think, worn out with the amount of social media and email and we also realised that we weren't reading things as we used to. ... Reading off a screen was a different reading experience and we weren't enjoying the prose or absorbing the details as we had when we read it off print.

He decided to make the Review a quarterly publication so as not to overload his audience. "People didn't really have the time to read a lot, and so it had to be infrequent so people wouldn't feel too guilty if they couldn't read it in a week or in a month", Bui Jones says. He also knew it couldn't leave out politics, despite the sensitivities of the region. "Even though it was a literary magazine, it had to be very political because that's what everyone was talking about in Southeast Asia, whether you were in Cambodia, Vietnam or Thailand or Myanmar or Malaysia."

The key factor in the Mekong Review's take-up has been its quality journalism. Each issue brings a new lineup of reviews, essays, poetry and fiction. One article in particular got the magazine on to readers' radar: American academic Thomas Bass's review of the acclaimed 2017 Ken Burns-Lynn Novick ten-part documentary on the Vietnam War for US public broadcaster PBS. Bass's piece was an erudite, stinging indictment of the war itself and slammed the series as a product of conservative forces that largely ignored important sources and facts that contradicted that view (Bass 2017). Bass's article got 30,000 readers in a week. "That made people take notice, especially in the US and elsewhere", says Bui Jones. "That review was mentioned in *Newsweek*, in *The New York Times*, and I think it's probably arguably one of the first reviews of that series that was really critical."

Bui Jones says the job of getting Mekong Review out is so full-on that he doesn't have time to think about a business model, not to mention the fact that "I am really bad with numbers" or the impulsiveness of the whole thing ("done on the spur of the moment, on the smell of an oily rag", as he says). Perhaps the playing down of business nous is a little exaggerated because there is clearly good financial thinking behind the outlet. Bui Jones says his initial plan was to give up if it didn't break even after three years, but it did so after two, and he used the extra money to expand from 20 to 40 pages and have more colour, illustrations and photos. He pays his freelancers (unless they have "tenured" positions at universities or other publications) as well as the photographers and artists.

Income came first from payment for the physical copies – one of the advantages of print over digital, Bui Jones points out – and this remains one of the magazine's staples. But its largest revenue source is now the paywall, with subscriptions between US$25 and US$70 a year depending on whether you take print or online. The two are linked, says Bui Jones.

"Newsstand sales are very important because they serve as a first step towards subscription sales", says Bui Jones.

> Because people travel through Southeast Asia and they pick up a magazine at a shop or at the airport and they like what they read and then when they're back in Boston or in Sydney or in London they subscribe to us.

Even though the coronavirus has stopped people moving around for the time being, the journal has more or less held its ground.

Bui Jones has pursued advertising, though more as a service and content component than for revenue. "In the first year, as any magazine person will tell you, you don't get any money from advertising because you're a new business", he says. The potential was small anyway, with most ads coming from arts organisations and other community-oriented outfits. One very enthusiastic commercial advertiser dropped out due to political considerations. Knowing he had to create a new market for advertising, Bui Jones focused on small publishers. "I wanted to get all the local publishers into the pages of Mekong Review so the ads become part of the content", says Bui Jones. "It's important for the design of the magazine that these ads break up the endless wall of text and also that they provide extra reading material for our readers." He charges these advertisers very little.

The question now is, can Mekong Review survive? The key is Bui Jones's continued willingness to be the driving force. He wrote in a 2019 article published in Splice Media how, with no money and near burn-out, he had taken a new job in Hong Kong and been on the point of shuttering the magazine and then, finding himself in the middle of the pro-democracy protests in Kowloon, noticed how life continued despite the chaos – and journalists were "risking life and limb" to cover it. He resolved to keep Mekong Review going (Bui Jones 29 October 2019).

SOUTHEAST ASIA

New Naratif

New Naratif runs on two tracks, neither of them easy, though for different reasons.

On the one hand it's about Singapore. Started up in 2017 by three Singaporeans, two of them critics of the government, it had its legal base in a company in Britain, but when the pair tried to register a local subsidiary in their home country they were rejected because authorities claimed its activities were political in nature and its overseas income constituted foreign interference. NN still has its largest audience in Singapore and continues to cover Singapore politics from its office in Kuala Lumpur. It also continues to have run-ins with the Singapore government.

At the same time, it has much wider ambitions for the whole region. New Naratif is, according to its website, "a movement for democracy, freedom of information, and

FIGURE 7.22 Thum Ping Tjin. Supplied by Thum Ping Tjin.

freedom of expression in Southeast Asia". It provides thoughtful in-depth journalism that finds solutions "to inspire people to believe in their society and work collaboratively for the greater good".

How can such an idealistic site thrive in such a hostile environment? It not only draws censure from its founders' own government but is trying to cover a hugely diverse set of countries where its ambitions are generally not welcome. Moreover, it's specialising in a journalism genre that is expensive to implement and difficult to fund. It has no big backers and relies on donations, grants and membership fees, the latter requiring a paywall, something known to deter readers.

Yet New Naratif seems to have struck a note among Southeast Asians keen to see an Asian-based outlet that expresses their yearning for the kind of freedoms that are so lacking in the region. When NN foundered during the coronavirus pandemic in spring 2020 it put out a call to raise US$75,000 by the end of June – and it succeeded. That move also brought membership up from 700 the year before to about 1,200 by early 2021. It must be doing something right.

New Naratif's initial founder is Thum Ping Tjin, a scholar with a doctorate in history from Oxford University, where he is part of an academic group called Project Southeast Asia. He wanted to find a way to bring important academic research on the region out from behind paywalls and make it accessible to the public. In around 2012, he approached Kirsten Han, a freelance journalist who has long campaigned against capital punishment in Singapore and who was also living in Britain at the time, about setting up a site. Han suggested pairing up academics and journalists to do the job. She returned home in 2014, and in 2016, when Thum was on his way back, they decided to go into action. The third founder is renowned graphic novelist Sonny Liew, whose cartoons would add an extra dimension and who saw the opportunity as a chance to create a space for Southeast Asian artists.

Thum registered the parent body, Observatory Southeast Asia (OSEA), in Oxford as a private company limited by guarantee, with no owner or shareholders – essentially a nonprofit. There was good reason to base it in Britain, according to Han, who was editor-in-chief in 2019 when interviewed but has since stepped down to focus on her own writing and reporting: "[T]he publishing is all done in Oxford because we wanted to … protect it as much as possible from any government or laws that would try to compel us to stop publishing, or stop doing anything". The company registered in Kuala Lumpur was designated as providing consultancy and editorial services to the parent in Oxford.

Once the New Naratif site was launched, Thum, who became managing director, posted video talks explaining complex issues of Southeast Asian history and politics while Han ran a group of high-quality freelancers to produce and process content. She also organised and often conducted discussion forums on democracy and freedoms round the region. The two were determined to be transparent – they published company accounts every six months – as well as egalitarian – they paid themselves on the same freelance basis as everyone else.

Within a year they had more than 400 members, each paying an annual subscription of between US$52 and US$552, the higher options giving no extras but included for those who wanted to contribute more. The goal was eventually to get 2,500 members, a number that would allow them not to need other funding sources. What members get for their money is a unique member token URL that gives them access to all content as well as to the forums held round the region, and also contacts with the outlet's writers. But in order not to completely bar non-members and ensure that content gets a wide audience, a back door was left open for sharing free on social media.

Han pointed out that having NN membership is different from subscribing to mainstream media like *The New York Times*. "It's not about paying money to get past a paywall", she said. "You actually want people to feel that they are part of a community for democracy, freedom of information and freedom of expression in Southeast Asia." The founders are keen to emphasise that these goals do not put them in the "western" camp. One recent cartoon explainer starts off with:

> Many people are quick to tell you that "rights" are a "western" thing and not "Asian" or whatever other markers or identity they highlight. This is not the case. In a social context, rights are simply the basic principles you accept for yourself and which you extend to others, without exception, in order to live together.
>
> *(Tang 11 June 2020)*

The outlet itself progressed smoothly, but it has evoked some strong responses. "Our editors and correspondents frequently face harassment online", says Thum, some receiving death threats. Thum himself has been at the centre of controversies in his home town.

The first time was when he got involved in the debate over the setting up of Singapore's law on fake news, eventually passed as the Protection from Online Falsehoods and Manipulation Act (POFMA) in 2019. In early 2018, Thum made a submission to the parliamentary Select Committee preparing the law. In it he provided a set of suggestions for dealing with fake news, mainly by lifting Singapore's many restrictions on press freedom (Thum 26 February 2018). Even more critical of the government was his statement that by far the largest and most impactful generator of fake news in Singapore was the ruling People's Action Party itself. He accused the PAP of deliberately spreading falsehoods over the years for political gain, dating this back to the sensitive Operation Coldstore in 1963, when, under founding prime minister Lee Kuan Yew, many opposition party members were detained without trial under the security law of the time. Thum said there was no evidence for the charge that they were part of a communist conspiracy.

It was the Coldstore reference that hit a nerve. Invited to speak to the Committee in person, Thum found himself on the receiving end of a harangue from Law & Home Affairs Minister K. Shanmugam. The minister first questioned Thum's credentials, pointing to Thum's description of his position at

Oxford as a "research fellow in history" rather than his actual job title – "visiting fellow in anthropology" – as proof that he was being deliberately deceitful. Then Shanmugam spent the next five hours attempting to demolish Thum's points on Coldstore (Tan 31 March 2018). Thum says that the minister failed to do so.

> I'm very proud of the fact that my work stood up to his questioning, as I expected that he would pull out some previously classified official document to disprove me. The fact that he didn't, I think, shows that the government has no evidence to contradict my arguments.

It was an extraordinary performance designed to question Thum's academic standing. Thum says the distinction between the job descriptions is "meaningless" and wasn't designed to deceive. A petition signed by over 300 academics from round the world, including Thum's colleagues at Oxford, condemned the Select Committee's treatment of him and demanded an apology. In response came another onslaught from the Select Committee chair, Charles Chong, who said that Thum may himself have had a hand in drafting the petition, constituting, according to a story in government paper *The Straits Times*, "possible involvement in 'a coordinated attempt, with foreign actors involved, to try to influence and subvert' Singapore's parliamentary processes" (Au-Yong 1 May 2018).

It came as no surprise when the application to register an OSEA subsidiary with Singapore's Accounting & Corporate Regulatory Authority (ACRA) was rejected in April 2018. ACRA said the proposed company's aim to hold democracy discussion forums and to support New Naratif, which had been publishing "critical" articles about countries in the region, meant that its purpose was clearly "political". ACRA's statement also referred to a US$75,000 grant the parent company had received from a body linked to George Soros's Open Society Foundations, saying the funding body had "a history of involvement in the domestic politics of sovereign countries". The company would allow foreigners to interfere in Singapore, it concluded, and so its registration would be "contrary to Singapore's national interests" (ACRA 11 April 2018). A response submitted by the founders mentioning that its members came from 17 countries brought a rejoinder from ACRA saying that the company was therefore foreign-funded (ACRA n.d.). The failure to register in Singapore meant that NN's live forums had to be abandoned there, though they continued elsewhere.

Once POFMA was passed into law, it was on the cards that Thum would be an early casualty. When he criticised it on NN's YouTube channel in May 2020, the government responded by saying he had been wrong on four points: that POFMA was so strict that almost any statement could be found to be misleading, that the law made all criticism of the government illegal, that it was impossible to overturn a POFMA direction through legal means and that the law allows the PAP alone to define truth. The government directed NN to issue a correction notice – which it did, though with many riders – but allowed the video to remain where it was. The government statement also clarified that POFMA doesn't cover opinion and "fact-based criticism", so other matters mentioned by Thum in the video were not relevant (gov.sg 13 May 2020; Thum 8 May 2020).

Yet the fact that Singaporeans continue to support the outlet shows that at least some of them value NN's firm stand on democracy and freedoms and Thum's willingness to put his neck on the line when many others daren't do so. Oddly, herein lies one cause of NN's difficulty in growing bigger. Many of its Singaporean members are willing to pay the higher subscription rates to support it, but they themselves are often too busy to read it. Meanwhile people in neighbouring nations like Indonesia or Vietnam want to read it but may not be able to pay – not so much because they can't afford it but because bank transfers are needed, and with NN having no official presence there it can't open bank accounts. "Interestingly for us it seems that there isn't necessarily a direct correlation [between] people who are paying and people who are reading", Han said. She hoped new payment systems and opening offices in other countries would even out the situation.

There are no plans to move NN to a commercial basis. "We quite deliberately structured it this way because we wanted it to be accountable to members and people who read us", said Han.

> Because we've seen in Southeast Asia that a lot of the governments can go after you by the business and funding angle, so ... they can lean on investors, they can lean on advertisers, or they can make life so difficult that owners sell up.

NN's principle, she went on, was "to do something that was much more grassroots and dependent on the people".

While building up member numbers, New Naratif has applied for grants. During the coronavirus pandemic it received US$5,000 from the Google News Initiative Emergency Relief Fund and the same amount from the Splice Lights On Fund. However, their applications to the GNI Innovation Challenge and Luminate's Membership Puzzle Project failed, and funding received in 2019 from the Taiwan Foundation for Democracy for staging live events had to be returned when such events became impossible.

The cancellation of its forums was nearly a death blow to New Naratif. The emergency funding came to the rescue, and NN was also able to capitalise on the situation with its successful fundraising push. It appointed one of its correspondents, Aisyah Llewellyn, as editor-in-chief after Han's departure, later replacing her with Bangkok-based Jacob Goldberg; it also appointed one of its freelancers, Matt Surrusco, as deputy editor. A new post for marketing and outreach was created, fulfilling a need Han had pointed to earlier, the position being given to Indonesia-based Erik Nadir. With the increase in members NN was able to launch its events online, and start a new trajectory into 2021. Thum himself, who was still teaching at Oxford, was planning to return to Singapore at the end of the 2020–2021 academic year to take up full-time work with NN.

New Naratif's business model isn't really a business model at all, but it has shown that high principles and quality journalism can engender a substantial level of audience engagement and, as a result, payment. Now to see if it really can reach the 2,500 members it needs to keep it going in the long term.

CHINA

Qdaily

As an entrepreneurial media outlet, Qdaily did everything right. When it started its site and app in Beijing in 2014 it had solid initial investment and a leadership of experienced and dedicated journalists. Its lively, original business coverage quickly gained an admiring audience and plenty of advertisers. Over the next couple of years, it opened another office in Shanghai, built up a team of 80 and received a large new injection of funding from its appreciative main backer. It expanded its coverage to areas beyond business, including many new columns and a well-liked reader survey app, and attracted so much advertising that it had broken even by 2017. In 2018 it was on target for a profit of RMB20 million (about US$2.8 million).

Which is when things started to go wrong.

In August that year, the site suddenly shut down. Later, visitors were redirected to a statement by the outlet saying it had "violated the news information regulations and … damaged the order of online information dissemination", as well as broken internet laws and regulations. SupChina reported that the Shanghai Internet Information office had announced that Qdaily's reporting team was illegal, and that it should refrain from covering politics, the economy, the military and many other sensitive topics (Feng 13 July 2018).

FIGURE 7.23 Yang Ying. Supplied by Yang Ying.

A line had been crossed: in China, only official media may produce original news. And Qdaily had even been covering stories that were not being reported elsewhere, such as a major fire in Beijing in late 2017 and the forced movement of people out of Shanghai to "clean up" the city. Another reason was a change in the law regarding registration. When the outlet started, regulations for digital media were quite loose, and Qdaily set up its first company in Beijing as a technology outlet and its second in Shanghai as an advertising firm. In May 2017, the Cyberspace Administration of China (CAC) updated the 2005 Regulations on Administration of Internet News Information Service (News Regulations), extending compulsory licensing of news media to internet outlets. It also restricted news collecting, editing and publishing, whatever the platform, to state media and their subsidiaries alone (Smith Freehills 4 Sept 2017).

Qdaily just went on publishing news as before. The authorities eventually set a trap, according to chief editor Yang Ying. When the much-loved Shanghai independent Jifeng (Monsoon) book shop was forced to close at the end 2017, other media received a notice that the 31 December final event was not to be covered as a story. When the party was marred by the sudden shutting off of water and electricity, Qdaily, having missed the message, blithely posted its stories. A few days later it received a direct order to delete them. After that, the authorities wouldn't leave the outlet alone. Its editors were "invited for tea" to be told off and were regularly asked to report on what they planned to publish as well as update full details of the company. Yang got messages to her private QQ account telling her to delete articles, and, when she didn't reply quickly enough, would get a phone call. And on multiple occasions officials thought the outlet was taking things too lightly, officials asked for a written explanation of its "mistakes", sending the resulting statements to the central government.

Qdaily seemed contrite. Its mid-2018 statement said that it would "carry out comprehensive and thorough rectification" and reappear at 3 pm on 2 September (Koetse 4 August 2018). And indeed it was back right on schedule. But the authorities didn't let up. Requests to delete articles came thick and fast, sometimes within ten minutes of posting, even if that was at 6 am. "It was like torture for us," says Yang. "You are still doing so-called media, but if you post an article … someone will delete it. And you wrote the article for whom? It's like, for no one!"

Then on 4 June 2019, the anniversary of the 1989 Tiananmen Square crackdown, they published in their regular "News in History" column a short bio of Hu Yaobang, the popular president whose death had fuelled the protests that led up to the disastrous event. All the information they used was from official sources, but that didn't matter. As soon as it went up automatically on Weibo at 6.04 am, their app disappeared from the app store and the site was closed.

This time it was much more serious. They opened their website three months later (their app remained available to those who already had it, but not for new downloads), but by then they had lost their Beijing office and many staff. They staggered on but morale was low. "We feel we're not doing media, we're doing fighting, and our intention is not to fight with anyone", says Yang. People have suggested they could go on by sticking to lifestyle or business reporting, as many other outlets do – and their investors would support them if they took that route. "Yes, of course we can do that,", Yang says. "But we know we are not for that. That's not important for us any more, that kind of content."

It's clear that independent media cannot win when the odds are so stacked against them. One China media watcher said: "For me, Qdaily is very strange because they seem so mindlessly brave. ... They were supposed to distance themselves from journalism, hard news, but somehow they just keep doing that." But many people have great admiration for this outlet because it keeps going through thick and thin.

Even though politics got Qdaily into trouble, its business model was highly successful, and is worth looking at. There were several reasons it did well.

One was that, having been started by three experienced journalists – Yi Xianfeng, former chief editor of China Business Network Weekly, along with Huang Jingjie, CBN's former tech editor, and Yang herself, who was lifestyle editor there – it had a commitment to quality content. All reporters were trained, whether experienced or not, and required to write in clear language, avoiding jargon, and show readers what the importance of the story was and why they should read it. In the newsroom they had a guide you would expect to find in the United States rather than China: the Associated Press Reporting Handbook. It was used "to train our reporters how to write as simply as possible", says Yang. Staff also had to avoid plagiarism and cite sources for all content taken from the internet.

Then there was subject matter. Yang said they didn't want to cover macroeconomics but "lifestyle economics", stuff people are actually interested in. Indeed, the "Q" in Qdaily stands for the first syllable of the English word "curiosity". So when they started in 2014, they set up a column called "Big Company Headlines", for which they picked 15 top companies that they saw as setting both industry and lifestyle standards, among them Apple, CocaCola and Muji. Then they widened the field by scouting out all their competitors. That gave them a list of about 300 companies "that we should care about in our daily life", says Yang. Reporters were put into groups to scout out stories about these companies for the budding site.

Another contributor to Qdaily's success was a clever tool called Qdaily Labs. At first called Life Research Lab and then renamed Curiosity Research Lab, it is a reader survey mechanism that came out of the market research done while setting up the site with the help of US-based design company Frog, a contact they knew from CBN Weekly. Users were asked what Yang calls "daily life questions", such as their attitude to a certain brand or what they thought of the "Me Too" phenomenon. Usually more than 2,000 responses would come in, and sometimes as many as 15,000. The answers were summarised and published, evoking further discussion. The Lab served another purpose: the brand questions brought in advertisers, who valued it as a channel to communicate with young consumers.

Design was another factor in Q Daily's success. Initially it was similar to the layout used by big companies like Sina.com and Tencent. "It's very ugly, and it's very crowded too," says Yang. "You can't find the useful information." So they took up the Microsoft "Metro" user interface, which splits the screen into squares. This was very different from other websites in China at the time, says Yang. "The first group of readers were those who do creative work because we introduced something very new and we focused on creativeness, innovation and some new business ideas." Also they didn't overwhelm their readers, putting up 30 to 35 articles a day rather than the thousands posted by bigger sites, leaving the interface relatively uncluttered.

All these factors – strong journalism, lively new topics, interactivity and an attractive interface – made the site very popular among China's young urban élite. Eighty per cent of users were aged from 18 to 30, most living in "Bei-Shang-Guang-Shen" – the well-off major cities of Beijing, Shanghai, Guangzhou and Shenzhen – or overseas, and 70 per cent had a degree.

The company grew from 10 staff in Beijing to a total of 80 staff in both offices, of whom 40 were reporters and 8 editors. The rest comprised technical staff (ten people) and advertising and marketing personnel, and one accountant. Recruits were treated well, with reporters being sent out after training to do stories all over the country and sometimes even overseas, usually at the invitation of big tech companies like Apple, Microsoft or Amazon or of governments in Europe, but also on trips paid for by the company to cover art and design fairs.

Advertising was the planned source of income from the start, and Qdaily found it easy to attract big names, some of them in the Fortune 500; half were car companies, who valued Qdaily's quality lifestyle content. Unusually, Qdaily only sold banner ads, with the price determined by the position on the site. "We're not that mainstream and we care more about the quality and taste more than the clicks", Yang says. If they sold ads by clicks they would have earned even more, she thinks. The site had another means of getting an income through partnerships with aggregators. Baidu, Jinri Toutiao, Netease and others all paid Qdaily to publish its content. The revenue was very small, but the added benefit was the extension of the outlet's influence through these massive portals. Qdaily also had partnerships with seven other major online operations and as many as 100 small ones.

Qdaily's faithful main funder was Trustbridge Partners, a Shanghai-based investment company with a US$5-billion portfolio specialising in media among other areas, according to its Crunchbase profile. Yang says Trustbridge has a special interest in culture and encouraged her and the other founders to set up Qdaily. It was the main investor in a US$2-million "angel" round, about one-sixth of which was put in by individual media investor Li Ruigang. Even before that amount had been used up, Trustbridge added another US$6 million to the pot. Yang Ying says the deal was that they never had to pay the money back. She also says the funders continued to support Qdaily through its trials and tribulations, making it clear that tweaking content would be a good idea but never forcing the issue.

By 2020, says Yang, she and her partners were tired and ready to call it quits on Qdaily. "I think it's done its own responsibility enough for … society", she says. "I can say, it's done all it can do." She is sad that circumstances overtook what was a very successful business, and sees Qdaily as the last entrepreneurial media outlet in China that wasn't about lifestyle or tech or startups. At the end of the year they stopped updating the site altogether, though they left it in place – "frozen … not dead but not alive" – and it was still getting "tens of thousands" of hits a day, especially when controversial issues they used to report on cropped up. One such was the "MeToo" case of state TV intern Zhou Xiaoxuan against a senior programme host – Qdaily had interviewed Zhou when she went public with her complaint in 2018. Yang and Yi have a new project for 2021, an app called Aves which covers non-fiction and literature. But they still haven't given up hope of reviving Qdaily should circumstances change.

CAMBODIA

Sabay

"Our company name is Sabay, and 'sabay' means 'happy'", says Chy Sila, the outlet's CEO. "We are living our mission to make people happy." The younger generation deserves a better life after the terrible tragedy Cambodia has been through, he believes. Regular media try to capture audiences with graphic visuals of traffic accidents and gruesome illnesses, but Sabay News focuses on "good news" across a range of topics – entertainment, celebrities, technology, health and sport. Today the site is one of the most popular digital outlets in Cambodia, with 2.2 million UVM and 5 million Facebook followers.

FIGURE 7.24   Chy Sila. Photo credit: Author.

Getting to the top came from being first on the scene and taking the big risks that go with it. Sabay started out as an early local online games company called CIDC Information Technology, which was established by Chy Sila in 2007, a time when the internet in Cambodia was so slow that it seemed impossible to make anything that relied on it work. CIDC invested in their own ISP, fibre optics, cables and even a dial-up service to make it happen.

The market was very ready, and in 2010 CIDC had made enough to expand into media, changing its name to Sabay Digital Corporation (SDC) and creating Sabay News. It was still a tough challenge. At the time there was only one Khmer-language font and it wasn't recognised by Microsoft, so Sabay used Khmer Unicode, which appeared on screen as a row of squares. "And they said, what a stupid website!" says Chy Sila with a laugh. "Cannot read, only see the pictures!" But six months later Windows was upgraded to recognise Khmer Unicode and the site was all ready for it.

In two years the company was turning a profit, and today the gaming outlet and Sabay News have been joined by more services: an internet TV channel (Sabay TV), a film distribution arm (Sabay MVP), a city guide (Sabay Der – though this has been dropped since), a multimedia news and entertainment site (30 Daily), a short-news app and website (Kley Kley), a site for women (Kanha), a site for fiction (Enovel – connected with Sabay Write, which encourages readers to become authors) and, since 2017, a streaming video-on-demand service called Soyo with all content dubbed in Khmer. It has a large office in Phnom Penh with 170 staff as well as an office in Singapore, which is where SDC owner Sabay Digital Group is based.

Sabay's success attracted investors. In 2017, local mobile operator Smart Axiata, majority owned by Malaysia-based telecoms company Axiata, bought a stake in Sabay's media operations, the goal being to invest in more local content. In 2018, the company received an investment from local firm Belt Road Capital Management, but mainly for its gaming operation. Sabay prefers the details of these deals to remain private.

Advertising provides the company's main income. Chy Sila remembers that it was difficult at first to persuade advertisers to come on board because of the newness of digital, but business has built up. While most Cambodian news sites flooded their home pages with layers of bright, bold banner ads that dazzled the eye, Sabay's front page was more sophisticated, with clickable top stories and banners placed instead at the top and bottom of articles. More importantly, Sabay was first to use impressions as a measure. Some advertisers were not happy with that. "They said, where the hell is my advertising?" says Chy Sila, and he had a hard time explaining to them that the method was in fact more effective than just paying for ads to appear for a set time.

The company also does well with content paid for by advertisers. The idea is to move one step further from the common practice of publishing unchanged press releases, which, Sila says, makes for boring copy. Sabay's branded ads need to promote the product but also provide a service for the audience: "So in all articles the readers gain certain knowledge, information, plus they learn about the company or product that you want to promote." Sabay attracts sponsors by focusing on a particular business sector for a period of time – one campaign they did on the real estate business in 2016 brought them 50 sponsored articles.

The branded advertising is done in-house. "That's why I need to groom a new kind of people, so-called PR journalists, that means, they are going write articles about a certain company but in the journalist way," says Chy Sila. "They must try to dig down into the details about the whole industry and make them blend into the story." Understandably he's having difficulty getting that point over to his team of 25 journalists, many of whom are well-established professionals with experience in respected mainstream media and don't want to be "PR journalists".

> When I convince them to write an article … about certain things that will change the world, they [are] very [inspired] to write about it. But when I tell them to write about a beer company that has just won a medal from Germany …, they would be very sceptical to do that because they say, oh this is a beer company.

Chy Sila thinks that they should be proud of the beer company, but his journalists don't see it that way. The answer has been to split the writers into two teams, one news and one commercial.

Another ethical worry is that it's difficult to resist pressure from sponsor companies. In 2016 one of Sabay's biggest sponsors, Samsung, called several times and asked the outlet to drop the news about its Galaxy 7 model's overheating problems. Chy Sila found himself with a dilemma: this was a genuine news story that had gone viral. In the end, he removed one article to appease the company because he didn't want to endanger relations.

One of Sabay's secrets to success is that it provides an easy means of payment in a country where credit cards and other modern methods are not widely available. This was a concern they had to address when they set up their online games business long ago.

> We figured out that if there's no payment gateway, how will people play the game if they [have] to pay online? How do they pay? We can't go and collect the money from their home, right? So we had to develop our own [gateway].

The answer was a deal with the telephone companies which allowed customers to pay Sabay along with their phone bills.

Another system the company developed was the "Sabay coin", which is sold by agents, mostly in internet cafés, round the country – 1,000 locations in all – and can be used to purchase Sabay services. Coins cost only 100 riel (US$0.025) each, which will buy you entry into a special room in your game. This micropayment system opened the market to a much wider demographic – and today is still in use but in an up-to-date way under the company's state-of-the-art payment settlement system, ssn.digital, which is run through blockchain.

Sabay has also been a pioneer in reaching out to its audience. One unusual feature is Sabay Enovel, which is both a service and an income earner. The best fiction entries each month receive between US$30 and US$50 per chapter, and the company publishes them on its website and phone app. They hire script writers to turn the winning novels into plays, and then record them in audio format. There is no charge for people wanting to read them, and income comes from ads and from Facebook, where they put up sponsored posts and ads – the page has been very popular and in 2021 had more than 5.5 million Facebook fans.

Sabay also goes out to meet its readers. In 2017, the staff did a 90-day journey round Cambodia called The Road Home, with a team of journalists and photographers to take pictures and make videos of places of interest. The content was featured in an exhibition in Phnom Penh and gathered into a book, for which sponsors were found. Sila says the objective was to show people the beauty of Cambodia, to publicise people's hometowns and make them proud, and to promote Sabay in rural areas, where Facebook has become very popular.

Every step Sabay has taken has contributed to its commercial success, but the idea of social benefit is still important. "We really want people to read", says Chy Sila. "We write [things] that people want to read. ... I believe [the] more [people] read ..., [the better] their knowledge ... That's my dream also. People make the right decisions when they read." The company also gives free ad impressions to NGOs and to the government for health and welfare announcements.

The company ran a contest for films about traffic awareness and provided prizes totalling US$6,000. It sponsors a number of organisations and events, including Barcamp Phnom Penh, an annual gathering of young people in the IT and web business field, as well as the Bopea Music Festival, which combines the promotion of "charity culture" (funds are raised for projects like rural schools) and live rock bands, and JCI International, a nonprofit organisation that brings together young people who want to make an impact on their communities. Of course, there's a marketing side to all this, but there is also much good coming out of it.

Chy Sila's choice of "Sabay" as a theme harks back to his own experience of Cambodia's tragedy. He was born in 1974 during the Khmer Rouge period he is keen for Sabay's readers to forget. In 1979 he and his parents were among a large group herded into the Dongrek escarpment on the northern border with Thailand as Vietnamese troops swept the Khmer Rouge out of the country. The group was pushed back by the Thai army, resulting in many deaths from falls as well as starvation for those who survived. Chy Sila, weak and not expected to live, was given a last name, Thmor, meaning "rock". He doesn't like to use it today. He and his family came through the tough times, and now it's his time to make life happier for others.

HONG KONG

The Initium

When Yang Shaoming took over as CEO of Hong Kong-based The Initium in May 2017, he wasn't doing it for the money. The Chinese-language in-depth outlet was highly respected for its journalism, but it was deep in debt after only two years in existence. Yang was an e-commerce entrepreneur raised in Beijing who had seen through three startups of his own and also worked at tech giants Huawei and Alibaba. Now he was being asked in to rescue the outlet. He had little idea how to approach the task. "I was from a completely different planet! I didn't know the company and

FIGURE 7.25 Yang Shaoming. Photo credit: Author.

I didn't know the business", he says. "I mean, I loved to read the articles, but I didn't know how they were produced." But at the end of the next year, when Yang moved on, the company was back on an even keel.

Initium Media was the dream of Will Cai Hua, a lawyer from mainland China. Having lived overseas for many years he had come to admire quality western outlets like *The New York Times* and *The Economist* and wanted to set up a Chinese one that would provide equally good reporting for others like him who lived outside China. He hired a young high-flying journalist to lead it and they set up in a large office in Hong Kong with 70 staff, of whom 40 were the reporting team crucial to turning out the in-depth reporting The Initium would specialise in. The website was smart and serious and had a button that could toggle between the simplified characters used on the mainland and the traditional ones used elsewhere, making it readable to Chinese everywhere. The equation seemed perfect: good funding, lively reporting and a huge audience. The outlet won many awards and quickly built a good reputation.

These achievements gave The Initium a very high profile, but they had literally come at a huge cost: there was nothing left in the kitty. A reported US$11 million – US$10 million of Cai's money and another US$1 million of debt – had been used up. One problem was that the site was blocked in mainland China, meaning its biggest audience only had access via VPNs, and these were becoming more and more difficult to use. The main miscalculation, though, was in relying on advertising for income, which was much harder to earn than expected due to the outlet's lack of any single local audience. Many staff were laid off, reportedly reducing overall numbers to 25, and a subscription mechanism was started on but not implemented.

That's when Yang came in. He had met Cai through a mutual friend on the mainland a year earlier. He hadn't heard of The Initium, but when he got back home – at that time in Shanghai – he looked it up and was impressed by its articles about media, in particular an in-depth story about a monthly journal called *Yanhuang Chunqiu* (China through the Ages) which had been run by a group of former government officials with enough weight to publish liberal articles. The journal's closure was the peg for The Initium's story. "I read it and I was so touched", said Yang. "And then I sent a WeChat Moments [message and] said that there are more than 10,000 people wanting to do e-commerce and get to IPO, but there's no one who wants to broadcast the truth."

Yang learned that Cai was trying everything to make The Initium work. In early 2017 Cai had said he was in talks with Richard Li Tzar Kai, younger son of tycoon Li Ka Shing and head of local telecoms company PCCW. He asked Yang to join him at this stage and Yang agreed, but before he got there Li rejected the deal and Cai went bankrupt. With no salary in sight, Yang put off the move. But in May Cai asked him again, reasoning that his presence might bring in some new investors. "I really didn't want this company to die because it produced really high-quality articles, especially for people like me", said Yang. Another factor was that his elderly parents were living in Shen Zhen, next door to Hong Kong, and he wanted to be nearer them. So he sold his apartment in Shanghai and took his wife and children to Hong Kong. He did get a salary, he said – joking that it was the same as he had had at Alibaba except that one zero was missing.

Yang may not have had any background in media, but he quickly diagnosed The Initium's problem: lack of financial nous. There wasn't even a business model for the operation. Yang wasn't sure his ideas would work, but he knew he could bring some business sense into play. He took a three-pronged approach.

The first was to find a suitable business model. Yang said he listed all the possibilities he could think of, including e-commerce and even travel. Indeed, the outfit ran some tours to northeast China and North Korea – high-end trips inspired by *The New York Times's* Times Journeys travel outfit. Participants loved them but no profits resulted, and Yang realised a media outlet didn't have the skills to organise travel, so this idea was dropped. Advertising was de-prioritised, with the ad team being put on part-time on a commission basis. Native advertising wasn't suitable, Yang said. It was not only disliked by the journalists who had to produce it but it would bring down the tone of the high-quality outlet. "Advertising is not the right way for the media business in my opinion", said Yang.

Yang's focus moved firmly to subscription, the best form of income for The Initium, he said, because people will sign up to get high-quality articles. He knew this had worked well for many western media and The Initium had already made a start, though the IT systems in place were not suitable. Yang instructed the IT team to do the job properly and in July The Initium became the first Chinese online media outlet to launch a paywall. At the end of the year Yang brought off a cooperative deal with *The Wall Street Journal*. A subscription to The Initium cost US$64 a year but for just double that subscribers could read *WSJ* as well, for which they would otherwise have had to pay US$370 alone.

The Initium didn't have any marketing staff and had to rely on their old reader database to get the word out about the new paywall, though they did a little Facebook promotion. In 2018, Yang set up a subscription team to convert the old free audience to a paying one. Team members came from both editorial and business sides. "This is not very common in the media industry because usually they are completely separated", Yang said, but it worked. Old readers were emailed details of good deals and subscription campaigns were launched, including a three-day drive before Taiwan's local elections offering "real news, in-depth news, not fake news" at a discount. After that event they had 30,000 paying subscribers, nearly 50 per cent from Taiwan and about 25 per cent from Hong Kong, the rest coming from the US, Japan and Australia – accounts assumed to really be from people in China using VPNs. These fees were bringing in 90 per cent of income at that point, with the rest from ads.

The second prong was plain cost-cutting. The Initium had rented two spaces in an office building in North Point, a high-end location on Hong Kong island, when most startups would choose a cheaper building in an industrial area. Yang pointed to the offices' upmarket Macintosh computers, bought for around US$2,500 each, noting that his predecessors didn't cut corners. "They burned money in every aspect", he commented. He shut down the bigger of the two offices to save the rent. Then he worked on putting in place the kind of working processes any company needs: "I built up systems – financial systems, human resources systems, KPI [Key Performance Indicator] systems, everything to turn the company from randomly working based on their passion into an organised company based on a system", he said. "I mean, this is not something creative because I've done this in other companies … many times. I just copied it into this company, that's all."

The third prong was fundraising. Yang knew he couldn't promote investment in The Initium as having much profit potential, so he sought out people who liked the product. "I told every investor that I met that, if you want to make money, don't invest, because the best I can do is to keep your money [and] I can't make more", he said. "But if you have passion, please invest in us." Cai's good connections and his own passion soon brought in a couple of big investors and another couple of smaller ones, most of them people who had made money from the internet business. In late 2018 Yang, about to quit the company, could say that all the debts had been paid off and the company had broken even for one month.

On an additional note, Yang, who has co-founded a club for Chinese e-commerce enthusiasts, says he is happy to provide advice to any media startup that needs some business nous. He can be found on LinkedIn.

MALAYSIA

The Malaysian Insight

When The Malaysian Insight opened in 2017, it already had a history. Ten years earlier, a similar news site, The Malaysian Insider, had been launched to compete with the established Malaysiakini and the many new outlets appearing as the 2008 elections loomed. In 2014 Insider was bought by The Edge, a business newspaper and website. In 2015, the two outlets joined in uncovering the emerging story of then-prime minister Najib Razak's corrupt use of the 1MDB state fund and other matters kept close by the government. This got them into trouble.

FIGURE 7.26 Jahabar Sadiq. Supplied by Jahabar Sadiq.

Insider's leading editors were detained briefly on suspicion of sedition after a raid in early 2015, and in 2016 both companies had their products blocked. The Edge fought its case and re-opened after three months, but Insider folded in March that year, citing financial problems due to persistent government pressure on advertisers to ignore it (Holmes 16 March 2016).

The Malaysian Insight was started by Insider's leading editors, bringing with them the goodwill the old outlet had accumulated for its strong stand (Najib was later convicted for corruption). Jahabar Sadiq, a former Reuters journalist who was Insider's CEO and editor-in-chief (and one of those detained in 2015), took on the same two roles at Insight. The initial funding of US$1.1 million came from friends of his, according to Jahabar. Insight has a rather larger remit than Insider's political focus: its promise, according to its website, is to provide "an unvarnished insight into Malaysia, its politics, economy, personalities and issues of the day, and also issues sidelined by the headlines of the day". That means a wider potential audience, says Jahabar.

Insight differs from Insider in another aspect: its income is not from advertising alone but from subscriptions as well. However, the paywall's rollout didn't go smoothly. It was all ready to go in March 2018 when the site was suddenly suspended, Jahabar announcing that traffic hadn't reached high enough levels to proceed. With a general election approaching as well as rumours of a complaint to the government that Insight was foreign-funded, not to mention the fact that it was continuing Insider's path and publishing 1MDB revelations, it seemed as if the site might have closed (*Straits Times* 23 March 2018). But in May it was up and running again and the paywall went into effect in July. It is still doing well today, with its 60 staff, nearly half of them journalists, producing a very professional news site in Bahasa Malaysia, Chinese and English.

Insight's paywall is very strict. Non-subscribers can only see the lead paragraphs of each story and the rest has to be paid for – the equivalent of US$35 a year or US$3 a month. It's a good deal, Jahabar says: "You can't get a cup of coffee for that!" He had hoped for 10,000 subscribers in the first year, but by mid-2019 there were fewer than 7,000; a year and a half later the figure had dropped to 6,000. Still, he said he was very grateful to have got that many considering the economic situation and the many free alternatives.

Subscriber income is far from enough to cover costs – it provides only about 25–30 per cent of what's needed to pay staff, rent premises and cover the US$7,000 a month needed for outsourced IT services, which the ringgit's decline is increasing. So other revenue sources come into play, mostly from partners and advertising. Audiovisual output on Spotify and YouTube, where income is based on reach, brings in US$2,000 a month, and Google AdSense and Ad Manager together make up 15–20 per cent of revenue. Jahabar has a love-hate relationship with Facebook because of its algorithm preference for personal posts and the limits of Instant Articles, so he only uses it for putting up stories. Another 40–50 per cent of income comes from direct advertising – mainly campaigns from local banks and a few government institutions, who deal with Insight's sales team. Smaller advertisers can get technical help with videos and graphics from Insight's audiovisual staff, who also work on news. Native advertising and events also provide a small proportion of income.

With the 2018 opposition win in the Malaysian general election producing a freer climate for the media, Jahabar said it was a relief that "you don't have to look over your shoulder to think whether someone's going to call you in and question you over your articles", but that didn't mean life was easy. "It's so much more about, you're looking at your numbers and seeing whether you can sustain yourself in the next three months or six months." Though the new régime was more friendly and treated media more even-handedly than the old one, it did little to support the media. When the government was ousted, its successor proved more prickly about reporting but more willing to engage behind the scenes. But Jahabar doesn't see this as the main issue: "Our problem isn't the government of the day. Our problem is revenue, to sustain ourselves as we go along."

The challenge of how to stay in business in the digital age plagues every startup, with the new ways of distributing information throwing up new problems. "The biggest enemy form for paywalls is a subscriber copying everything into a WhatsApp group, and then it spreads like wildfire", says Jahabar. "I think the reality is ... people want the news for nothing." Moreover, ad money has many new destinations to choose from that are better than media. "You know, we are like Hong Kong and Singapore, we are a country where everyone is going online to purchase things", he goes on. "People bypass online media because they can. There are so many e-wallets and so many apps, so it makes sense for advertisers to go straight to the e-wallet and put in their ads there."

Jahabar says Insight's speciality is that it holds "the middle ground", covering all sides of the political spectrum. It also takes strong editorial stands on issues of the day. But its focus on news brings in a more mature audience, mid-20s to mid-60s, with two-thirds of them men and their preference being for English, the language of the older generation. The challenge is to bring on board the younger crowd. "I think people below 24, the millennials, they don't have a habit of reading news", he says. "They are on social media, they are more prone to just opinions and chat apps and all that." So the outlet has put in place a strategy of reaching out, with its video team posting short videos on YouTube and podcasts on Spotify, places that might be more attractive to youngsters than the website, as well as on Facebook and Instagram, even though neither brings many users to Insight's own site or app – the chances are about one in 100, Jahabar says. And all this distributed content is available free without subscription.

In early 2019 came some unexpected revelations about Insider. The Edge, having lost its investment when Insider had closed, produced a report on it. It said Insider had been set up by its wealthy investors to support the incumbent PM in the 2008 elections, a surprise given its later anti-government stance. Even more unexpected was the claim that in 2010, after Najib came to power, Insider had received US$9 million in funding from Jho Low, the infamous fugitive financier who masterminded the 1MDB scheme. However, with Insider turning against Najib, it was sold to The Edge in 2014 for just under US$1 million (Ong 15 January 2019).

Jahabar, who joined Insider in 2010, says he knew nothing about Low's investment and has some doubts about the claims, pointing out that the evidence came from affidavits. If it did happen, he said, the possible explanation is that people were just happy to have news without paying for it:

I don't think they bothered where the money came from before … It could come from Soros or Trump, it doesn't matter, they were just hungry for news. As long as the news is seen as impartial and covers all the bases, they're fine with that.

While Jahabar says the reports made no difference to him or Insight, they did add to questions about his initial source of funding for the new site. Jahabar remains unwilling to give full details about his "angels". "It's a bunch of the Malaysian diaspora who, at that point in time, when we started in 2017 under the previous government, didn't want to be identified", he says. "They still don't want to be identified, but basically they're … people I went to school with." He says the terms of the deal were that if he didn't repay them in three or four years, they could take over the company and do what they liked with it.

However, in 2019 he says, he received more funds from them, and this time they cut the budget, "making it tight for us". At that point, with Insight just breaking even, Jahabar had some plans for improving income, such as increasing podcasts and videos, which cost far more than text to produce, and putting them behind a paywall as premium content. Meanwhile a daily report service was set up to reach out to the Chinese and Malay markets at first on WhatsApp but eventually on Telegram, which Jahabar found more flexible and at the end of 2020 was "getting some traction". The next plan was to seek sponsored content in 2021.

TAIWAN

The News Lens

When The News Lens started in 2013, Taiwan's traditional news market was already saturated and digital-only was an unknown quantity. Finding no interested investors, founders Joey Chung and Mario Yang had to launch on their own savings. A slow start, but once they got going interest perked up. By the end of 2020, they were on their fourth funding round, having attracted more than US$10 million in venture capital investment. They had also become multi-vertical by taking over four other media companies and multi-functional by taking

FIGURE 7.27   Joey Chung. Supplied by Joey Chung.

over two tech companies. With two more acquisitions in sight and IPO just over the horizon, in 2021 TNL is one of the region's most successful VC-invested entrepreneurial journalism endeavours.

It all goes back to 2008, when Chung was studying business at Harvard University. At that time the new entrepreneurial media were bursting on to the US scene – HuffPost, TechCrunch and so on – and Barack Obama was the first to use

Facebook in a big way for a presidential campaign. At that point, Chung didn't take up the idea of a media business but moved to Shanghai, where he spent two years as head of Japanese firm Sanrio's China operations. When he returned to Taiwan, he noticed that no one was doing much in entrepreneurial media there. An audience of millions of young people wanting non-partisan digital news was waiting to be tapped. He teamed up with media industry contact Yang, an editor with a background in national and international media, and in 2013 they decided to set up TNL as an independent news site that would appeal not only in Taiwan but beyond to Hong Kong, Southeast Asia and to Chinese people the world over.

They had huge difficulty getting investors interested. Chung's Harvard background and business connections were enough to get him initial business meetings, but no further. "They'd look at my résumé and say, you've never had a startup before, you've never led a new company from zero all the way to exit", he says. Investors also had a preconceived idea about the kind of media that would do well, and TNL didn't fit. After their pitches, according to Chung, he would be told,

> You know that the public wants more fun pieces, more sensational pieces, more gossip, even though that's not what everyone ideally imagines news to be, but that's what's popular, and you're saying you're going to go in exactly the opposite direction and you're going to take my money to do that? No.

Chung and Yang traipsed from boardroom to boardroom with zero success. Finally, they gathered all their savings, a total of around US$100,000, and started anyway. They hired their IT person on the first day to get the website up and running, and then recruited a small staff. They gave themselves a year and a half to prove their business model. Chung says:

> The worst-case scenario was, if we ran out of money in 18 months, and we were never able to get traction, then we would have to honestly tell ourselves, hey, we were not meant to do a startup, you know, we have no capacity nor skillset to do this.

They would have closed it and gone back to their day jobs.

Then, Chung goes on, out of the blue came an email from American media investor Marcus Brauchli. After working for *The Wall Street Journal* for many years and later becoming editor of *The Washington Post*, Brauchli was joining Sasa Vucinic, a Serbian journalist and media investment veteran, in setting up North Base Media, a US-based venture capital company specialising in independent digital media outlets in emerging markets (see p. 45). Brauchli had learned of TNL when he had been giving a talk at a conference and a Taiwan business person had approached him and told him he should check out the budding startup. Brauchli, who had worked in China and Hong Kong for many years with *WSJ*, did some homework and zapped out the message, introducing himself to Chung.

"Serendipity" is how Chung describes it. Arriving just a few months into TNL's 18-month runway, the email presented the perfect opportunity. North Base wasn't connected to the complex politics and business of the region, and it would boost TNL's ambitions to be an international site. NBM made an angel investment of US$300,000, kicking off the small media outfit's rise. The partnership has lasted: to this day Brauchli is a member of TNL's company board and Vucinic a member of its advisory board, and NBM has continued to invest. Fellow investors include individuals like Taiwan-American investor Charles Huang, Kevin Lin, formerly of Twitch, and YouTube co-founder Steve Chen, as well as VC companies including US-based Walden International, Taiwan family firm Dorcas Investments and, for the most recent injection, New York-based Palm Drive Capital. TNL got totals of US$1–2 million in Series A in 2015, US$2 million in Series B in 2017, US$3–4 million in Series C in 2018, and was building up its Series D at the end of 2020.

The outlet aims for broad content coverage rather than niche: "We want to be that one-stop shop, if you will, the voice of the digital generation", says Chung. Of the 60–80 items posted every day, about a third are original TNL stories, another third are summaries of domestic and international news based on a collation from published sources, and a third are commentaries and analysis from think tanks, NGOs and about 800 columnists. There is also a wide range of original video news. The site has separate Chinese editions for Taiwan, Hong Kong and Southeast Asia, and, since 2015, an international site in English, aimed at second-generation overseas Chinese and others round the world who want to know more about the region. But there are some challenges in their market, with Hong Kong and Southeast Asia having their own strong Chinese-language and English-language media that are much closer to home, while mainland China bans the site altogether. Company information shows that the majority of TNL's audience – 70 per cent – is in Taiwan, with 15 per cent in Hong Kong, just under 5 per cent in the US and 3 per cent in ASEAN.

TNL's main income source is advertising. Chung says they offer progressively more services to clients as they gain their trust. The outlet can assure them that in its homeland it reaches almost one out of every two highly educated people in the 15–45 age range. They don't have the massive range of eyeballs the big players like Google do, but boast 16 million UVM, with their high-quality content reaching a well-off audience. They run plenty of native advertising and it's designed to blend in with the regular content though always clearly marked. However, with the VC investors injecting more capital and hurrying the company along to their desired exit, it was becoming clear that a single independent media outlet could not produce enough income.

Chung had noticed that, in the west, platforms and media were increasingly coming together (e.g. Apple with Apple News) while major news outlets like Bloomberg and *The Economist* have their own production facilities that work for themselves as well as for paying clients. "Whoever has content, a platform and their own in-house tech capabilities to actually monetise and optimise all these services, that will be the future", he says. So, from 2018, TNL started making acquisitions. First came the media verticals: INSIDE, which covers digital tech trends; Cool3C, with new product information; comprehensive sports site Sports Vision; every little d, which has inspirational stories; and movie site Agent Movie. Then came the purchase of big-data market research firm TNLR and, next, of the largest mobile ad tech company in Taiwan, Ad2iction. TNL has also launched its own ticketing system. An AI business and two more unspecified targets are to follow. The services TNL now incorporates are for both in-house use and for sale to other businesses.

One rule TNL observed from the start was not to splash the cash. "Most of the digital media startups that failed did so because they had too much money initially, were burning through it like crazy, and ran out before they could build a big enough audience and then monetise it", Chung says. In TNL's first Taipei office they used cheap or hand-me-down furniture, and in its second the ceiling leaked when it rained, and when they branched out to Hong Kong there was no office at all at first. "When you're lean, it forces you to focus", says Chung. The only exception was salaries, but even then TNL avoided hiring costly big-time journalists. The first major name was TV news star Jennifer Shen, who hosted a livestreaming show for the outlet in 2017.

One thing Chung has been grateful for is the support of co-founder Yang, who takes complete responsibility for the media content. "I always joke that his job is to make sure that the dream survives, and my job is to make sure the dream has dinner on the table tomorrow", he says. The core DNA of the company is always going to be the media business, he goes on, but the bulk of the revenue will come from the complementary tech services and data analysis platforms. It's been an exhausting process, Chung says, but today TNL is in its fifth (more salubrious) office and is planning to move to a sixth, while its small staff of the early days have become 215 in both Taipei and Hong Kong. On the horizon now is finishing Series D and moving towards IPO. No definite predictions, but the underwriter is already on board.

TAIWAN

The Reporter

The "received wisdom" in entrepreneurial journalism is that you can't earn enough to survive from in-depth and investigative content. Stories are costly and time-consuming to produce and rarely attract paying advertisers. Also, it's difficult to build up enough of a reputation to persuade audiences to pay – least of all the elusive younger generation, who are supposed only to respond to short videos, memes and listicles and pay for them through catchy ads or influencer sales. But Taiwan's The Reporter has shown that a serious journalism outlet not only can succeed on donations alone, but can attract younger readers too.

The site is part of The Reporter Cultural Foundation, set up on Reporter's Day

FIGURE 7.28 Sherry Lee Hsueh-li. Supplied by Sherry Lee Hsueh-li.

(1 September) 2015 by former *China Times* editor and first president of the Association of Taiwan Journalists Ho Jung-shin, who became CEO. He brought in Sherry Lee Hsueh-li, a long-time journalist with *Commonwealth* magazine and its first Beijing correspondent, as deputy CEO, and the two of them invited ten more board members from professional fields – academia, law, NGOs, media and enterprise management. Then they launched The Reporter itself later that year as Taiwan's first nonprofit media outlet. Such was the promise of this setup that even before starting it secured a no-strings donation, via the Foundation, of NT$90 million (about US$3.2 million) spread over three years from Tung Tzu-hsien, founder of Asus computers and owner of the Pegatron electronics business.

Even though The Reporter was already financially viable, the founders still debated over the new publication's positioning in Taiwan's highly competitive media market, where many daily news providers were going all out to get clicks. According to Lee, who is also The Reporter's editor-in-chief, they decided that the main goal should not be popularity but quality journalism. "We thought we should have our focus on, and we should be confident to do, investigative reporting because we felt the audience had the need."

And The Reporter has come up with the goods. By 2021 it had won 55 local and international awards for journalism excellence. That in turn has allowed the publication to pursue its second source of funding – reader donations. By the end of the first year they had 300 regular donors, building to more than 2,000 in early 2020; after the addition of podcasts that August, the number bumped up to 4,400, with 7,000 donors in all. "If you give the public a very good article, a very good project, when we deliver the project they will see the influence and donate", says Lee. Readers' contributions now total NT$20 million a year (US$714,000), providing 40 per cent of the publication's income.

Unusually, the preponderance of The Reporter's audience and supporters are under 35. Lee puts this youth appeal down to what she calls "new media imagination". While stories are generally lengthy – 3,000–8,000 characters – they also incorporate attractive multimedia features such as video games and motion graphics. Readers were soon sharing these stories as much as they did shorter items on news sites. In 2018 a "Mini Reporter" feature was added to appeal to the younger generation with articles of around 1,000 characters about popular science and knowledge to give hardcore facts at a time when fake news was taking a firm grip. The new podcasting service was another success, so popular it went straight to the top tier of Google's rankings.

What put The Reporter on the map was an investigative story done in its first year. The team had learned about the terrible abuse of Indonesian forced workers in the Taiwan fishing industry – one man had actually died – and spent five months investigating the situation in collaboration with Indonesia's respected *Tempo* magazine. At the time, Lee says, she worried endlessly that they were putting too much effort and money into something that might not be well received. The story, "Slavery at sea, the exploitation of the far sea fishing industry", was put together as a striking online multimedia product. It appeared on their site on its first anniversary, and was also republished by the major mainstream outlet *Apple Daily*.

Lee needn't have worried. The effect was "like a bomb", she says. Taiwan's legislators and officials were so shocked that they pressured the government to change conditions in the industry. The story won multiple honours from the Society of Publishers in Asia (SOPA) and a Human Rights Award. And readers started pouring money in spontaneously. "We didn't push them to donate, we didn't say anything", says Lee. Sixty new regular donors signed up in the days following the appearance of the story. Soon after this, The Reporter became the first Chinese-language outlet to join the Global Investigative Journalism Network, which undertakes international investigations through the network of its members worldwide.

While the big story had been brewing, Lee had been working on promoting the outlet. The first effort was an attractive video clip featuring nine celebrities – who volunteered their services, Lee emphasises – stating on camera they were fans of The Reporter and why they liked reading it. Then in 2016 and 2017 the team started doing roadshows, hiring coffee shop venues in major cities where their journalists covering the locality came to talk directly to their audience. The public appearances have continued since then with the reporters sharing their experiences in cafés and bookstores across Taiwan as well as on radio shows. Taiwan's avoidance of the coronavirus epidemic has allowed these events to keep going.

The Reporter's audience are "very intellectual young people" who are interested in big issues like the environment and human rights, says Lee. Fifty-five per cent of the site's readers are women (though 55 per cent of its podcast listeners are men). The principled stand of the outlet doesn't seem to have filtered out to a wide audience yet, though, with Reuters' 2020 digital news survey placing it at the bottom of the top 15 list of most trusted media in Taiwan, with only 21 per cent of respondents saying they trusted it – but then only 15 per cent said they didn't trust it, the majority neither trusting nor not trusting (Newman 2020). That probably just reflects the fact that its audience is still a relatively small group of digital-savvy people. "On the internet we are very famous", says Lee. "But in the real world most people don't understand and don't know The Reporter." The challenge is "to get the virtual and the real world together and to make the connection".

The Reporter's method of getting its small but loyal audience to pay is through its "ding si ding er" – regular donation – scheme (Lee emphasises that it is not membership or subscription, purely donations). Anyone can give any amount they like as a one-off or repeated payment, but the scheme allows them to sign up for three tiers of regular payment – NT$1,000 (US$35) a month, NT$500 a month or NT$300 a month. The most expensive includes two books the outlet has put out in collaboration with local publishers, plus two notebooks, a canvas bag and free entry to activities, and the less costly ones have correspondingly fewer perks. The huge boost in donor numbers after the addition of podcasting is a sign that The Reporter is becoming more widely known, says Lee. "That means we are breaking our echo chambers and reaching out to more readers."

Even the smallest donation is treasured. "Every time when the money comes in, no matter whether it's NT$10 or NT$2,000, or a regular donor giving only NT$300 a month, I feel overwhelmed by this kind of passion," Lee says. "It's that people really feel the importance of your existence and they really read your articles." However, all donors have to understand that their funds are accepted on a "three no's" basis – "no intervention, no ownership, and no return". The donor can have no influence over or role in the publication and the amount is non-refundable. The outlet rejects donations from politicians and money offered to produce specific stories, and any amount over NT$1 million (just under US$33,000) has to be examined by the Foundation's board.

Tung Tzu-hsien has continued to be the outlet's financial anchor. At the end of the initial three-year period, in 2018, "he appreciated our work and achievements", says Lee, and he made a second commitment of the same amount for the next three years. Tung is one of the few "charity entrepreneurs" in Taiwan, she goes on, and his interest in media goes back to his youth, when he wrote for and edited his school newspaper and harboured an ambition to be a reporter. It was he who established the "three no's" rule, applied first to himself: "He does not participate in the board of directors, he does not intervene in the editing desk, and he will not reclaim his donations", Lee says. "This has set an example for [our] donors, allowing reporters to make news independently without being influenced by sponsors."

Tung's support has given The Reporter the opportunity to expand. It has a lot more content than before, most notably the successful podcasting service, which is called The Real Story. Also newsroom staff have increased from 25 to 31 – 12 are journalists, 4 (including Lee) are editors at various levels, 3 are art designers, 3 are software engineers, and 3 work on photos. With the site publishing at least three in-depth articles a day, it relies on outsourced contributions from another team: 80 to 90 freelancers and columnists, many of them aspiring young journalists. This is somewhat like the Huffington Post model, but these contributors get "decent" pay, according to Lee, as well as feedback on their work and invitations to seminars and training sessions. The Reporter, she says, is dedicated to contributing whatever it can within its means to educating a new cohort of professionals adept at multimedia storytelling.

What of the future? With The Reporter expanding its products and audience, and with all those awards in hand, Lee is expecting Tung to continue his donation after the current three-year period has ended. However, she hopes too to diversify the donation pool with more "big angels", as well as increase its regular donations.

SINGAPORE

TheSmartLocal

"The thing that has set us apart is our ideation", says Bryan Choo, founder and managing director of Singapore travel and lifestyle outlet TheSmartLocal (TSL). "To convey any message, you first need attention", he goes on. "Ideas give you attention." It's not easy: you need to work hard and be persistent. "Content is always changing, so ideation requires constant calibration," says Choo. That means constant experimentation, and that in turn means mistakes are bound to happen. But you should take errors in your stride, Choo advises: "Just calibrate and always have the mindset that there is still a lot you don't know".

FIGURE 7.29 Bryan Choo. Supplied by Bryan Choo.

That focus and philosophy have taken TSL from a tiny review publication started from Choo's Singapore bedroom in 2012 to a multi-platform, multinational set of hyperlocal outlets with a staff of 150. The sites attract more than a million unique visitors a month and hundreds of thousands of social media followers, most of them millennials. Choo has never been a journalist, and his qualifications – a degree in finance – and skills – he is a champion gamer who used to run a gaming site and has been an events organiser for games companies – aren't the obvious ones for a media boss. But they give him business savvy and tech knowhow, along with the inspiration needed to find ideas that the younger generation are interested in.

The business driver for most media startups is advertising, he says: "It is the same concept as mobile games – a good amount of them are 'free-to-play', which is great for the user, but the price of that is the ads that come with the games". The ad model underpins all four media companies Choo now runs under the TSL Media umbrella – the other three being "wholesome news and current affairs" outlet MustShareNews (opened in 2014), food blog Eatbook.sg (2015) and women's site Zula.sg (2016). The popular MustShareNews, which gets by far the most traffic with 100 million page views a year, does well from display ads, but for the other three branded content is the main earner. "The beauty of branded content ... is that it allows you to create content that can still add value for readers and not look like an ad", says Choo.

Choo has invested a lot in the all-important ideation process that makes the site's branded content stand out. Nearly all work is done in-house, with 70 per cent of staff assigned to content production. A dedicated ideation team comes up with the bright ideas and then a production team carries them out, calibrating to make sure they are in tune with the young users TSL wants to attract. "The reader experience with TSL is less jarring [than other sites] as our ads are more aligned with our audience," says Choo. Content sponsors include "government agencies from various countries as well as many major MNCs", Choo says, because "the biggest demographic they have trouble reaching is our demographic – the millennials".

The style of TSL's content is very much localised BuzzFeed-type listicles ("10 Singlish words and phrases with origin stories you didn't expect"), many clearly sponsored ("9 aesthetically pleasing IKEA kids items from $7.90 for your child's bedroom"), and there is a TSL YouTube channel with videos of young people doing fun things (it has more than a quarter of a million subscribers). Choo sees one of the outfit's main competitors as SGAG, another local site that puts out memes, videos and listicles – though he says the two companies get on well (they actually shared office space overseas before the coronavirus). The formula has worked so well that in 2019 TSL set up versions of itself for Thailand, Malaysia, the Philippines, Vietnam and Indonesia.

Choo started the outlet on income from his earlier business and has received Singapore government startup fund grants, though won't say how much they amount to. He says TSL has been profitable from day one, but again is reluctant to give any figures. An interview done with him by a local blogger quoted him as saying the company had made "> a million dollars" in 2015 and was making double that in the next year (Tan n.d.).

As TSL has diversified, so too have its means of making an income. The site boasts 14 different revenue streams, including regional marketing, event organisation, workshops and custom publishing. The company started e-commerce in 2020. It has also added new service brands: Wiki.sg, a version of Wikipedia for Singapore; InsightsRN, which does data analytics; TSLoffice.com, which provides HR and project management technology; and promotional outlet TelegramCo, which offers deals to its 350,000 followers. The company has never had outside investment but Choo has recently started looking. "We are open to listening to any investment/acquisition opportunities, and have shared our investor deck with big name global and local players who have sought us out", says the TSL site. "If the right offer comes along, we'll be interested to discuss terms." Choo has no plans for subscription or membership. "Content should always be free so you can reach the largest audience", he says.

TSL steers clear of politics and news, and so hasn't been required to register for a licence with the Infocomm Media Development Authority. To the question of whether TSL is doing journalism or content or marketing, Choo says: "We are a lifestyle/entertainment brand. We aren't trying to do investigative journalism or tackle politics. We produce light-hearted and positive content."

If TSL has anything to worry about in the long term, it's the aging of its users. The millennial audience who loved it from the start have stuck with it, taking the average age upwards – now pushing into their mid-20s and 30s. To keep going, Choo says, the outlet needs to capture the next age group down, Generation Z, the people who are growing up on social media and may not be interested in reading content. He is capturing this audience by expanding current platforms – the website, YouTube, Facebook, Instagram – and into TikTok, the latter already having 70,000-plus followers.

Choo acknowledges that it's getting tougher to get into the media business. Social media's algorithm tweaking makes it ever harder to get traffic organically (i.e., free), and, with many businesses already up and running for years, the competition is fierce. With four thriving media brands already under his belt, Choo sees the best route to success as coming from starting a new company. "However", he says, "you need a truly differentiated product with a demand or it will not be easy". He points to new brands like The Woke Salaryman, which uses cartoons to educate Singaporeans on how to make good decisions on life and finance, as an example of a site that uses innovative content and ideation to "serve an underrepresented finance market on social media through relatable comics and clever storytelling". As a media entrepreneur, you need to create content that stands out, he says. "Do it once and you have viral content. Do it consistently and you have a brand."

THAILAND

The Standard

The Standard was launched in 2017. Inspired by American digital pioneers HuffPost, Business Insider, Vox and VICE, its market positioning was "creative" news for young urban adults – political, business and sports stories with an edge, though with a strong emphasis on being unbiased and trustworthy. Four years on, not only is the outlet wildly popular but it has sprouted three new verticals: one for lifestyle (aimed at "Gen Z"), one for business and finance and one for podcasts. The latter, developed out of the site's focus on podcasting from the very beginning, has been a huge success: it gets 20 million downloads a month. 20 million!

FIGURE 7.30 Nakarin "Ken" Wanakijpaibul. Photo credit: Author.

The outlet had a single initial investment, was already in the black in its first year and has been profitable ever since. What are its secrets?

It has to be acknowledged first that The Standard didn't appear out of nowhere but came from a thoroughbred bloodline in modern media terms. Way back in 2000, two of its owners co-founded Thailand's first younger-generation lifestyle monthly magazine, a free-sheet with the unusual name of A Day. The pair, Wongthanong Chainarongsing (nicknamed Hnong, and known as "Hnong A Day") and Nitipath Suksuay (nicknamed Pingpong), developed the publication under the umbrella of their company, Day Poets, and expanded it over the years to produce A Day Bulletin – the "urban current magazine", also free – and entertainment outlet Hamburger, among others.

In 2015, A Day caught up with the times and set up a digital-only news site called The Momentum. Within a year, however, a dispute broke out when some Day Poets shareholders wanted to put the company up for sale. Hnong and Pingpong disagreed but didn't prevail, and eventually resolved the situation by leaving. Along with them went many A Day staff along with all those from The Momentum, some 80 people in all, including Momentum executive editor Nakarin Wanakijpaibul, known as Ken. The decision to leave Day Poets was a matter of principle for the owners, says Ken: "They feared if it went on the market they would lose control and have no independence". He joined Hnong and Pingpong in co-founding The Standard in March 2017 and became its chief editor. As for Day Poets, it didn't get sold and runs The Momentum to this day. The separation was quite a scandal at the time, evoking a lot of support for the leavers and giving the new publication a boost.

However, lineage is far from The Standard's only reason for success. It stepped up with a whole new take on the news. "We try to make the serious issues sexier, to be more attractive to the readers", says Ken. "We have four pillars of DNA – the 'four I's': first is insightful, second is inspiring, third is intellectual, and the last is intimate." Every story has to contain all four. Another factor is its look and feel, which are very different from other Thai media. Taking its cue from western digital outlets, the site has a clickable menu of short and long articles with the main points of each listed alongside plus the time needed to read them. And its design is different too, using clever graphics to bring the stories alive – for which Ken gives a nod of appreciation to Hong Kong's *South China Morning Post*. "We focus on infographics a lot, five or six pieces per day, from sport to world politics to business", he says. Moreover, the site is designed for mobile first, acknowledging the viewing preference of today's audience.

Ken has been the power behind the policy of diversification into specialist sections. The first emerged from the realisation that the site was getting a lot of hits from the 25+ age bracket but not so many from teens and early 20s. "This group are interested in culture, K-pop, lifestyle, they want to go out and have entertainment", says Ken. So in 2018 The Standard Pop was set up to focus on this kind of content. Pop now not only gets more than 5 million UVM to its site and its Facebook and Instagram pages, it has helped boost visits by its young fans to the main news site. Then in 2020, as the coronavirus spread, Ken identified a need for a business outlet. "Thai consumers wanted to invest more because COVID-19 shows that you cannot just deposit money in a bank account and you have to invest in the stock market or something else, right?" he says. Inspired by the likes of Bloomberg, The Standard Wealth came into existence late that year and was soon getting attention.

A couple of months later, at the start of 2021, The Standard Podcast was set up, formalising the site's already established place in the field. Ken puts down its spectacular success to being the earliest to start on podcasting in Thailand. "If you compare to social media ... podcasts are one of the rising stars, and we were the first mover in this market, so we could gain audience because they stuck to us first." The 15 podcasts a week cover topics for all their audiences – business, lifestyle, English lessons, health and wellness among them.

The Standard's initial investment was Baht 30 million (about US$1 million) from a businessman (who wants to remain anonymous) who liked what they were doing. He is the third owner of the company, along with Hnong and Pingpong. For this investor, says Ken, the amount is a drop in the ocean and he is not in it to make money. He also takes no part in the running of the outlet – in fact Ken has a plea many editors in his position would envy: "I want him to be involved more!"

The goal at the start was to rely on advertising for an income, and the company set up its own in-house production department – something completely new for Thai media. The team produces advertorials and sponsored content highly customised to clients. This allowed The Standard to get premium advertising for a mass audience, putting it on its fast track to profit. But the rule is that all advertising is clearly labelled as such. "I think integrity is one of the keys", Ken says. "We try to be sincere to our readers, so every content item that is an advertorial, we will mark it and you can see it obviously, advertorial." And if the editors don't like an advertisement they reject it. Ken works closely with the advertising team so that he can ensure that the company's branding is properly maintained.

After the first year they wanted to explore new revenue sources. Ken would like to have put up a paywall, but knew that Thais weren't willing to pay for news. "Everything is free – television, newspapers, everything online is free for them," says Ken. "They don't want to buy content – this is not our culture." So the next move was to organise events. The Standard set up workshops, masterclasses and even a mini-marathon, which was sponsored by an insurance company. Packages were offered to advertisers that included advertorials and sponsored podcasts along with the event itself. "I think it's the new way to sell", said Ken. It also allowed The Standard to reach out to readers in person.

When the coronavirus put paid to in-person gatherings in 2020, The Standard didn't miss a beat. In February it set up The Standard Economic Forum to put on virtual conferences. The first featured a variety of well-known speakers talking about "the new normal", a topic expected to pique interest. Tickets were put up for sale, the first time the outlet had sought income directly from the audience, and nearly 4,000 people bought them – many more than could have attended at a real venue. That revenue, along with sponsorship, resulted in a healthy profit, which in turn led to ten more virtual conferences put on for advertisers. Ten per cent of The Standard's income now comes from events.

The expansion has seen an increase in staff to 120. They are based in a modern, airy, four-storey office in the trendy RCA district of Bangkok, setting the tone of the publication. It has plenty of desk space, large meeting rooms and even beds for people who want to stay overnight. But very few come from a journalism background. Ken himself trained as a pharmacist and doesn't even call himself a journalist. The outlet hasn't joined the Thai Journalists Association, though Ken says he gets invited to speak at its events. The team of 15 doing journalism work are called "content creators" and only a couple have formal journalism training; the rest come from a range of backgrounds – architecture, political science, law and liberal arts. The main thing, says Ken, is that they must have passion because journalism isn't a respected job in Thailand and can get you into trouble. "They have to want to tell the stories they feel, stand up for the people", he says. "For me, it's a job that can make an impact on society, on the country. That's why I'm here."

Despite a sometimes cheeky take on political news, little trouble came their way. However, in October 2020, during the anti-monarchy protests in Bangkok, The Standard was one of four local media threatened with closure. Ken received a letter from the Ministry of Digital Economy & Society saying the site would be shut down. "At the time it was very difficult for us", he says. Three days later he got called in for a meeting only to be told it was all a mistake. He speculates on why the outlet was singled out. "Our audience is … young urban adults, the same group as the protesters", he says. "So maybe our government thought that we supported the protests. But it's not true." Ken emphasises that their coverage was balanced and unbiased – and if officials did try to close them their supporters would be very angry.

Perhaps that experience coloured already-brewing plans for the future. The site's legions of podcast fans have set Ken thinking about a new revenue stream. "They listen to us not just to inform or just to inspire themselves, but they listen to us because they look at us as a solution", he says. He himself hosts a podcast called Secret Sauce, where he interviews business owners who talk about the secrets of their success. He noticed how keen listeners were to learn. "Our audience wants to engage with us, wants to know more, not just knowledge, not just information – they want wisdom", he says. So he has set up an experimental event called the Secret Sauce Club, which people can join to learn leadership skills, the idea being to educate rather than just entertain them.

He hopes to create more in the same vein. "We're trying to reimagine ourselves as not just a media company", he goes on. So the plan is to develop an education hub providing events, workshops, talks, seminars, books and classes in areas where they have expertise – something they hope people will eventually pay for, as with the first virtual conference. "This model can generate more revenue and build us more trust," says Ken. One of the planned subjects: podcasting. "Everyone wants to do a podcast, right?"

The outlet's success has led to Ken being promoted to managing director, with Hnong and Pingpong still in charge but stepping back a little from day-to-day operations. It has also brought forth a host of VCs wanting to invest. But they have all been rejected in favour of going it alone. "I think we're not ready", says

Ken. "If you look at our financial model or our balance sheet we're doing very well, so we'll try to expand gradually, not too fast."

CAMBODIA

Thmey Thmey

In 1992, a year after the Paris Peace Accords officially ended the long-running conflict in Cambodia, the government of the former colonial power, France, set up programmes to restore the French language. One project was a course for journalists at the Royal University of Phnom Penh (RUPP), which was later incorporated as an elective into the French language undergraduate programme. Accomplished professionals graduated, ready for jobs at the government TV station's French programming department and in local French-language publications, which were provided with a little support from the French government's organisation to promote the use of French round the world.

FIGURE 7.31 Ky Soklim. Photo credit: Author.

However, by the 2000s it was clear that Cambodia's international language was English, and French no longer had much traction. In 2009, the last French publication, the respected *Cambodge Soir* (Cambodia Evening) newspaper, closed. The only remaining French outlet is Radio France Internationale (RFI), but its local broadcasts – still highly regarded – are in Khmer, not French. It says a lot for the high quality of the graduates of the French degree that, faced with a complete lack of the jobs they were trained for, they were able to transfer their skills to Cambodian and international outlets.

But two veterans of the RUPP programme and the French media took a different route. They decided to set up a news outlet of their own, one which would be predominantly in Khmer but have companion sites in French, English and Japanese. Ky Soklim and Leang Delux founded Thmey Thmey ("New New") Online News in 2012, along with a former senior RFI journalist, Pen Bona, though he soon dropped out to become editor-in-chief at a new TV outfit. They invited a third colleague with a French background, Ung Chamroeun, then at the *Phnom Penh Post*, to become editor-in-chief. The company was opened under one owned by their investor, Cambodian-American doctor, educator and businessman Mengly J. Quach, and was registered with the Information and Commerce Ministries. Mengly had no influence over the editorial operation, but he helped find advertisers and sat on the board with the three journalists.

Given their French connections and the fact that many respected media in Cambodia had been started by foreigners, they saw a gap in the market. "We decided to set up a newspaper in a neutral way with Cambodian journalists, with Cambodian perceptions, Cambodian ideas, targeting the Cambodian public and foreign public", says Soklim, now the outlet's senior journalist. True to their professional background, they eschewed the eyeball-catching diet of crime, gore and scandal favoured by the mainstream media. They focused instead on publishing quality news and analytical articles covering society and trends, sometimes with a critical element, and presenting them in text and video.

The aim is to be balanced, a foil to outlets close to the government like Fresh News. They pride themselves on having decision-makers and officials among their readers – even Prime Minister Hun Sen apparently reads their news because they have detected Thmey Thmey information in his speeches. They are careful not to openly attack anyone, and couch their criticism in soft, diplomatic language, which Soklim thinks the government accepts. Their efforts have earned some respect from their colleagues. In a 2017 survey of local journalists, Thmey Thmey was considered among the most independent local media; RFI came top and Fresh News came bottom (CCIM, 2017).

Being frugal was the key to getting through their initial stages. Soklim called Mengly the "money investor", while he and his senior colleagues were "intellectual investors" because they were happy to take low pay. "If we worked for other media outlets, maybe we'd get a big salary, but here we don't want to get much, just ok to survive," he says. Their office is in a small sports complex next to gym rooms with a swimming pool downstairs. It's owned by a friend who charges a reasonable rent. They have 14 editorial staff and three technicians working there. Things became difficult when Mengly pulled out in 2017 to set up his own TV station. He had up to that point been making up any losses on a monthly basis. The outlet had just about been breaking even, though the bottom line had been stretched by the hiring of new journalists. But they managed to bring in new shareholders – senior journalists and overseas friends. They don't want to be identified publicly.

Thmey Thmey's main income comes from advertisements, though its good reputation hasn't necessarily helped. "Getting advertising is easy for those who try to get support from politicians, but for us we want to make our website professional", says Chamroeun. Still, they attract a good amount of banner ads as well as what Soklim calls advertorials – native or sponsored advertising. They either keep the paid content in a separate section labelled "commercial" or clearly display their sponsor's name, such as Mercedes Benz in the motoring section. They encourage their journalists, who are forbidden to take the cash handouts event organisers routinely offer, to make connections with companies who will sponsor content, for which they get a cut of the resulting income.

The editors have found some original ideas to expand the site's audience. One popular feature is their cartoons, which cover politics, society and "everything", says Soklim. Another is a column to help readers improve their Khmer, a response to their perception that people's knowledge of their own language's grammar has weakened since English became used for business. One column became popular for its critical content – it used as a substitute for "Cambodia" the term "romdoul country", the romdoul being a flower that symbolises Cambodia, and the phrase meaning a place where the government does "wrong things".

They have also strived to appeal to people nationwide. With a subsidy from the French Foreign Ministry's media support outfit CFI they have designed their app so that it can be used in every province and they have provided training for rural reporters (CFI 6 September 2018). To this they've added a campaign to bring local vocabulary into their writing to get on board new readers from those localities. "If you write [in local] dialect in Battambang", Cambodia's second city, says Soklim, "the people in Battambang see that and they share. It's a kind of marketing."

The site, which publishes 35–40 articles a day reported by their staff or from other sources such as Xinhua and *China Daily*, has an average of 20,000 unique visitors per day, and its Facebook page boasts nearly 800,000 followers. Facebook has been the key to getting their content shared, and their page on the social media outlet is very important to them. They have in the past paid to boost their posted articles, but decided to stop because they were already getting a lot of attention.

In 2019 they launched the planned English-language site. Called Cambodianess, it is put together by two new foreign staff and some freelancers. It uses stories translated from the Khmer site and some from international news agencies Agence France Presse and Xinhua, and runs a section with branded content. The French and Japanese versions have yet to appear. Thmey Thmey has also published two books.

INDONESIA

Tirto

Sapto Anggoro has been involved in entrepreneurial journalism from way back. Since the 1990s, he has been part of three media startups, and on the way has also set up with his partners a successful data monitoring business. Today he's head of Tirto.id, the respected investigative journalism site he launched in 2016. His long career reflects the ups and downs of Indonesia's media in the digital age.

He grew up in Jombang, East Java, and did a journalism degree in Surabaya, graduating in 1990. He joined the local newspaper there as a reporter and later

FIGURE 7.32 Sapto Anggoro. Supplied by Sapto Anggoro.

moved to Jakarta to work for the long-established *Republika* newspaper. In 1998, the media were suddenly freed up after the fall of long-time president Suharto, and Detik, a paper set up as an investigative outlet in 1992 but banned in 1994, was relaunched as an online-only site, the pioneer of digital news in Indonesia. Sapto was brought on board as vice chief editor by one of the founders, Budiono Darsono.

Detik.com survived by itself for more than a decade, but in 2011 was bought out by local megabusinessman Chairul Tanjung's CT Corp. The outlet's top journalists quit in droves. Budiono and others eventually went on to set up the hybrid news-and-social-media outlet Kumparan in 2016, supported by local investors and today one of Indonesia's most popular platforms. But Sapto and two other Detik colleagues, Teguh Budi Santoso and Nur Samsi, had already started a move into a different side of the journalism business.

"We had a new idea, a new dream, not to be just publishers, we wanted to move to become entrepreneurs", says Sapto. In 2010, the three had set up Binokular (as its name suggests, it means "binoculars"), a media monitoring business providing services for paying clients. Its speciality was social media monitoring, using an artificial intelligence language program to find out for corporate customers what was being said about them on popular platforms, giving them insights into how to improve themselves as well as how to beat the competition. It was an immediate success – and still is: "From when we started until now, Binokular has never been in the red, always in the black", Sapto says.

Even so, he was persuaded back into the news business by Steve Christian, CEO of the news portal KapanLagi, started in 2003 but at that point launching new verticals. According to Sapto, Christian asked him to set up a new news site called Merdeka.com (Independence). Sapto took up the challenge and launched the outlet in 2012 into an increasingly crowded online scene. However, history repeated itself: in 2015, KapanLagi was bought out by the Singapore government's MediaCorp. Sapto wasn't happy to "share" Merdeka with the new owner, he says, and wanted to do something different instead. "I offered my idea, which was in-depth content, investigative reporting, to my partner, Mr Steve Christian, but he didn't like our proposal", says Sapto. He guesses Christian probably thought it too expensive.

So Sapto exited Merdeka (KapanLagi and its subsidiaries were sold to local conglomerate Emtek in 2018) and went ahead with his two Binokular partners to launch his proposed outlet independently in 2016, calling it Tirto.id. "We think the Indonesian online digital scene has too many media with just upbeat news and breaking news", says Sapto, among them the long-established magazine *Tempo* and daily paper *Kompas*, as well as Detik.com. They were all doing the job very well but none had much in-depth coverage. "We think Indonesia needs … investigative reporting", Sapto says, "because one of the functions of the media is to control the government".

The name Tirto has two derivations. It is Sanskrit for water or liquid, and the significance of this is that the site's work can be fluid and not confined by established perceptions. Then it is also a tribute to Tirto Adhi Soerjo, a journalist active in the late 19th and early 20th centuries who established several newspapers and resisted Dutch rule; he died in his 30s in 1918 but was recognised as a national hero in 2006. Tirto "made the media deliver content quality so that it can be insightful for the people, especially for the local people in Indonesia", says Sapto. The new outlet aimed to do just the same, he goes on: "We have the soul of Mr Tirto Adhi Soerjo". The country suffix ".id" adds the Indonesian identity to the official name. Tirto.id is not following an easy path, Sapto says, "because many people tell us that the millionaires don't like our in-depth content, but it is our challenge".

Sapto is the outfit's CEO and chief editor, Teguh is COO and Nur Samsi is CTO, all three of them having a share in the company. Tirto.id has close links with the already successful Binokular, which acts as its "back end" for data, according to Sapto, but the two remain separate companies. Binokular is still owned by the three partners and a fourth, a local company which Sapto will not identify but says holds 5 per cent of shares, while Tirto.id has issued a convertible bond to the same company. The three partners are still shareholders but no longer majority owners.

Tirto.id has a staff of more than 100 to process the 40–60 stories it publishes every day. It has a section on news called Current Issues just to keep up with the news, but the rest diverges from the usual. Jelajah ("Explorer") features one of the site's specialities, fact-checking – Tirto.id has been certified by the International Fact-Checking Network. Meanwhile, its main "selling point", as Sapto puts it, is Mild Report, which, far from being mild, has business insider stories unpublished elsewhere. The section has an enthusiastic readership and clients are happy to place advertising there. But what has made Tirto.id famous is the InDepth section, which features data journalism. The outlet subscribes to Binokular for its raw data as well as to other services including Statista. A team of six researchers seeks out content from these and other sources, and eight journalists follow up with reporting and interviews. Each week they work on two themes and produce three to five investigative stories on each, presenting them with multimedia and animation. "Infographics are our strength", says Sapto.

They have produced some major stories. In 2017 they revealed that dredgers belonging to a China-based operation were being used to cut up and remove dozens of World War II shipwrecks in Southeast Asian waters for scrap metal. This caused great consternation to the western countries the ships belonged to and the story was picked up by international media. The main company involved protested to President Joko Widodo, resulting in Sapto getting a phone call from an official asking him to hand over Tirto.id's sources to the police. He refused. "The data, the raw material data, it's owned by me, by Tirto", he says. "We cannot share it with the police." The same year Tirto.id republished an article from The Intercept by investigative journalist Alan Nairn which said that Indonesian associates of Donald Trump were conspiring with Islamic gangs and army officers to overthrow President Widodo. Trump's main business partner complained to the Indonesian Press Council and Tirto.id was ordered to apologise, but efforts to sue failed because the article had originally appeared elsewhere.

Tirto.id's engagement rate is very high – according to Sapto, up to 7,000 people open a story within a day of its posting on the site. Since the site's fare is on the serious side, people think it is for older folk, he goes on, but he was surprised (and pleased) to find from Google Analytics that 60 per cent of readers were millennials. Less surprising, given the long and complex stories published, was that 80 per cent were university-educated, and nearly half were in "greater Jakarta" – the capital and its surrounding towns. One appeal to younger users may be the sophisticated infographics, which help stories spread on Instagram, where Tirto.id has 1 million followers.

Tirto.id's business operation is based on advertising, including what Sapto, in a harkback to the old days, calls "the advertorial model". The weekly themes provide the field and the editorial team creates sponsored content for advertisers, including infographics, all clearly labelled and usually placed in the Mild Report section. Sapto gives as an example a story done on the history of Samsung where the company supplied the raw information – he was bemused to find the Korean giant had started out as a fruit seller – and Tirto.id journalists wrote it up and got it checked by the company. Then the outlet also takes display advertisements alongside.

Tirto has yet to make a profit and Sapto has been looking for a new investor. This is difficult because the outlet not only has risky content but is a high-cost operation. "It's challenging for us", he says. He has been considering subscriptions – in Indonesia only print outlets *The Jakarta Post* and *Kompas* have them so far – but on the lines of the freemium model, that is, putting the high-quality stories behind a paywall. He thinks things will work out anyway. "We should be optimists … with the business and the model of content we have chosen", he says. He has faith an investor will eventually appear.

What Sapto hopes for most is that Tirto.id will inspire other media, making them ask, "Why are we not like Tirto?" What's important, he says, is not so much the investigative work but keeping a clear mind and staying independent. "In my humble opinion, we have a dream, we have hope for the future that we should be the legacy in media in Indonesia", he says. "Tirto is not just … content … or journalism, but Tirto, we hope, can be part of the new civilisation of trust of Indonesia."

THE PHILIPPINES

VERA Files

Every media outlet strives to be truthful, but truth alone doesn't pay the rent. In the Philippines, VERA Files turns that idea on its head. "Vera" means "true" in Latin, and the nonprofit was set up to tell the truth through its investigative reporting, getting its income from project grants. Since 2016, a big part of that funding has come from its sponsored work as a fact-checker of Philippine news. While reliance on grants may go against the grain for journalism entrepreneurs, fake news is a huge issue and verifying what's true and what isn't may well turn out to be at least a medium-term job and even a viable business model in the long run. The small but high-profile outlet's motto, "Truth is our business", is literally true.

FIGURE 7.33   Ellen Tordesillas. Supplied by Ellen Tordesillas.

It would be hard to find a more illustrious group of journalists than VERA Files's six founders, some of whose careers date back to Ferdinand Marcos's martial law régime in the 1980s. Ellen Tordesillas, president of the Board of Trustees, started out in those days as an education reporter for the alternative newspaper *Ang Pahayangan Malaya* ("The Free Newspaper"), which became mainstream after Marcos's unceremonious ouster in 1986. Yvonne T. Chua also worked for the same paper, among others, and is now an associate professor at the prestigious University of the Philippines's College of Mass Communication (UP CMC). The others were print and broadcast journalist Booma Cruz, who managed the TV show Probe; long-time editor "Chit" Estella, who also taught at UP; TV reporter Luz Rimban, who is today director of the Asian Center for Journalism at another top university, Ateneo de Manila; and Jennifer Santiago of the *Philippine Daily Inquirer*. Chua, Rimban and Santiago have left VERA Files, while Estella died in a traffic accident in 2011, a tragedy that took the publication into road safety promotion in a project supported by the World Health Organization and Bloomberg.

FIGURE 7.34   VERA Files logo. Supplied by Ellen Tordesillas.

The group got to know each other as reporters working on the same beats. In 2008 they were at a stage in their careers, says Tordesillas, where they felt they had benefited from the profession and wanted to give something back. Money had never been their reason for entering journalism, and it was the same when they set up VERA Files in 2008. "We wanted to do more in-depth reporting, which cannot be done in mainstream media", says Tordesillas. "We also wanted to help in promoting excellence in journalism in the Philippines." Their original plan was to set up a magazine like *George*, the glossy political magazine put out by the late John F. Kennedy Jr. in the US, but they couldn't secure financing.

They already had stories ready to go, however, so, meeting over coffee and cakes, they decided to put up a website. They wanted their name to include "truth" – "because that's what journalism is all about: truth-telling", says Tordesillas – and they plumped for the Latin version of the word, vera. They pooled their own funds (a "minimal" amount, says Tordesillas) to launch, using the money mainly to pay for registration as a nonprofit with the Securities & Exchange Commission. They had no office at first, meeting instead in restaurants. They sold their stories to other publications, but that didn't bring in much. "I think we were paying more for our meals than the fees we were charging for our articles!" laughs Tordesillas. They all kept their day jobs and paid their own expenses while producing stories for the site.

So they still needed to find an income to keep going. It was going to be hard to go the commercial route with their investigative and critical journalism. They did consider ads but were wary of conflict of interest, and they weren't keen on sponsored content for the same reason, says Tordesillas. So they started looking for grants. The Asia Foundation (TAF), a US funder (see pp. 81–82), was their first big supporter, giving them financing for a multi-year project on Reporting on Persons With Disabilities, with which the Australian embassy in Manila also helped out. The British Embassy gave them a grant to conduct investigative journalism training for NGOs. The American media training organisation Internews also provided funding to promote environmental protection. VERA Files also became the Philippine partner of the German branch of the French watchdog Reporters Without Borders in a global media ownership monitoring project, in which they revealed the powerful families behind the major news organisations of their country.

The fact-checking work only started in 2016. It came about during the campaign for the presidential election, when Chua asked her students at UP to check some of the candidates' statements. That experience gave the outlet enough standing to win a grant from the National Endowment for Democracy (NED), an aid organisation under the US Congress (see p. 81). Since then, VERA Files has gone through three more funding phases with the NED, receiving in total US$272,000, according to the NED's site. The grants allowed VERA Files to set up an office and hire a fact-checking team.

NED gives them a free hand to decide who and what to check. "What we do is we monitor speeches and statements of public personalities – it could be government officials, or private officials as long as they are people of influence", says Tordesillas. The team does deep research to corroborate or give the lie to a story according to a rigorous six-step checking procedure. "And then if we spot false statements, we debunk them with verified data", she goes on. The results are written up as stories and posted on the site, appearing with a red stamp across them branding them according to a five-category fact-check ratings system: "false", "fake", "misleading", "needs context" or "satire".

The outlet won its credentials in 2017, when it was accepted as a signatory of the International Fact-Checking Network, set up by the Florida-based Poynter Institute. Then in 2018 it became one of three media outlets – the other two were the for-profit startup Rappler (also an IFCN signatory) and the French news agency AFP – chosen by Facebook as third-party fact-checkers of the social media platform's Philippine content. For this contract, the VERA Files team rates the accuracy of posts – articles, status updates, photos and videos – according to the ratings system mentioned above. They do not block or delete posts, Tordesillas emphasises. Facebook takes action by placing stories rated as false lower in news feeds and reducing the ability of pages repeatedly sharing false news to monetise and advertise. It also notifies users who have shared reports rated false and gives them links to articles which point out what was wrong with the posts. There's a complaint process for those who think they've been labelled incorrectly. VERA Files does not reveal how much Facebook pays for the service, but the outlet now has a bigger office and a fact-checking team of ten and is able to give competitive pay and benefits to its young and talented staff.

VERA Files was also part of Tsek.ph, a pioneering collaborative fact-checking project composed of academe and media set up to counter disinformation during the Philippines' 2019 elections and provide the public with verified information. The project was supported by Facebook and San Francisco-based Meedan, an outlet that builds open-source digital tools for fact-checking.

The fact-checking function has not made for good relations with the government. Many of the stories that appear on the VERA Files site rated false as a result of their checks involve statements by President Rodrigo Duterte, who was no fan of the outlet in the first place. It's no surprise that the site has faced attacks, along with fellow Facebook checker Rappler. Yvonne Chua wrote in an article for the Poynter Institute that, when the Facebook effort started, "[d]iehard Duterte supporters, digital influencers and trolls launched a fresh round of attacks on the two organizations, which by then were no strangers to the stream of invective, threats and unfounded accusations of political bias, corruption and unpatriotism" (Chua 17 December 2018).

VERA Files has been accused of bias in its judgment, and was one of the organisations reported by the president in 2019 to be in the pay of the CIA and involved in a plot against him. Tordesillas emphasises that VERA Files has no links whatsoever with the CIA. TAF has been charged with having been set up by the CIA in the 1950s (see p. 81), but she says the funding it gave VERA Files for disabilities reporting was purely for that purpose. NED has been similarly labelled as a CIA front without justification. VERA Files funders let the team act independently and have no influence over them, Tordesillas goes on, and this is clear from their work: "I think the only, to us the most effective, counter to all the accusations of partisanship is good journalism, good fact-checking, because our work will speak for us".

She says she respects the right of anyone to criticise VERA Files, but she worries about the effect of the vicious onslaughts on its staff.

> I have been a journalist since the Marcos years, I worked during martial law, so these things are not new to me, but we have young reporters, they are fresh from college, who were not born during the martial law years … The threats that we get have a different impact on them, and I, as head of the organisation, am very concerned about that.

With the office having been visited by "members of the authorities," the staff have been given safety training.

In the belief that anyone can – and should – be a fact-checker, VERA Files conducts fact-check training in universities in different parts of the Philippines. One of the most memorable sessions was at the University of Antique on Panay Island in the country's west. "They gave us 350 senior students taking their Bachelor of Science in Education", recalls Tordesillas. While the journalists taught the students how to fact-check, the event quickly became a two-way process. "We also learned a lot from them because they are teachers", she says. "During the workshop they used their teaching skills on how to fact-check, and some of those skills were new to us." They also realised the youngsters could pass on their new fact-checking knowledge to their own students as well. "From then on, we have told school officials, 'Give us your education students'."

Reliance on grants allows VERA Files not to have to worry about making money by other means. It still sells its stories for "minimal" amounts or gives them away free ("many media outlets don't have the resources to pay") for translation from English into Filipino and other languages, and refuses to take ads. Costs are kept down in a number of ways. The three remaining founders have stuck to their commitment to work in other jobs for their bread-and-butter income. The full-time team works on fact-checking, which is paid for by the project funding, but other stories come from a pool of freelance reporters, keeping costs down. They have a full-time administrator but no marketing or technical staff (they contracted professionals to set up the website).

They still have to work hard at finding new projects. "All of us, trustees and even the employees, we're always on the lookout for grants", says Tordesillas. One of her fellow trustees, Rosario Laquicia, a former Reuters journalist, has a particular talent for writing proposals and usually does that job. Tordesillas knows that continued reliance on grants has its downsides. One is that it discourages commercial growth, which could be a problem in the long run. But the time limits on funding also make staff a little nervous, she says: "Our employees cannot really plan very long-term, because these grants are only good for the short-term usually".

Tordesillas's dream is to get long-term support from a philanthropic family or organisation, but she knows that's not realistic.

> Our problem is if you approach rich people here to put up an endowment fund, these rich people are usually business people, and they are into telecoms, mining, big businesses, which means they might want to compromise with the government.

So, for the foreseeable future, project grants are going to be the main source of income. "That's the reality we have to accept," she says. "Yes, it's really a choice."

See online site (www.routledge.com/9781138283091) for Chapter 8 with the following case studies: Bioscope, Katadata, News Lab, Splice Media, The Diplomat.

References

Accounting & Corporate Regulatory Authority (ACRA) (11 April 2018). Rejection of application by OSEA Pte Ltd to register as a private company limited by shares. Retrieved 1 February 2021 from https://www.acra.gov.sg/docs/default-source/news-events-documents/2018/11042018_media-statement_rejection-of-application-by-osea-pte-ltd-to-register-as-a-pte-ltd-company-by-shares(web)

ACRA (n.d.). Rejoinder to statement from New Naratif. Retrieved 1 February 2021 from https://www.acra.gov.sg/news-events/news-details/id/440

Agung, Bintoro (27 December 2019). Sebelum tahun berganti kami membuka lembaran baru untuk masa depan yang begita dekat (Before the next year we turn to a new chapter for a very near future). *Daily Social*. Retrieved 25 August 2020 from https://dailysocial.id/post/lokadata-rebranding-beritagar

Altermidya (1 December 2020). On the red-tagging of Altermidya network at the Dec. 1 senate hearing. Retrieved 22 January 2021 from https://www.altermidya.net/on-the-incredulous-red-tagging-of-altermidya-network-at-the-dec-1-senate-hearing/

Au-Yong, Rachel (1 May 2018). Historian suspected of engineering academic support for himself. *The Straits Times*. Retrieved 17 June 2020 from https://www.straitstimes.com/singapore/historian-suspected-of-engineering-academic-support-for-himself

Bandurski, David (1 September 2018). Highs and lows for "WeMedia" in China. China Media Project. Retrieved 31 May 2020 from http://chinamediaproject.org/2018/09/01/highs-and-lows-for-wemedia-in-china

Bass, Thomas A. (2017). American's amnesia. *Mekong Review*, Issue 8. Retrieved 21 September 2020 from https://mekongreview.com/americas-amnesia/

Brooten, Lisa, McElhone, Jane Madlyn, & Venkiteswaran, Gayathry (2019). Myanmar media historically and the challenges of transition. In Brooten, Lisa, McElhone, Jane Madlyn and Venkiteswaran, Gayathry (Eds.). *Myanmar media in transition: legacies, challenges and change*. Singapore: The ISEAS Yusof Ishak Institute. 1–59.

Bui Jones, Minh (29 October 2019). After struggling for 5 years, Minh Bui Jones almost shut Mekong review down this month. *Splice Media*. Retrieved 6 February 2021 from https://www.splicemedia.com/mekong-review-almost-unpublished/?fbclid=IwAR0ktjMqjzk69WySSxCnaUsV-5LQ2u4J2aGF4Tx6yST6A3h14XzFyIUyvuI

CCIM (Cambodian Center for Independent Media) (2017). *Challenges for independent media*. Phnom Penh: CCIM.

Chua, Yvonne T. (17 December 2018). Fact-checking under pressure: how Vera files has dealt with the Duterte regime. *Poynter.* Retrieved 9 September 2020 from https://www.poynter.org/fact-checking/2018/fact-checking-under-pressure-how-vera-files-has-dealt-with-the-duterte-regime/

Deng, Iris (28 May 2018). Chinese blog Chaping to refund 30 million yuan investment from Tencent after outcry. *South China Morning Post.* Retrieved 22 May 2020 from https://www.scmp.com/tech/china-tech/article/2148172/chinese-self-media-account-chaping-refund-30-million-yuan-investment

Ellao, Janess Ann J. (24 February 2020). Alternative media groups, IT companies settle cyberattack case. *Bulatlat.* Retrieved 21 January 2021 from https://www.bulatlat.com/2020/02/24/alternative-media-groups-it-companies-settle-cyberattack-case/

Feng, Jiyun (13 July 2018). Online press Q Daily cuts down coverage on public affairs to stay alive. *SupChina.* Retrieved 31 March 2020 from https://supchina.com/2018/07/13/online-press-q-daily-cuts-down-coverage-on-public-affairs-to-stay-alive/

gov.sg (13 May 2020). Corrections and clarifications regarding falsehoods and misleading statements by Mr Thum Ping Tjin. *gov.sg.* Retrieved 17 June 2020 from https://www.gov.sg/article/factually-corrections-on-falsehoods-about-pofma-by-thum-ping-tjin

Holmes, Oliver (16 March 2016). Independent Malaysian news site closes amid government clampdown on media. *The Guardian.* Retrieved 25 July 2020 from https://www.theguardian.com/world/2016/mar/15/independent-malaysian-insider-news-site-closes-government-media-clampdown

Jiang, Sijia (28 May 2018). Tencent pulls investment in content start-up after online backlash. *Reuters.* Retrieved 22 May 2020 from https://www.reuters.com/article/us-tencent-investment/tencent-pulls-investment-in-content-start-up-after-online-backlash-idUSKCN1IT12B

Jikkham, Patsara, & Thip-Osod, Manop (21 October 2015). Isra News defends spending of ThaiHealth funds. *Bangkok Post.* https://www.bangkokpost.com/thailand/politics/737076/isra-news-defends-spending-of-thaihealth-funds

Koetse, Manya (4 August 2018, updated November 2018). The sudden suspension of news site Q Daily has attracted the attention of Chinese netizens. *What'sonWeibo.* Retrieved 12 April 2020 from https://www.whatsonweibo.com/chinese-online-news-outlet-q-daily-shut-down/

Malaysiakini (27 March 2019). M'kini wins Google News Initiative innovation grant. Retrieved 24 July 2020 from https://www.malaysiakini.com/news/469764

Newman, Nic (2020). Reuters Institute digital news report 2020. Reuters Institute for the Study of Journalism. Retrieved 18 July 2020 from http://www.digitalnewsreport.org/

Noor, Sabrina (30 July 2020). Dr Mahathir's cousin? DAP man? We fact check viral claims about Najib's judge. *Cilisos.* Retrieved 31 July 2020 from https://cilisos.my/dr-mahathirs-cousin-dap-man-we-fact-check-viral-claims-about-najibs-judge/

Ong, Justin (15 June 2019). Report reveals how Jho Low funded The Malaysian Insider. *Malay Mail.* Retrieved 25 July 2020 from https://www.malaymail.com/news/malaysia/2019/06/15/report-reveals-how-jho-low-funded-the-malaysian-insider/1762426

Pongutta, Suladda, Suphanchaimat, Rapeepong, Patchranarumol, Walaiporn, & Tangcharoensathien, Viroj (2019). Lessons from the Thai Health Promotion Foundation. *Bulletin of the World Health Organization,* 97/3, 213–220. https://www.who.int/bulletin/volumes/97/3/18-220277/en/

Reuters (31 July 2014). Shanghai Husi rotten-meat scandal blows the lid on a huge problem for China's food processing industry. *South China Morning Post.* Retrieved 31

May 2020 from https://www.scmp.com/news/china/article/1562922/shanghai-husi-rotten-meat-scandal-blows-lid-huge-problem-chinas-food

Sainul, Abudheen K (2 October 2020). Cambodia's Mediaload raises Series A from True Digital to expand into new markets. e27. Retrieved 14 October 2020 from https://e27.co/cambodias-mediaload-raises-series-a-from-true-digital-to-expand-into-new-markets-20201002/.

Santos, Jamil (10 May 2019). Editor says 58 tagged in 'oust-Duterte' matrix remind him of Maguindanao massacre. *KBK, GMA News*. Retrieved 22 January 2021 from https://www.gmanetwork.com/news/news/nation/693954/editor-says-58-tagged-in-oust-duterte-matrix-remind-him-of-maguindanao-massacre/story/

Smith Freehills, Herbert (4 September 2017). China tightens control on internet news and content. Lexology. Retrieved 24 May 2020 from https://www.lexology.com/library/detail.aspx?g=b2aa77aa-0270-40f8-9f18-ad65b6130259

Straits Times (23 March 2018). The Malaysian Insight to suspend publishing from next week. Retrieved 25 July 2020 from https://www.straitstimes.com/asia/se-asia/the-malaysian-insight-says-to-stop-publishing-from-next-week

Tan, Adrian (n.d.). How start-up TheSmartLocal disrupted lifestyle publishing in Singapore. *Adrian Tan Blog*. Retrieved 13 June 2020 from https://adriantan.com.sg/the-smart-local/

Tan, Martino (31 March 2018). Why historian PJ Thum was Shanmugamed for nearly 6 hours. *Mothership*. Retrieved 17 June 2020 from https://mothership.sg/2018/03/pj-thum-k-shanmugam-fake-news/

Tang, Xiao Ming (11 June 2020). NN explains: rights and what you ought to have. *New Naratif*. Retrieved 17 June 2020 from https://newnaratif.com/comic/nn-explains-rights/

Thum, Ping Tjin (26 February 2018). Submission to the Select Committee on Deliberate Online Falsehoods, Parliament of Singapore. Medium. Retrieved 17 June 2020 from https://medium.com/submissions-to-the-select-committee-on-deliberate/submission-to-the-select-committee-on-deliberate-online-falsehoods-parliament-of-singapore-984a7a2d6ee3

Thum, Ping Tjin (8 May 2020). How bad laws are created and abused in Singapore (a POFMA case study). *The Show with PJ Thum*. Retrieved 17 June 2020 from https://www.youtube.com/watch?v=AWjPx48lRVM

Wahyudi, Eko (21 October 2019). Bantah Beritagar tutup, pemred: 17 karyawan di redaksi dirumahkan (Editor in chief denies Beritagar is closed: 17 employees in the editorial staff dismissed). *Tempo*. Retrieved 25 August 2020 from https://bisnis.tempo.co/read/1262529/bantah-beritagar-tutup-pemred-17-karyawan-di-redaksi-dirumahkan

Yu, Ivy (28 May 2018). 'Article laundering'? [update.] *SupChina*. Retrieved 22 May 2020 from https://supchina.com/2018/05/28/why-did-tencent-just-invest-in-article-laundering-account/

Zhao, Juecheng, Li, Fengxiang, & Ling, De (18 August 2018). Hong Kong opposition-camp media confuse right and wrong. *Global Times*. Retrieved 11 July 2020 from http://www.globaltimes.cn/content/1161826.shtml

Zhao, Xiaochun (23 May 2018). China dealbook: Tencent's TOPIC Fund bets on self-media Chaping; Qifeng Caijing rides the blockchain wave. *KrAsia*. Retrieved 22 May 2020 from https://kr-asia.com/china-dealbook-tencents-topic-fund-bets-on-self-media-chaping-qifeng-caijing-rides-the-blockchain-wave

INDEX

100 Most (Most Kwai Chung) 24, 41–42
500 Startups (also 500 Durians, 500 TukTuks) 41, 151

Accelerated Mobile Pages (AMP) *see* Google
accelerators 39
ad blockers 67, 68, 70, 76
Ad Manager *see* Google
AdSense *see* Google
ad tech companies 68, 101
advertising 66–72, 95; affiliate advertising 69, 101; display advertising 67, 124, 127, 134, 194, 205; ethical issues of 101–102, 113, 179, 207; programmatic advertising 68–69, 93, 101–102
Agence France Presse (AFP) 28, 98, 100, 202, 208, 222
aggregators 72–73, 98–99, 121
algorithms 59–60, 150, 157
Alibaba 7, 24, 45, 59, 115, 117–118; Alipay 78; Ant Finance 124; and digital advertising 67; startup funding 123
AMP *see* Google
analytics *see* metrics and analytics
Anchor 56, 74
"angels" *see* investors
Anggoro, Sapto 61, 215–219
Apple 3, 57, 67, 69, 115; Apple News 73; App Store 67; iTunes and Apple Music 74, 77; and podcasts 56, 74–75; Safari browser 68

Apps 55, 142, 155; Cambodia 130; IDN-planned "super app" 146; Khmerload-planned "super-content" app 149–151; messaging apps 32–33; Qdaily 174–175, 178; Sabay 179–180; and security 57; Thmey Thmey 202
Arao, Danilo 112–115
Arkadia Digital Media 41, 43
art4d 15, 23, 80, 86, 107–109; DesignNation 97, 109
artificial intelligence (AI) 59–60; and Binokular 203
The Asia Foundation (TAF) 81–82, 207
theAsianparent 22
Asmarani, Devi 156–157, 159
The Associated Press (AP) 59, 98
Audible 74–75
audience 20–24; audience engagement 91–97
Automattic 53, 73, 93; Parse.ly 33, 93

Belt & Road Initiative (BRI), China 8–10
Belt Road Capital Management 41, 157, 189
Beritagar.com *see* Lokadata
Binokular *see* Tirto
Bioscope 23, 42
Bishop, Bill 74
Blendle 77–78
blockchain 60–61
Blognone 23, 25, 42, 110–112; Blognone Jobs 112; Blognone Tomorrow 112; Brand Inside 97, 111–112

blogs 3, 22–24, 27, 34, 48, 53, 74, 76, 97, 110
Bloomberg 23, 59, 75, 189, 197, 206; Bloomberg Beta 44
"boosting" social media posts 32; Cilisos 120; Thmey Thmey 202
bootstrapping (self-funding) 36–37
brand-building 24–26
branded content *see* paid content
Brauchli, Marcus 44–45; and The News Lens 188–189
Briggs, Mark 4, 62, 68, 91, 102
Bui Jones, Minh 36, 165–169
Bulatlat 24, 30, 112–115
business coverage 23
business model 29–30
business plan 30–31, 39, 103
buyouts: Bioscope 23, 42; Blognone 23, 42, 110–112; DealStreetAsia 23, 42
BuzzFeed: early entrepreneurial outlet 3, 5, 24, 69, 149; as inspiration 119, 143, 195
ByteDance 7, 24, 40, 59; and copyright 99; as investor 41

Cai Hua, Will 20, 37, 182, 184
Canadian International Development Agency (CIDA) 84
Cashmore, Peter 3
Chainarongsing, Wongthanong "Hnong" 196–199
Chandran, Premesh 61, 134, 149, 160–165
Chaping 33, 41, 86, 94, 97, 99, 116–120; Chaping Black Market 119
Charoen Pokphand 80, 150, 153
Chen, Steve 200
China Business News Weekly 185–186
Chinsupakul, Yod 112
Choo, Bryan 196–200
Chrome *see* Google
Chua, Yvonne T. 206–208
Chung, Joey 36, 187–190
Chy Sila 20, 61, 178–181
Cilisos 24, 70, 95, 118–121
Civil (Civil Media) 54, 60–61
Ciwei Gongshe 24, 122–124
Coconuts 22, 24, 96, 124–128; events 86, 125; Grove 97, 126; membership 96, 125–126; and sales 85
coding 54, 62
comScore 93
consultancy 85
content: quality content 91–92; sourcing 27–28

content management systems (CMSs) 33, 53–55, 62
The Correspondent, De Correspondent 48, 96, 137
crowdfunding 36, 47–49, 78–80; Hong Kong Citizen News 136–137; Hong Kong Free Press 139–142
CT Corp 203
Cuaca, Willson 41, 150

Daily Social 154
DAP News 21, 98, 128–131; DAP Advertising Co. Ltd. 130; DAP Business 130; *Deum Ampil* 128–130; Deum Ampil Media Center 129, 130; FM93.75 Mhz 129; *Looking Today* 129–130; Morakot 129
data journalism/data-driven journalism 24, 62–63
Day Poets 196–197
DealStreetAsia 45, 76, 86; business news 23, 25; buyout 42, 45
De Correspondent, The Correspondent 48, 96, 137
Diani, Hera 156–160
D-Insights *see* Katadata
The Diplomat 25, 27, 166
distributed denial of service (DDoS) attacks 114, 157
distributing your work 31–34
donations 30, 36, 78–79, 95; Bulatlat 113; Frontier Myanmar 133; Hong Kong Citizen News 136; Hong Kong Free Press 140–142; Isranews 148–149; Malaysiakini 160; New Naratif 170; The Reporter 190–193
Dorcas Investments 200
"doxxing" 58, 164

e27 23, 39, 41, 76
East Ventures 41, 145
e-commerce 7, 53, 69, 85, 86, 97; Chaping Black Market 117; DesignNation 109; TheSmartLocal 195
email newsletters *see* newsletters
Emerging Opportunity Fund (EMOF) *see* Media Development Investment Fund (MDIF)
entrepreneur: definition 4–5
entrepreneurial journalism: background and emergence 1–4; nature and definition 4–6
ethical issues 98–102; codes of ethics 98, 141

events 27, 86; art4d 107–109; Ciwei Gongshe 123; Coconuts 125; Magdalene 158; New Naratif 173; Sabay 181; The Standard 198, 199
"evergreen" stories 92, 127
exits 41–42

Facebook: and advertising 66–68; change of algorithms to downplay news 33, 73, 138; for distribution 32–33; Facebook Instant Articles (IA) 32, 71–72, 120, 127, 150, 185; Facebook Journalism Project 80; Facebook Live 56; Facebook Messenger 32; and fact checking 100–101, 208; for finding users 33, 127; and governments 73, 99; hogging ad income 66, 149; for monetisation 71–72; popularity of 14, 31, 94; and third-party cookies 67
fact-checking 60, 62, 100–101, 206–209
Factcheck.org 101
FactWire 24, 47–48, 78, 136, 137, 142
fake news 6, 14, 29, 57, 76, 100–101; Singapore 171; VERA Files 206, 208
Fang Kecheng 85
feedback *see* metrics and analytics
FHI360 84
first-party data 69
focus groups 96
Fojo Institute 82
foundations 42, 45–46, 54, 62, 79–80, 83; government-sponsored 81–82
"freemium" model 76, 125, 205
Friedrich Ebert Foundation 82
Friedrich Naumann Foundation (FNF) 82, 84
Fringebacker 48–49, 136–137, 140
Frontier Myanmar 20, 22, 25, 46, 76, 80, 131–135; Black Knight Media Group 97, 133; membership programme 96

Gan, Steven 61, 134, 149, 160–165
Garena *see* Sea
GDP Venture 41, 150, 169–170
General Data Protection Regulations (GDPR) 68
Ghost 54, 74
Global Investigative Journalists' Network (GIJN) 28, 137, 203–204
Google 3, 31, 33, 56–57, 127, 135; and advertising 66–68; GNI Innovation Challenge 80, 134, 141, 164; Google Accelerated Mobile Pages (AMP) 33, 71; Google Ad Manager 71, 185;

Google AdSense 18, 71, 149; Google Analytics 92, 205; Google Chrome 57, 67; Google Earth Pro 10; Google Fact Check Tools 101; Google Fusion 63; Google Image Search 101; Google Launchpad Accelerator 111; Google News 72, 99, 120; Google News Initiative (GNI) 49, 54, 60, 62, 80, 92, 173; hogging ad income 66, 149; News Consumer Insights 92; News Tagging Guide 92; Reader Revenue Playbook 79; Realtime Content Insights 92
GoTo (merger of Gojek and Tokopedia) 7
"government-linked companies" (GLCs) 38
grants and sponsorships 79–85; Bulatlat 113; Frontier Myanmar 134; Malaysiakini 163; New Naratif 170, 173; VERA Files 206, 207, 209–210
Grundy, Tom 48, 59, 92, 139–143

Han, Kirsten 169–174
hate speech 6, 29, 76
"Hedgehog Commune" *see* Ciwei Gongshe
Ho Jung-shin 191
Hong Kong Citizen News (HKCN) 24, 25, 91–92, 135–139, 142; Civic Journalists Ltd. 141; crowdfunding 49, 78; data journalism 63; newsletter 95; and SEO 33; as social enterprise 30; veteran journalists 61
Hong Kong Free Press (HKFP) 24, 25, 59, 92, 95, 139–143; and crowdfunding 48–49, 78; as GNI Innovation Challenge winner 80; as Newspack user 54; registration 30
Huang, Charles 200
Huang Jingjie 185
Huffington, Ariana 3, 27
Huffington Post 3, 23, 24, 27, 144, 162
"hyperlocal" news 22, 124, 127, 144, 194

Idea River Run (IRR) 122
IDN Media, IDN Times 21, 55, 61, 103, 143–146; Creator Network 97, 144; Duniaku.com 143; GGWP.ID 143; IDN Creative 144; IDN Pictures 143; investors 45, 154; mission statement 20; Popbela 143; Popmama 143; UGC 29; use of AI 29, 59; Yummy 143, 144
IJNet *see* International Center for Journalists (ICFJ)

216 Index

"impact investors" *see* investors
income 66–87
incubators 39
Indiegogo 47–48
infographics: The Standard 21, 197; Tirto 204
Initial Public Offering (IPO) 38, 111
The Initium 20, 24, 37, 77, 86, 181–184
Instagram 31–32, 56, 71, 160; IGTV 71; Instagram Reels 31
Instant Articles (IA) *see* Facebook
instant messaging 32, 94
International Center for Journalists (ICFJ) 44, 83–85; IJNet 56, 62, 85, 93; and Malaysiakini 163
International Consortium of Investigative Journalists (ICIJ) 39, 46, 63, 78; FinCEN Files 63; Panama Papers 45, 78; Pandora Papers 46, 63; Paradise Papers 46
International Fact Checking Network 204, 208
International Media Support 82, 134
Internews 62, 84, 207
investigative and in-depth journalism 24, 91, 96, 131, 138, 143; data stories 63; funding 22, 48, 78–80, 101; Isranews 146–148; The Reporter 190–192; sensitiveness of 15; Tirto 202, 204; VERA Files 206–207
investors 37–47; "angels" 37–38, 130, 165, 197; "impact investors" 42–47; specialist investors 42–47; venture capitalists (VCs) 38–41
In Vichet 41, 155–159
Isranews Agency 25, 61, 80, 146–149; Isra Institute 147; Issara News Center 147

Jinri Toutiao 25, 33, 40, 122, 124; copyright issues 99; for distribution 123; income sharing with contributors 72
journalism skills 61–63

Katadata 24, 43, 53, 76, 80; D-Insights 76; Katadata Insight Center (KIC) 97
Khmerload 25, 41, 55, 130, 149–153; Groupin 151; Mediaload 151; Myanmarload 151, 153
Kickstarter 47–48, 74
The Knight Foundation 54, 83, 86
Konrad Adenauer Foundation (KAF) 34, 62, 82; Asia News Network (ANN) 34, 82; *Entrepreneurial journalism*

handbook 98; Konrad Adenauer Center for Journalism 82; Media Programme Asia 82
Kwik, Derek 37, 39, 40
Kwok, Herman 154, 155
Ky Soklim 200–202

Lau Chak Onn 118–121
Lee Fook Long, Vincent 119
Lee Hsueh-li, Sherry 61, 190–193
Lertrattanawisute, Prasong 61, 146–149
Lin, Kevin 189
LINE 32, 145
LinkedIn *see* Microsoft
livestreaming 56–57, 109
Li Yuet Wah, Daisy 30, 34, 61, 63, 91, 135–139
Lokadata (formerly Beritagar.com and Lintas.me) 24, 153–156; Lintas Cipta Media (LCM) 154
Luminate 42, 43, 45–48, 96; and Frontier Myanmar 134

machine learning 59–60
Magdalene 15, 25, 44, 156–160; Working Room 85, 158
MailChimp 94, 138
Malaysiakini 15, 21, 25, 61, 95, 160–165, 184; and AI use 60; and FG Media 97, 161; Frontier Myanmar 134; funding 80, 83, 84; GNI Innovation Challenge winner 80; and Isranews 149; Kini Academy 163; Kinibiz 165; Kinibooks 165; Kini "community" 164; KiniTV 97, 161, 163; mission 19–20; paywall 76
The Malaysian Insight 21, 25, 38, 61, 76–77, 184–187
Mandel, Harlan 42, 170
market research 26–27
Mashable 3, 5, 23, 24
Media Development Investment Fund (MDIF), formerly known as Media Development Loan Fund (MDLF) 41–44, 46, 80, 96; Emerging Opportunity Fund (EMOF) 42–43; and Frontier Myanmar 134; and Magdalene 158–159; and Malaysiakini 162–163; MDIF General Fund 42; MDIF Media Finance 42; MDIF Ventures 43; Myanmar Media Program (MMP) 42, 170; Southeast Asian Technical Assistance Initiative (SEATAI) 43, 46
Medium 36, 53, 73
Mekong Review 25, 27, 36, 165–169

membership 95–97; Coconuts 125–126; Frontier Myanmar 132–135; New Naratif 170–171, 173
The Membership Puzzle Project (MPP) 96, 134, 173; Membership in News Fund 96
metrics and analytics 92–93; algorithmic or digital feedback 75, 92–93
micropayments 77–78
Microsoft 3, 37, 124, 176–178; Firebase 55; GitHub 54; LinkedIn 31
mission 25–26, 153, 161, 178; mission statement 19–20, 55, 96, 102, 103
Mo Runhuo 115–118
Most Kwai Chung *see* 100 Most
Myanmar Media Program (MMP) *see* Media Development Investment Fund (MDIF)

names 24–25
National Endowment for Democracy (NED) 81, 163, 207
native advertising *see* paid content
New Naratif 25, 86, 169–174; donations 95; registration 30, 80; transparency 55
News Lab 85
The News Lens 15, 21, 25, 45, 80, 187–190; Ad2iction 97, 190; Agent Movie 189; and AI 60; Cool3C 189; funding 36, 41; as GNI Innovation Challenge winner 80; INSIDE 189; Sports Vision 189; TNLR 97, 189
newsletters 23, 34, 94–95, 103
Newspack *see* WordPress
niche 19–24, 47
nonprofit business model 29–30; Bulatlat 114; New Naratif 170; The Reporter 191; VERA Files 206
North Base Media (NBM) 42, 44–45; and IDN Media 145; and The News Lens 188
Nugrahadi, Didi 153–156

OhmyNews 28–29
Omidyar Network (ON) 45–46, 83, 87, 134; ON Democracy Fund 96
Open Society Foundations (OSF) 42, 79–81, 84; and New Naratif 172

paid content 70–71, 102; branded content 70–71; Cilisos 119; Ciwei Gongshe 123; Coconuts 124; Frontier Myanmar 134; Lokadata 155; The Malaysian Insight 185; native advertising 70–71;
The News Lens 189; Sabay 179–180; TheSmartLocal 194–195; sponsored content 70–71; The Standard 198; Thmey Thmey 201; Tirto 205
"paid online knowledge" 85
Paireepairit, Isriya 23, 110–112
Patel, Rishad 85, 138
Patreon 73
paywalls *see* subscriptions
Peretti, Jonah 3
Perry, Byron 124–128
philanthropy 79–80
Philip, Joji 23
pitch: "elevator pitch" 39; making a pitch 39–40; pitch deck 39–40, 48
plagiarism 28, 98–100
podcasts, podcasting 53, 55–56, 62, 74–75; Frontier Myanmar 134; Magdalene 158–159; The Malaysian Insight 186, 187 The Reporter 191–193; The Standard 196–199
"product thinking" 25, 78, 79

Qdaily 15, 23, 41, 174–178; Qdaily Labs 176
Quach Mengly 38, 200–201

Rappler 92, 112, 114, 115; fact-checking 208; and Frontier Myanmar 134; investment and grants 43, 45, 46, 80, 81; Rappler PLUS 96
registering as a company 34, 127, 130, 153; "nonprofit" options 30, 112, 129, 136, 141, 169–170, 172, 200, 207
The Reporter 15, 24, 25, 61, 190–193; donor funding 78, 80, 95; events 86; nonprofit status 30; The Reporter Cultural Foundation 190
research 26–27
Reuters 44, 62, 98, 102; Reuters Institute for the Study of Journalism 83; Thomson Reuters Foundation 28, 62, 83
Revue *see* Twitter

Sabay 21, 25, 61, 70, 98, 178–181; initial funding 85; Kanha 179; Kley Kley 179; Sabay coin 78, 180; Sabay Der 178; Sabay Digital Corporation 178; Sabay Digital Group 179; Sabay Enovel 95, 179, 180; Sabay MVP 178; Sabay News 178; Sabay TV 178; Sabay Write 95, 179; Soyo 179; ssn.digital 180; 30 Daily 179; values 20

218 Index

Sadiq, Jahabar 38, 61, 77, 184–187
sales 85–86
Samsi, Nur 203
Santoso, Teguh Budi 203
scaling a startup 97–98
Sea (formerly Garena) 7
search engine optimisation (SEO) 33–34, 53, 54, 127, 138
security 57–58, 62
seed funding 37–38
self-funding *see* bootstrapping
Shi Can 123
Siam Cement 80, 107, 148
Siam Commercial Bank 148
Signal 32, 57
Sirisukwattananont, Prommate 110
Slack 54, 58–59, 97
SmartNews 72, 150
SoftBank 7, 38
Soon, Alan 30, 85, 134
Soros, George 42, 79–80, 163, 172, 187
Southeast Asian Technical Assistance Initiative (SEATAI) *see* Media Development Investment Fund (MDIF)
Southeast Asia Press Alliance (SEAPA) 170–171
Soy Rithy 128–131
Soy Sophea 128–131
Soy Sopheap 128–131
specialisation 22–23
Special Purpose Acquisition Company (SPAC) 38
Splice Media 27, 30, 54, 62, 85, 95; and Frontier Myanmar 133, 134; and Mekong Review 169; Splice Beta Fund 27, 133; Splice Frames 95; Splice Lights On Fund 80, 173; Splice Slugs 95
sponsored content *see* paid content
sponsorships *see* grants
Spotify 56, 74, 159, 185, 186
Squarespace 54
staff 97; art4d 108; Cilisos 120; Ciwei Gongshe 123; DAP News 130; Hong Kong Citizen News 138; IDN Media 146; Magdalene 159; Malaysiakini 161; New Naratif 173; Qdaily 177; The Reporter 193; The Standard 198–199

The Standard (Thailand) 15, 21, 25, 55, 97, 196–200; events 109; Secret Sauce podcast 199; The Standard Economic Forum 86, 198; The Standard Podcast 197; The Standard Pop 197; The Standard Wealth 197
Stitcher 74–75
Storyful 101
Stratechery 23, 34, 76
Stripe 73
Suara.com 41, 43
subscriptions (paywall) 75–78; Coconuts 125–126; Hong Kong Citizen News 137, 139; The Initium 183; Malaysiakini 161–162; The Malaysian Insight 185; Mekong Review 168
Substack 36, 73–74
Suksuay, Nitipath "Pingpong" 208–210
surveys 26–27, 63, 75, 123, 186; Cilisos 119, 120; Frontier Myanmar 96, 134; Qdaily 174, 176
sustaining a startup 91–97
Swe, Sonny 96, 131–135
"SWOT" analysis 31
syndication 114
Tanjung, Chairul 203
Taobao 86, 97, 117, 150
Tao Weihua 33, 94, 115–118
Tech in Asia 23, 25, 26, 85, 86, 95; GNI Innovation Challenge winner 80; investment in 41; subscription 76
technology news 15; Blognone 23, 25, 97, 110–112; Chaping 16–120; The Information 76; Mashable 3, 23; investment in 44–45; Stratechery 23, 34, 76; TechCrunch 23; Tech in Asia 23, 25, 85, 86; Unbox 25
technology skills 52–61
Teeratada, Pratarn 107–109
Telegram 32, 57, 187
Tencent 7, 24, 40, 67, 78, 123; and Chaping 116
Thangnitirat, Khitichai 110
TheSmartLocal 25, 97, 194–196; Eatbook.sg 194; InsightsRN 195; MustShareNews 194; Telegram.co 195; TSLoffice.com 195; Wiki.sg 195; Zula.sg 194
third-party cookies 67, 68
Thmey Thmey 25, 38, 200–202; Cambodianess 202
Thum Ping Tjin 169–174
Tickled Media 41
TikTok (Douyin) 31–33, 40, 123, 150, 196
Tirto 24, 25, 61, 85, 159, 202–205; Binokular 24, 203, 204; Current Issues

217; InDepth 204; Jelajah 204; Mild Report 204
Tordesillas, Ellen 61, 206–210
transparency 66, 98, 101, 102; Coconuts 127; of finances 46; Malaysiakini 84; New Naratif 170
True, True Digital 41, 145, 151
Trustbridge Partners 187
Tung Tzu-hsien 80, 191, 193
Twitter 31–32, 56, 71, 73, 94, 123; for news coverage 140; Periscope 56; Revue newsletter 74

Ung Chamroeun 200
United Nations 83; UN Democracy Fund 83; UN Development Programme 83; UNESCO 83, 84
US Agency for International Development (USAID) 84
User Generated Content (UGC) 28–29, 144–145
Utomo, William and Winston 20, 61, 143–146

venture capitalists (VCs) *see* investors
VERA Files 25, 30, 61, 80, 81, 206–210
verticals 97, 129, 189
Virtual Private Networks (VPNs) 12, 57
Vucinic, Sasa 42, 44–45, 162, 188–189

Walden International 189
Wanakijpaibul, Nakarin "Ken" 55, 61, 209–212
WeChat (Weixin) 33, 78, 116, 122, 123; use for distribution 55, 94, 115, 117, 126; use for e-commerce 97, 117; WeChat Pay 78
Weibo 33, 78, 123, 175
WeReport 78, 138
WhatsApp 32, 33, 57, 71, 78
Whitehead, Peter 43
Wix 54
Wondery 75
Wongnai 23, 111
WordPress 53–54, 72, 93, 121, 127, 134; WordAds 72; WordPress Newspack 54, 140, 141
working from home 86, 95, 97, 109
Yang, Mario 36, 187, 188, 190

Yang Shaoming 181–184
Yang Ying 174–178
Ye Tieqiao 122–124
Yi Xianfeng 176
YouTube 31–32, 45, 56–57, 85, 125; The Malaysian Insight 185; New Naratif 172; YouTube Creator Academy 32; YouTube Live 56; YouTube Partner Program 71

For Product Safety Concerns and Information please contact our EU
representative GPSR@taylorandfrancis.com
Taylor & Francis Verlag GmbH, Kaufingerstraße 24, 80331 München, Germany

www.ingramcontent.com/pod-product-compliance
Lightning Source LLC
Chambersburg PA
CBHW051356290426
44108CB00015B/2043